Creating Value
Through People

Discussions with
Talent Leaders

Creating Value Through People

Discussions with Talent Leaders

MERCER

FOREWORD BY M. MICHELE BURNS, CEO

WILEY

John Wiley & Sons, Inc.

Published by John Wiley & Sons, Inc., Hoboken, New Jersey.
Published simultaneously in Canada.

For general information on our other products and services, or technical support, please contact our Customer Care Department within the United States at 800-762-2974, outside the United States at 317-572-3993 or fax 317-572-4002.

Wiley also publishes its books in a variety of electronic formats. Some content that appears in print may not be available in electronic books.

For more information about Wiley products, visit our Web site at www.wiley.com.

Library of Congress Cataloging-in-Publication Data:

Creating value through people: discussion with talent leaders/Mercer.
  p. cm.
ISBN 978-0-470-12415-4 (cloth)
  1. Leadership. 2. Personal management. 3. Employee motivation. I. Mercer (Firm)
HD57.7.C734 2009
658.4'092—dc22

2008040275

Printed in the United States of America

10 9 8 7 6 5 4 3 2 1

Contents

About the Authors

MERCER

Mercer is a leading global provider of consulting, outsourcing, and investment services, with more than 25,000 clients worldwide. Mercer consultants help clients design and manage health, retirement, and other benefits and optimize human capital. The firm also provides customized administration, technology, and total benefit outsourcing solutions. Mercer's investment services include global leadership in investment consulting and multimanager investment management. Mercer's global network of 18,000 employees, based in more than 40 countries, ensures integrated, worldwide solutions. Our consultants work with clients to develop solutions that address global and country-specific challenges and opportunities. Mercer is experienced in assisting both major and growing, mid-size companies. For further information, visit www.mercer.com.

M. MICHELE BURNS

M. Michele Burns is Chairman and Chief Executive Officer of Mercer, a global leader in human resource consulting, outsourcing, and investments, and a subsidiary of Marsh & McLennan Companies (MMC). Prior to being named Chairman and CEO of Mercer in 2006, Ms. Burns held the position of Chief Financial Officer for MMC.

From 2004 to 2006, Ms. Burns served as Chief Financial Officer, Chief Restructuring Officer, and Executive Vice President of Mirant Corp., where she was responsible for directing the company's corporate and operational financial functions, and investor relations. As Chief Restructuring

Officer, she spearheaded the development of a new capital structure and plan of reorganization—two vital components in Mirant's emergence from Chapter 11.

Previously, she was Executive Vice President and Chief Financial Officer of Delta Air Lines, Inc. from August 2000 to April 2004. She held various other positions in the finance and tax departments of Delta beginning in January 1999.

Ms. Burns' roots are within the consulting industry. She began her career with Arthur Andersen, and over the course of a successful 18-year tenure rose to Senior Partner, leading Andersen's Southern Region Federal Tax Practice, headed its U.S. Healthcare Practice and its South-eastern Region Financial Services Practice, and served on its Global Advisory Council.

Ms. Burns currently serves on the board of directors of Wal-Mart Stores, Inc., and Cisco Systems, Inc. She also serves on the Board of Directors for the Elton John AIDS Foundation, where she holds the title of Treasurer. She graduated Summa Cum Laude from the University of Georgia with a bachelor's degree in Business Administration and a Master's degree in Accountancy.

Acknowledgments

Many people had a hand in creating *Talent Leaders,* but a few deserve special recognition. Joel Kurtzman and the team at the Kurtzman Group played a crucial role at every stage in the project—from identifying candidates, to conducting interviews, to distilling hours and hours of conversation into a collection of memorable stories you will find here. Steven Faigen at Mercer also deserves special mention. He was the first to see the potential of grouping diverse perspectives under the umbrella talent innovation, and lead the project from beginning to end. A special thanks to our editors at John Wiley, John DeRemigis and Judy Howarth. Both displayed inexhaustible patience, professionalism, and judgment in bringing this book to life. Finally, we would be remiss without explicitly acknowledging the talent leaders themselves, whose collective wisdom we have been fortunate enough to capture in these pages.

End Note: We think you'll agree that it is the diversity of views in these pages that makes this book unique. But, please bear in mind, as you read through the 20 interviews, that observations, opinions, and insight expressed here come from the talent leaders themselves, and not Mercer. To view the firm's thought leadership, we encourage readers to visit mercer.com.

Foreword

M. MICHELE BURNS

Why do some organizations get better results than others? It's an age-old question but, in today's business environment, an especially vital one. Not surprisingly, the answer has to do with people. During a number of different chapters in my own career, I've seen how talent innovators consistently win.

I have seen how dedicated teams of people worked diligently to turn around an independent power producer that had gone bankrupt, quickly breathing new life into the company. I saw how the focused power of people allowed an airline that was hit hard in the aftermath of 9/11 to persevere, and ultimately, thrive. I've seen these changes firsthand because I was part of the teams that made these changes happen. As a result, I have long believed that talent innovators, no matter where they sit in an organization, make lasting differences.

But, as is so often the case when you get deeply involved in all-consuming challenges, I had little time to reflect on the larger themes that connected the remarkable performance of my former colleagues. When I joined Mercer as its CEO in 2006, and became affiliated with some of the top minds in the human capital consulting business, the mental framework guiding my talent decision-making all these years came into crystal-clear focus: Whether it is in a crisis situation, or in the day-to-day operations of a successful enterprise, people can make a powerful difference when an organization's business strategy, workforce strategy, and HR strategy are closely and carefully aligned to work together as a focused, integrated system.

How many times have we all heard that people are every company's most important asset? Often is the answer. The fact is that many companies make that statement, but either don't believe it, or don't deliver on it.

The truth is, people not only make a difference, they *are* the difference between one company and the next. In Mercer's view, how organizations manage their people is what makes the difference between failure and success. Effective talent management is about creating and engaging the right workforce to meet business objectives and achieve sustainable competitive advantage. It is about getting the right people in the right place at the right time and at the right cost. When people are engaged, and are given clear direction and the right kind of support—everything from effective leadership to valuable training to rewards that drive the right behaviors and results—there is nothing they cannot achieve.

This book gives you an opportunity to view how talent innovators innovate. To do that, we interviewed CEOs of Fortune 500 companies; well-known heads of HR at innovative, outperforming companies; researchers at some of the world's best business schools; heads of associations and foundations; and people who have had success in difficult and stressful circumstances—the military and in sports. Despite their different roles and backgrounds, they have something in common: a reputation for being innovative and effective in how they manage talent.

This book is part of Mercer's commitment to developing world-class strategies and solutions. More importantly, it is part of Mercer's commitment to world-class thinking. We wanted to convey how talent innovators think, in their own words, which is why we chose to use an interview format. Among the topics covered:

- *Managing and rewarding talent.* Different companies approach these issues differently. There is no one right answer. And yet, in each instance of talent innovation, these issues are not left to happenstance. They are important and treated as such, often with the full attention of the CEO. At Li & Fung, in Hong Kong, Victor Fung, the Chairman, created a system where his senior team is rewarded as if they were in business for themselves. Mr. Fung wants to create a culture of entrepreneurs. It may not work for every organization, but it's right for this one.

- *Keeping teams engaged and workers focused.* Companies like McDonald's have gone back to the basics—and it works. According to Jan Fields, McDonald's North American Chief Operating officer, the company has built new teams and created ways for them to keep in touch. They have even developed networks so people of diverse background can learn from each other about how to succeed. The reward for all this work? Many analysts once again view McDonald's as a growth company.

- *Creating tools to ensure retention of your best talent.* At Colgate Palmolive, a Fortune 500 company, when a highly valued, high-potential employee is threatening to leave, you pull out all the stops. According to Bob Joy, who built the company's centralized global HR function, the loss of such a person is so damaging to the organization that even the chairman and CEO need to be notified within 24 hours. In addition, a counteroffer has to be made to the high-potential person within the same time frame. New policies like that have enabled Colgate-Palmolive to keep its competitive edge against all competition.

- *Transforming underperforming teams into world-beaters.* Many organizations have taken a team approach. But in some instances the teams just don't perform. The USS *Benfold,* a U.S. Navy guided missile destroyer, not only contained more than its share of underperforming teams, it was one of the worst-performing ships in the Navy. Enter Commander Mike Abrashoff, who is interviewed in this book. Through the application of clarity, the right metrics, good communication, and what he calls, "grass roots leadership," the USS *Benfold* transformed itself into one of the Navy's best-performing ships. Not only that, but some of the procedures developed onboard that ship have now become standard Navy practice. Though the Navy is not a business, there are many compelling lessons to be learned from Abrashoff's experience.

- *Talent innovation lies at the point where strategy and execution meet.* It's where HR and all the other important functions join forces for the future. The innovators in this book are among some of the most renowned and accomplished people in business. We hope you will incorporate their ideas into your own thinking on these important issues.

Do not take their words as if they were written in stone. When it comes to talent innovation, one size never fits all.

CHAPTER 1

Mike Abrashoff

FORMER COMMANDER, USS *BENFOLD* (RETIRED U.S. NAVY)

It's Your Navy:
On Clarity, Metrics, Communications

The idea that companies can benefit from the management expertise of the military has been in practice for more than 50 years. Corporations, indeed whole industries, owe a debt to the top-down, command-and-control style of people management that is common in the military. But the immediacy of today's communication and information systems has military and private companies scrambling to embrace a new order. Captain Mike Abrashoff has a name for it: Grass Roots Leadership.

During the first Gulf War, Abrashoff took the guided missile destroyer USS *Benfold* from its position as one of the worst-performing ships in the Navy to the top of its class in only a few months' time. The lessons he learned from this experience are explained in his book, *It's Your Ship.* Now retired, Abrashoff helps companies and their executives understand and embrace this new leadership order.

In this interview, Abrashoff advances an approach that can best be described as "reverse logic." Solutions surface from the bottom up, not just the top down, in a world in which executives must earn credibility if they want their directives followed. In Abrashoff's view, "unity" replaces "diversity," and people must focus on their common purpose, not their differences. In his view, rank must be set aside in favor of aptitude, and companies must compete not as individuals, but as a powerful group. In Abrashoff's view, lessons from his successful turnaround of the USS *Benfold* should be applied to companies without delay.

QUESTION: When you were given command of the USS *Benfold,* it was one of the worst-performing ships in the navy. A few months later, during Operation Desert Shield, it was at the top of its class. Many of the changes you enacted became standard operating procedure throughout the Navy. For that, the Navy awarded you medals and promotions. Yet, you achieved these improvements from your crew in close quarters, under strict Navy rules, and without being able to change any of your sailors or rules. Much of the time you were understaffed, and you were in the midst of a series of conflict situations. What did you do first?

ABRASHOFF: The first 30 days after I took command of the ship were critical because people were just getting to know me and I was asking a lot of stupid questions. So, instead of sitting behind my desk all day long, I went out and about talking to the sailors every day.

From the beginning, I went to every nook and cranny in the ship. In the bowels of the ship there are eight sewage pumps: four aft and four forward. The subcontractor who made them used substandard materials in all the mechanical seals on the pumps. As a result, they were the weakest link on the ship. Not only were they breaking, but because they were breaking on all the other ships too, there weren't any spare parts in the supply system. That's a problem because you're out of business if you can't pump sewage or treat it.

Once a day, I would either go down to the forward pump room or the aft pump room. To do it, I had to climb down an escape trunk on a ladder. I went hand-over-hand four-decks down along this dirty escape trunk. There were cargo nets to catch you at every level in case you fell off the ladder. But I would go down there to talk to the guy who maintained the system to let him know how important he was and that we couldn't operate the ship without him. It was important for everyone on the ship to see I went down there.

QUESTION: Is there a parallel in businesses?

ABRASHOFF: Yes. I see a lot of businesses today where people think that everything revolves around them and they are better than anybody else. In financial services, it's sometimes the people executing trades. And yet, if the people doing the mundane work don't do their jobs—the nuts and bolts work of maintaining computers, paying the bills, and even cleaning the floors—those traders wouldn't be able to do all the great things they do.

So what I tried to do on the ship was to show the crew that no matter how mundane your job appears to be, you were valuable and the ship couldn't operate without you. That's true in the Navy, it's true in business, it's true everywhere.

QUESTION: How many sailors were on the ship?

ABRASHOFF: I had 310 sailors on the ship. There were 256 men and 54 women.

QUESTION: The military, like all but a few companies, runs on hierarchy. And yet, here you are, the person in charge, climbing those ladders. Were you concerned you might destroy your own authority?

ABRASHOFF: Not at all. It was all about showing everybody that, yeah, there are different levels of pay, different levels of rank, different levels of responsibility, but if the ship goes down, we all go down, regardless of our rank.

What I found out was that the crew didn't resent their officers for having extra perks like private staterooms or private eating quarters or getting paid more. They didn't resent us because they knew we didn't think we were better than them. That's the challenge companies need to come to grips with, especially with regard to CEO pay. If executives start to believe that they are better than everybody else, that's when the true problems are going to come in. So on the ship, what we tried to do was show that we're all in this together.

QUESTION: How else did you demonstrate that you were all in it together?

ABRASHOFF: Well, you can't command a ship by sitting behind your desk. I mean it's awfully inviting to sit there and hide behind your paperwork and wait for people to come in and tell you stuff. But if you do that, you won't know what's really going on and you especially won't hear the bad stuff.

What I wanted to do was set an example that said, look, I know bad stuff is going to happen. For me, the key was to get people to tell me about the bad stuff right away so I could be part of the solution. That meant communicating that I'm not going to shoot you if you tell me bad news. In two years, I never shot one person on that ship for bringing me bad news.

QUESTION: What's more important, receiving bad news or good news?

ABRASHOFF: Bad news. Absolutely. I don't need to know every good thing that's going on with the ship. But I do need to know the bad news. That's what will hurt us and it's where I can help.

QUESTION: Was bad news ever withheld?

ABRASHOFF: Yes. My biggest disappointment was from my best officer who was just an extraordinary leader. He had personality. His people loved him. He was technically gifted. One day, his sonar broke. We were in port and I didn't know it because we don't use sonar in port. We were getting under way to go out to sea to participate in a major fleet exercise with the aircraft carrier battle group when he came to me and said, "Captain, the sonar's broken."

Now, whenever bad news happened, the first question I asked was, "How long have you known about it?" He said, "Two weeks." In two weeks I could have helped him get it fixed. That's part of my job. I could have picked up the phone and gotten technicians out to help him. His problem was that he took so much pride in his work that he was afraid to ask me for help. There's a lesson here. People need to be on the lookout to make sure that the best people know they're the best, but are not so overconfident that they think they don't need to ask for help.

QUESTION: Could he have been afraid to ask for help?

ABRASHOFF: Yes. But I actually think it was simpler than that. He just thought he could fix it. Period. Now, it wasn't his fault it broke. Complex machinery breaks. But he thought he and his people could fix it. It turned out they couldn't and so we missed a commitment. We couldn't participate in a major fleet exercise. It was overconfidence and it took away all my options. Confidence is good. But overconfidence is an enemy.

QUESTION: How did you handle the problem?

ABRASHOFF: We were in my cabin and I looked him in the eye and I said, "John, I've never been more disappointed in anybody than I am with you right now." I said, "Two weeks ago, I could have been part of the solution. I could have gotten somebody out here to help. But because you chose not to include me in the solution, we're going to miss a commitment and it's your fault." He was ready to slit his wrists. I could have yelled and screamed and hollered, but the fact that I did it this way just devastated him. And the message got out to the crew that bad news does not improve with age.

QUESTION: If you're seeking out bad news, how do you make certain that people who do good things day in, day out are not overlooked?

ABRASHOFF: You don't seek out only bad news. You need to be on the lookout for people who are responding to breakdowns and you need to be on the lookout for people who never have any breakdowns, since they are doing things right. You need to take both of those into account and then stroke them and communicate with them.

It's like my sewage pump operator. You never think about him when things are working well, and yet his equipment had the greatest propensity for breaking down. That's why I went down to visit him every day. I wanted him to know that I was interested in him and in how I can help. I went down just to make sure everything was working okay. That small act—climbing down four decks through a dirty trunk—showed him that I cared, and I think that means a lot to people. It shows them that their efforts are being recognized and that they know they're critical to the operation. That they are valuable and that you value their problem-solving abilities. Paying someone that kind of attention is a reward in itself.

QUESTION: You raise an interesting point. How do you balance rewarding the individual and rewarding the group?

ABRASHOFF: It is a fine line. One of the things we were lousy at was recognizing people in a timely manner. And in the Navy, if somebody does something great, a month later somebody will decide, hey, the person deserves a medal. Well, those medals are important because sailors gain bonus points in their advancement exams as a result. You see, I can't really promote them, but if they get a medal, they get a bonus point on their standardized exams and they can use those toward getting a promotion.

QUESTION: A captain can't promote people on a ship?

ABRASHOFF: No. But there is an exception. I can recommend them for promotion and that gives them the opportunity to take a standardized advancement exam. The entire promotion process is exam-driven. The exception is a program called Command Advancements. I'm authorized to advance three people a year to the next highest grade for meritorious conduct. But this is really important. If these promotions are not handled properly, they can cause a lot of heartburn among those who don't get it. The problem is that it can appear that you're giving it to a favorite person. When it's viewed that way, it ends up causing more division.

When that happens, a good program ends up causing divisions and even retaliation against the person that gets the advancement. I saw it myself coming up the ranks. So when I took command of the ship, I laid out the criteria and qualifications for Command Advancements. No requirements were listed in the Navy manual. It was up to me. Whomever the captain wants to advance is advanced. So I laid out my qualifications.

QUESTION: What were they?

ABRASHOFF: One of my requirements was how many times a person could take a test and not be promoted. You see, the advancement process throughout the Navy is numbers-driven. It's all about vacancies at the top. Somebody can take a test ten times and pass it every time but that person won't get promoted if there aren't any vacancies at the next level. In some areas, there are very few jobs. In other areas it's wide open, and if you take the test and get even a minimal rating you get promoted. Numbers drive the promotion process. It's all based on filling empty slots or billets.

QUESTION: Who did you advance?

ABRASHOFF: I'll give you an example. I had a sailor who was a machinery repairman. Each ship gets one machinery repairman. Contrast that with the fact that I would get 40 fire control technicians. As a result, there are only 300 machinery repairmen in the entire Navy— one per shop. So there's not much opportunity for advancement for a machinery repairman. And to top it off, the sailor on my ship was Filipino and English was his second language. As a result, he was stuck. He had been a second class petty officer for ten years. Normally you get promoted after two or three years. And this sailor would help everybody on the ship. He would stay late. If he could fabricate a piece of equipment that wasn't in the supply system to help somebody keep the equipment running, he would do it. So, my criterion was you've got to pass the test. He always passed the test, however, there were never any and there billets or opportunities for advancement. When I made this machinery repairman my first advancement promotion, the entire crew cheered. They cheered because they knew what my criteria were and that he fit it and deserved it.

QUESTION: What about simply recognizing good individual and group performance.

ABRASHOFF: Yes. We did that too. We instituted a program called Top Dog in the League. It recognized the best sailor and I was very careful to rotate it among the departments so that every department was being represented.

QUESTION: There's a lot of literature that says recognizing individuals can result in alienating others. Do you agree with that view?

ABRASHOFF: Well, even with the best of intentions, you can still screw up. We had a surprise dispersing audit. It resulted in 50% of the ship flunking this inspection.

QUESTION: What's a dispersing audit?

ABRASHOFF: It's when they come and audit your pay records to make sure everyone is drawing all the proper allowances and not over-drawing and that the records are being processed in a certain manner. We had a dispersing office and it got the best score in the Pacific Fleet, ever. So I got on the public address system and talked about how great the dispersing office was to have done this and how they're really taking care of the crew. I thought everybody would be happy.

Now the dispersing office works for the supply officer and then we have an admin officer that the personnel office works for. Within 30 seconds, the personnel officer was in my cabin. "Did you know that your personnel men are ready to quit right now?" I said, "What on earth for?" I asked. She said, "Don't you know that they are 50% of the dispersing audit?"

It turned out the personnel office processed the personnel forms before the dispersing clerks got them. I never knew that. I said, "Oh my God." I turned what should have been great celebration for everybody into one where 50% of the people were angry. So recognition has both upsides and downsides and you have to plan out very carefully how you recognize people and teams. You can make some awful mistakes. You also have to think carefully about what types of behavior you are rewarding. If you don't do it right, the downsides can outweigh the upsides.

QUESTION: As you settled into your command, the culture of the ship changed. Many companies want to change their cultures to enhance performance and increase employee retention rates and satisfaction, among other things. How did you change your ship's culture?

ABRASHOFF: It happened because of a lot of little things. There is no big silver bullet to changing culture. And I'm not here to bad-mouth my predecessor on the ship. But he sat in his cabin all day long with the door locked. It wasn't just shut; it was locked. If the major change agent is the person at the top—and I believe that's the case—then it's a pretty bad idea for that person to keep the door closed and locked. With my predecessor, the only people who could see him were the second-in-command and the five department heads. Nobody else ever saw him. So, just opening my door changed things.

Another tactic I used was to interview every crew member on the ship. I did it in my cabin one-on-one. When I did the interviews, I used something I learned from Defense Secretary William Perry, whom I worked for at the Pentagon. At the Pentagon, whenever a foreign minister or defense minister came by, the first thing Perry did was to take pains to put the visitor feel at ease. He would walk the person around his office—and it was a huge office—and he would show the visitor all of his pictures on the wall and explain their significance. For example, he had a series of pictures of nuclear tipped missiles that were taken as the former Soviet Union was breaking up. He would talk about them and their significance. That technique put everybody at ease.

I also had pictures on my wall and when sailors would come into my cabin, I'd walk them around the room and show them all these pictures of things from my career. Then I'd ask them to take a seat. You should have seen the looks on sailors' faces when they would come in and sit down in the chair across from me in the Captain's Room. The expression was like, "I've never known what was in here." These sailors didn't begrudge me for having beautiful quarters—my predecessor spent a lot of money outfitting the cabin—even though they lived in berthing apartments that could house 106 sailors in one space, sleeping in bunk beds triple deep. But despite the disparity in quarters, the sailors were happy to be in my cabin, sitting with me and having a conversation. Becoming accessible and demystifying the office resulted in having the sailors respect me but not fear me.

QUESTION: What else did you do to change the culture?

ABRASHOFF: Communicating is essential. Technology can be a curse because if you send an e-mail, you expect everybody picks up the same message. I found that was not true. If I sent an e-mail it would be interpreted differently by every person on the ship. So the challenge was to make sure the message was not being misinterpreted as it makes its way down the chain of command. The only way I could do that was to walk around and talk to the sailors and ask them about their priorities for the day. If they knew their priorities, great. If they didn't, I knew who was in their chain of command and who was falling down and blocking the flow of information.

I also had a tool called my "Command Master Chief." He's my senior enlisted advisor. He's kind of like the shop steward. He represents the enlisted people on this ship. He would be out there walking around as well. He had his own little network. They were people he could rely on to see if the message was getting through. He knew as well as I did that it was our ability to get the message out and have everybody playing and driving towards the same thing that improved our performance.

QUESTION: Did you use other tools?

ABRASHOFF: Yes. You can't smoke inside the skin of the ship anymore. There's a designated smoking area outside the skin of the ship. For us it was on the fantail, way back at the stern of the ship. Smokers know everything that goes on in an organization. It's because there's no rank structure involved in smoking. You're all up there, you're all equals, you can't smoke inside the building, so you have to go stand out in the cold.

Well, at night there were no lights on the fantail. I'd go out and just stand there on the deck and nobody would know I was there, and I would listen to the smokers. For reasons I said, smokers talk about everything that's going on in the ship and about everyone. I could just sit there picking up intelligence.

The challenge for leaders is to figure out where there are pulse points in their organization and then to figure out a way to tap into them, whether overt or covert. If you understand what people are talking and thinking about, you'll get a pretty good understanding of what you have to do.

QUESTION: What metrics did you use to make sure your change efforts were on track?

ABRASHOFF: On a Navy ship, you've got all these inspections you have to pass like the engineering inspection. It inspects thirteen major programs and is the most thorough and intrusive inspection ever known to man. In addition, every other function on the ship gets inspected. It's the way the Navy does things.

I had a post office and the Navy says it's supposed to have so many one-cent stamps and so many forty-one cents, and so on. And once a year, a Navy postal guy would come and do a surprise audit of our post office to make sure that the books balanced and that we had all the stamps we were supposed to have.

In addition, I've got two corps men on the ship who tend to the health of the crew. We have to have our teeth examined once a year. We would get rated by how many cavities our sailors had. I would always get furious with sailors when they came back with cavities because that meant we couldn't get the best dental rating that we could.

So the bottom line is we inspected and measured everything—laundry, the ship's store, and every financial function on the ship. In addition, how well we employ our weapon systems got measured, our maintenance programs got inspected, and our safety programs got inspected. So we have all the metrics in the world to determine how well a ship is doing.

We have all these metrics but the truth is they don't turn people on. So I started thinking about metrics that make more sense.

QUESTION: What did you come up with?

ABRASHOFF: Retention was one of my metrics. When I took over the ship we were at 71% of our operating strength. That meant that 100% of the work was being done by a crew that was only 71% of its full component. 29% of our billets—jobs—were unfilled. Before me, no one in the Navy really looked at retention.

I also looked at our disciplinary rate and at our Workmen's Compensation Rate. We have a form of Workmen's Compensation in the Navy called Limited Duty. And if you have a headache or a bad back—some malady like that—you get transferred to a hospital. And because the Navy doesn't have enough doctors, you're assigned to the hospital and it might take six months until a doctor can even look at you.

So during that time you're picking up trash in the parking lot of the hospital instead of working on a ship. Nobody ever checks these soft metrics. I never knew to check them either. And I started adding up how many sailors had Workmen's Comp in my predecessor's last year—31 sailors took Workmen's Comp in that previous year—whereas in my last year only two sailors took Workmen's Comp.

The other metrics that turned me on were the disciplinary statistics. Twenty eight sailors in my predecessor's last 12 months got placed on report. And of those 28 sailors, 23 got thrown out of the Navy; and 14 were young African-American males even though they only made up 10% of the workforce. And so you have a subset of the population that's getting placed on report 50% of the time.

What we tried to do on the ship was to get across to sailors that we're all in this together. We developed what we called a unity program instead of a diversity program. I wanted the crew to focus on our common purposes as opposed to our differences.

You can't legislate what people do in their off time, but I sure as heck can legislate what goes on in my workplace. And the crew knew that we weren't going to tolerate sexual harassment or racial prejudice. We had only five disciplinary cases on four sailors in my last 12 months in command—one guy went twice. And I was looking at who they were and they were all white males. And I went back to the last time a black male got placed on a report—it was 17 months prior to that. It was a statistic that I followed after I left the ship and it was ten months after I left the ship till the next black male got placed on report.

So for 27 months, a subset of the population that used to make up 50% of the cases now made up essentially none. And it wasn't because we lowered standards or told people not to put black men on report. It was, hey, we're all in this together—you treat each other with respect and dignity and everybody rises up to perform at a higher level because that's what the expectations were.

So when I left the ship, I sent an e-mail to the Three Star Admiral and I said to him, "Why don't you hold us captains responsible for these metrics?" And the Three Star comes out—he'd been in the Navy for 35 years—and turns to his assistant and asks, "How can we gather these statistics?" And the assistant said we already collect them. He said to the Three Star, "All you do is push this button, and you can get them for every ship." Though we collected the information, nobody had ever used it before. So the Three Star ran the statistics and looked at it and found there was a 100% correlation. Ships that had the highest disciplinary rates and the highest Workmen's Compensation rates had the lowest standings in the Fleet.

It was a direct correlation. A month later, the commanding officers' fitness reports were changed to include these metrics—their retention rates, their disciplinary rates, and their Workmen's Compensation rates. It's now a standard by which captains are getting judged. My point is, like a lot of companies, we collected all the statistics; we were just paying attention to the wrong ones.

QUESTION: Retention, disciplinary, and Workmen's Compensation rates are one thing. But in business, aren't the financial metrics the one's that really matter?

ABRASHOFF: The criticism from people who hear me speak is that, in the Navy, I never had to worry about a top line or a bottom line. And it's true—I didn't. I had a different type of pressure to worry about. What I had to live with was that if I didn't do my job correctly, I would have to write to parents and tell them their sons or daughters weren't coming home. My point is, you need to use metrics that matter in your line of work. Financial metrics are only one type of performance measurement.

QUESTION: You said you were at only 71% of your full component of crew. How did you deal with recruitment and retention issues?

ABRASHOFF: You can't just go out and pick somebody off the street. You have to recruit them, get them through nine weeks of boot camp, and get them through additional training for the job they're going to fill. It takes a minimum of nine months after you lose somebody to get a replacement. And then the replacement that you get is somebody that's eighteen years old and has no experience. So, what we tried to do was to recruit our people every day so that they would stay and allow us to focus our time and get it from the basic level to the intermediate level or even to the advanced level.

QUESTION: What do you mean recruit them every day?

ABRASHOFF: I mean give them recognition, talk with them, listen to them, and, most importantly, get them to engage their brains.

I would always ask sailors why we'd do things a certain way. And they'd always respond, "That's the way we've always done it."

And it got so repetitive I knew that if that was the case, nobody was engaged. They were just going through the steps because somebody was standing over them with a hammer.

So the biggest thing I had to get over with them was that we don't do things because that's the way we've always done them. We do things because we've examined every alternative and this is the best way. And so by changing that mentality, when they had to research things and find out why we had to do things a certain way, they started coming up with ideas of how we could do things better and then got invested in it. They got excited and engaged. I mean, if you develop a new process or procedure, you have a stake in it. It's yours. That's what I mean by recruiting them every day.

Let me give you an example. To shoot Tomahawk cruise missiles is a very laborious procedure where you get the mission via satellite and sometimes you get the missions at the last minute—like when Saddam (Hussein) was still in power. The way it works is you have to program the missile to get to the first land point then the next and so on. This process can take about two hours.

Well, we knew we were going to be targeting Saddam because he had just thrown the weapons' inspectors out back in 1997, and we were being given probable scenarios for launches. Back then, none of the ships could meet the time requirements because we were getting the missions too late and we didn't have enough time to program and execute.

So, my Tomahawk guys got together and researched every step of the launch procedures. And lo and behold, when the Tomahawk was first used in Desert Storm, it used a terrestrial navigation system. But, as the decade wore on, the missile was upgraded to a GPS Navigation system. But Navy had never taken the terrestrial navigation system steps out of the procedures! So when my sailors did their research, they said, "Gee, these procedures no longer apply." We then sent a rapid critique to the powers that be in Honolulu who said, "Hey, you're right—you're authorized to use these new procedures." Letting my guys figure it all out was recruiting them every day. By the way, the processes they developed are now called the Benfold Procedures throughout the Navy. Four enlisted guys who were Tomahawk technicians came up with it. And if we didn't have a culture that asks, "Where does every step come from and why is it there?" we would have never been able to do that. Letting people think is really important if you want them to stay.

What we tried to do was to constantly challenge every aspect of our job to see if we couldn't do it better and be more efficient or to get something done faster. And we also push responsibility down to the lowest level. That keeps people motivated. And, by the way, if somebody had the aptitude I didn't care what their rank was or how many years they had in the job. If they had the aptitude and wanted to do it, we'd train them for it. That created a lot of commitment.

QUESTION: Are you saying that to get the job done you would ignore rank and seniority?

ABRASHOFF: Yes. Absolutely. When we're at sea, we'd have to stand watch 24 hours a day. And there are many positions on the ship where previously, only officers or chief petty officers would sit in that position. But when I took command of the ship, in six or seven of these critical mission areas, we only had one trained officer or petty officer to do the job. If I lost that one person, I couldn't have gotten the ship underway. That's not good. So, my first job was to train a second backup team to my first string. It worked so well we trained a third string. Eventually, we were three deep in every critical position. It worked so well that I asked the question why we had a rank attached to this position in the first place. Why couldn't we just open it up to anybody who had the aptitude and ambition to do it? The answer was there was no reason. For example, the watch on the bridge is manned by the Officer of the Deck followed by the Junior Officer of the Deck. In the history of the Navy, these positions have always been manned by officers. But I qualified a Chief Petty Officer in the job and I eventually qualified a First Class Signalman to be an Officer of the Deck. He was the Officer of the Deck and he had Lieutenant Junior Grade underneath him as Junior Officer of the Deck. Now that's creative! And that's certainly not the typical Navy hierarchy. And the sailors loved it.

QUESTION: Did you get any pushback from your superiors on that?

ABRASHOFF: One of the lowliest jobs among all the high-level Navy commanders is the interception operations job where we would stop cargo ships going into and out of Iraq and inspect for contraband. It was hot, dirty, grimy work—none of the ships wanted to do it. And there was this squadron commander who was in charge of it. So, I said, "Well, you know, let's make him look good."

So we became the best inspection ship in the Gulf. And he flew over and we would communicate with him through a console on the ship that was traditionally manned by an officer. The day he came onto our ship, he said he wanted to talk to the person he'd been talking to on the radio for this operation. I said "Here he is," and it was a Second Class Petty Officer. He said, "Seriously, where's the officer?" I replied, "Well, I've got him standing the watch." He asked, "You mean that I've been talking to a Second Class Petty Officer for the last three hours?" I said, "Yes, you were."

I thought I was going to get reprimanded but instead he was utterly amazed because he thought the person he was talking to was an officer because of the quality of the work that the guy was providing. So, in my view, if you've got the aptitude, I don't care what your rank is. People feel that. They understand it.

QUESTION: What you have described is really a leadership story. Is that a fair way to characterize your message?

ABRASHOFF: Yes. We are talking about leadership. One critical component of leadership is how effectively the leader communicates with his or her people. Most importantly is what the mission is and whether people understand its importance. The problem is that a lot of people just aren't clear as to what the mission is. That leads to uncertainly and to conflicting priorities. Communicating with the greatest amount of clarity so that everybody understands where you're going, what you're doing, and why it's important, is critical.

The other critical thing is that your people have to respect your technical abilities in order to believe you have sound judgment and can lead them in the right direction. I was at one large aerospace company doing a presentation on the day the CEO got fired. Somebody asked me, "Do you think you could be CEO of the company?" I said, "No, I don't." I said it because I don't know the first thing about how to make a plane fly. I don't know how to make rockets go through space and I don't have the technical competence to understand how the aerospace industry works. So no matter how great a leader I might be, if I don't have the technical competence, I'll never gain the respect of the people.

When I took command of the ship, the crew thought that their mission was to get their captain promoted. That's wrong. The mission of the ship is to be able to defend itself and the country's interests. I tried to show the crew that I understood this and I gave them reason to be confident in my decision-making ability and my knowledge and understanding of where we needed to go. They "rogered out" and got behind it.

A lot of CEOs forget that their employees want them to be competent in the areas that their company does business, not just in specialized skills, like finance. Leaders have to be technically competent and then they have to be able to engage their people so that they understand where they are being taken and why. The bottom line is, a leader has to convey to the people why it's in their own best interest to support him or her.

CHAPTER 2

Jan Fields

EXECUTIVE VICE PRESIDENT AND CHIEF OPERATING OFFICER, MCDONALD'S CORPORATION

It's Back to Basics

Jan Fields, Executive Vice President and Chief Operating Officer for North America is a 30-year veteran at McDonald's. She began her career working in a restaurant as part of the crew, standing shoulder to shoulder with cooks and cashiers. Over the years, Ms. Fields never lost her belief in the people at the front counter. They are responsible for many of her best ideas.

That's not all that unusual for the world's largest fast food company. The meritocracy that McDonald's founder, Ray Kroc, built in the '50s, has remained in place. Many of the company's leaders—like Fields—began their careers making French fries and burgers. Jim Skinner, McDonald's current Chief Executive Officer, began his career on a restaurant crew. At McDonald's, having worked on a crew is a badge of honor.

With a culture like that, it is no surprise that McDonald's has moved ahead by sticking to—and in some cases returning to—the basics.

According to Ms. Fields, McDonald's is a culture of collaboration between the company, its franchisees, and its suppliers. In the '50s, Ray Kroc, called it the company's "three-legged stool." Today, that kind of collaboration is thought of as McDonald's "secret sauce." In the McDonald's culture, each of these groups must succeed for the company to consider it a successful year.

In this interview, Ms. Fields discusses employee networks and the metrics she uses to manage the operations of one of the world's most recognizable and valuable brands.

QUESTION: Talent innovators get superior, measurable results from their teams. What is it that makes someone a talent innovator?

FIELDS: That's a tough question. A lot of the things that we do we don't even consider to be *innovative*. So I argue with people about this word all the time. It happens to be a word that's on our performance reviews—innovation. And I always tell people to be careful with what that means because in many ways people think of innovation as something new and different. But it could also mean how do you execute the old things, but in a more impactful way. And so people a lot of times are looking for new ways to do something when in fact they just weren't doing the old way right.

QUESTION: Can you give me an example of what you mean?

FIELDS: In our culture, one of the things that we've used as a catch phrase is back to basics. When it comes to people, it can be very simple things that matter, such as treating people the way you want to be treated, and listening for understanding and for inclusion. That's not anything new and different. It's simply following the basic rules. But I will tell you, in my opinion, you could innovate to the nth degree, but if you aren't doing the core things necessary to motivate a person, like finding out personally what each individual needs, it's not going to make a difference.

QUESTION: You have a lot of capital investment and real estate expenditures in your business. But ultimately it's a people business.

FIELDS: Absolutely. That is our core asset, and I think it is what sets McDonald's apart from others.

QUESTION: McDonald's is a great company with a global footprint. It owns one of the world's most valuable brands. And, recently you made a very significant turnaround. What accounts for that?

FIELDS: Our turnaround has been global. And if you're in the people business, which is what I believe, then you have to think our people were an awfully big part of that turnaround. In fact, I would put the figure at 95% of it.

QUESTION: What are some of the people initiatives that you undertook?

FIELDS: There were a couple of things. One would be to make sure you recognize who it is that you interact with when you talk about people. There's the customer. The customer is a very important element. Then there's the employee, which for us is also a very important element. And then there's the staff at the center or home office. So you actually have three different groups that you're trying to balance.

Of these three groups, the one I think where we made the biggest impact was in understanding the customer better. When people say the business turned around, it's not that we did something that different with our employees other than clarifying what our customers want. Then we taught out employees to give it to them. Now, we believe that employees will do what we do. They follow what we do as role models. It's the theory that if the boss does it, it must be okay for us to do it, good or bad. And the higher up you are, the more they're going to look at you. So we've adopted phrases such as the "shadow of the leader." These phrases really ring true from a McDonald's standpoint. So we do what we say we're going to do and we hope others will follow. But another important element for us has been to develop unique networks of employees. We now have a full department that's called diversity and inclusion, to make sure we're not leaving anyone out.

QUESTION: What types of people are in these networks?

FIELDS: We have a network for the African American, Asian, Hispanic, Gay/Lesbian, women, and then all others. We do it to make sure we're listening equally to everyone and that everyone has a seat at the table. I think that that was an element in our turnaround. We also have that same structure for our owner/operators of franchise restaurants. They don't call them networks, they call them organizations. But they are more or less the same.

QUESTION: These networks give people the ability to communicate better with each other?

FIELDS: Yes, and to communicate with top management, also. We're all plugged in.

QUESTION: Do you see communication as the critical component?

FIELDS: I think it's listening, really. And I also think it's being very clear and articulate on regarding the goal of the organization. The better clarity you can provide, the more likely people are going to follow it. It's when they're confused over what the goals are that there are problems. But it all goes back to what the customer wants. For example, our research showed that chicken was growing faster than beef. In the U.S. the average person consumes more chicken than beef. So, if that's the case, we have to have our menu offerings represent the same thing. So, our innovation—and where we were somewhat behind—was chicken. We increased the variety of chicken products and at the same time, we increased the *perceived* quality, even though in our mind we felt it was high quality. Now let me give you an example of what would be considered innovation, but really wasn't. Chicken McNuggets. It turns out McNuggets taste better if they have a mix of white and dark meat. Dark meat is where the flavor comes from, but people don't like to see dark meat. They are used to seeing white meat as their idea of perceived quality. As a result, we had to get on track with what the customer perceived as high quality and then figure out how to get the taste back into it. Was it in the breading or in other ways, like the sauces? In any event, we had to get ahead of the curve.

QUESTION: What does getting ahead of the curve mean when it comes to helping the company listen to your customers?

FIELDS: I'll give you an example. We introduced a chicken product we call Snack Wraps. When we introduced them they came only crispy. But immediately customers said, "Do you have this in grilled?" So we went back immediately and figured out how to sell a grilled product the same way. That's listening to our customers.

QUESTION: And that's also back to basics since it's a new product made from ingredients that were already in the restaurants. You didn't have to invent anything.

FIELDS: Exactly. That's why I said you've got to be careful when you use words. Something that's innovative is not necessarily new and different. It might be executing what you already did, just in a better way. I think that that's kind of the answer at McDonald's—take what you already have, and ask, "How do we execute it better?" You don't have to create anything new to do that.

Along these lines, let me give an example regarding our people that I think is important. We haven't really changed who our core people are. We still start people in many markets at minimum wage or market wages. But we provide them with more clarity about what we're working on. We give them the freedom to satisfy the customer, because they know that that's what the ultimate measure is. It motivates them. And then having formats and forums where they can give feedback.

I do a lot of speeches to our people and when I'm out talking to them I'm listening too. And it strikes me that our people always have a lot of brilliant ideas. So, I always tell them that's where we get our answers from. I can't think of any time when I'm out there talking to people that I don't come back from a trip with a list of ten different things that somebody told me. I'm thinking, oh my God, that's so simple. Why didn't we do that before?

QUESTION: Does that go all the way down to the people on the line?

FIELDS: Yes. It goes back to my point that listening is really important. You can see how it works every day. In our business in the last five years, we've taken employee turnover—the front line—which is our starting level down to about 125% a year. Industry-wise, turnover is upwards of 250% a year.

QUESTION: That's an incredible result. How did you do it?

FIELDS: By satisfying employees. We didn't change the fundamental structure, but employees, let's face it, like to be on winning teams. And if you understand why it is they're leaving, and you talk to them, and you show them some love, sometimes that's all people need. It's true. Personally, I happen to be a kisser and a hugger, so I'm one of the odd ones in that regard. And I always have to watch where I'm at. But people need some very basic things in their lives. It's not anything that's that difficult. But when you don't give it they'll go somewhere else to look for it. They'll leave. So, we have always had flexible hours, and good benefits, and free food, and uniforms. That has always been the case. But what I don't think we necessarily had before was clear direction. I used to sit in meetings with people from France, China, and Des Moines. And we all thought we're very different. Well, we're really not that different. There are four things at McDonald's that are common across the world. One of them is the economy. It impacts your business. The second is nutrition. Everybody around the world is interested in nutrition. The third one is value. We're known for value. And the fourth one is people. Around the world, no matter where you are it's the same four things. And so, yes, the temperature may be different, people may look different, you may even have somewhat different kinds of food. But at the end of the day those four things are the major strategic issues the customer is looking for from our business. That's what I mean by clarity.

QUESTION: What about the upward mobility of employees within the organization?

FIELDS: About 40% of our top management came out of crew. Me included. I started working at McDonald's at the front counter. So did our CEO.

QUESTION: Is that widely communicated in the organization?

FIELDS: Yes. Anybody who's been with us for a while will know that there is a clear career path that's possible. And I think that motivates people, too.

QUESTION: That path is open to everyone?

FIELDS: Yes it is. Now, it's different for a franchisee than it is for the company as a whole. A franchisee is not going to have a COO in most cases. They might have a director of operations or an area supervisor. It all depends on the size of their organization.

QUESTION: What are some of the other innovations?

FIELDS: Well, we now have succession planning for every job. As you know, we had two CEOs die within a year. Probably no one understands the importance of succession planning quite like McDonald's does. So, within our job responsibilities, we must at all times have at least two qualified people to take our place. Now, there used to be a time when that scared people because, gosh, I don't want anybody else taking my job. Everybody wants to be indispensable, right? But we've done it and we're pretty secure. Our upper-level turnover is extremely low. At the restaurant manager level, turnover is less than 25%. At a staff level, which is our people who work in offices and above, turnover is 15% or less. That's very low. The average person here has 25 years. And I'm a baby with 30 years! A lot of people start here at 16, so they can have 30 years of experience and only be 46 years old.

QUESTION: Your turnover throughout the organization is well below industry average.

FIELDS: Yes. So we do succession planning for everyone, which is a very important element, and we have two people who can replace every one of us, including our CEO. And in fact, talent management is one of our CEOs three big initiatives. The initiatives are: shareholder value, talent management, and nutrition. That puts talent management at a pretty high level.

In addition, everyone in the organization gets an annual review, and a mid-year review. We also do reviews that are pretty broad. So in the one that I sit through, the China president, the European president, and me are all in there together. We get to know each other and each other's people. And so we do that from a pretty broad standpoint, which again, is a little bit different organization-wise because it broadens your reach which is motivating to a lot of people.

QUESTION: That sounds like the network idea you described earlier. Is it?

FIELDS: It is. And our leadership is very involved. Which is nice. You know, people want that. They want to know that management is involved. Another interesting thing is that our franchisee base is represented on all of our different committees. So we have franchisees that are involved in our people initiatives. In fact, we have a franchisee that leads it. We have 2,600 franchisees in the US, and we know that if we utilize our size then that's a real strength. Instead of acting as 2,600 individual businesses, if we act as one, we're far stronger. We're stronger than anybody. Our system knows that pretty well, but a group of franchisees, along with support from the company, determined last year what we are going to do from a people standpoint. And they asked, can we all agree to do a number of things which we call BHOT for benefits, hiring, orientation, and training? Our idea—which we worked out with our franchisees—is that if we get those four things right it will help all of us. Everyone. If we can all provide a minimum level of benefits—you can go higher, but everyone has to go to at least the minimum—we benefit, which is insurances, etcetera. If we can hire smarter by using our Web site, we all benefit. Last year we took in 1.2 million applicants at the Web site. And then there's orientation. If people get started with the company the right way, so that they really understand about the culture of the company, then the chances of them succeeding are far greater. So, in the orientation, we talk to them about the customer and why we're in business. And the last of the four items is training. We do a standardized training. And we have e-training that we can do in multiple languages. McDonald's is all about consistency from one site to the other. So that's another innovation which we call the "people team."

QUESTION: Having your franchisees as members of these committees is impressive. It's not the case in the industry. In fact, some franchisees are at odds with the companies. Isn't it a little risky?

FIELDS: Well, some people say it is. But in my view, we want them involved. We actually call franchisee involvement our "secret sauce." Let me give you an example why it helps us. We are selling a product right now in California called the Angus Burger. That concept came from a franchisee. They were looking to be competitive with other companies on the West Coast that sell a big 1/3 pound burger. They felt like they were at a disadvantage by not having one. So, they worked together. A big group of them came up with this. They showed it to us. Then we had our menu team do the research and development on it, and it's now selling in the stores. Soon, we'll be taking it to New York and Columbus, Ohio. That came from our franchisees.

QUESTION: And it's spreading across the system.

FIELDS: Yes. You know, our founder established what he called a three-legged stool, and it was the franchisee, the company, and the supplier. That idea is still alive and well. Ray Kroc said from the very beginning: If all three legs of the stool can stand strong we'll be successful. If one leg of the stool starts to falter we're in trouble. And so everything we do has to be with all three legs of the stool in mind. It's our culture.

QUESTION: Has that concept evolved over time?

FIELDS: It's pretty basic to us. I think it was there in 1955. The idea of making sure that all three parties have a seat at the table, and that we define success when all three parties are successful. Ray Kroc's said, "None of us are as good as all of us." That idea is as alive today as in the beginning. And so when we talk about how things have changed, what we mean is that we're going back to the basics. We sometimes get sidetracked along the way, and so by making sure that all three legs are strong, by making sure that we're listening, and actually taking care of the customer, giving them what they want, that is what makes us successful. But it doesn't happen by itself. It is the responsibility of the leader to set the tone. And we have to behave in the ways that we want our organization to behave. If we don't, they don't think it's real.

QUESTION: You've got to walk the talk.

FIELDS: Yes. That's what we mean by the shadow of the leader. If I want you to do this, then I've got to be doing it too.

QUESTION: How do you monitor the system to make sure the shadow is falling widely enough to be seen and that people really are following?

FIELDS: The system is kind of automatic. You can feel when things are not right. And because we're a very open culture, people will tell you real quickly. They'll tell you, you're not listening, or this leg of the stool feels a little short right now. And we pay a lot of attention to our customer count and our major numbers. You know, sales, profitability, and the success of all three legs.

QUESTION: Are there other metrics, people metrics, which you pay special attention to?

FIELDS: Yes. We have a lot of metrics. But I'll tell you the key one that I look at as the COO. I look at turnover. That one is very important and I monitor it closely. I do it annualized, but I also look at how many people left us in their first 90 days. It tells me if we're doing a good enough job in hiring and orienting. I monitor that figure—how many people left us in their first 90 days. It's a standard report that everybody gets. And actually it's low. It's much lower than it used to be. The second metric I pay a lot of attention to is how many we lost over the last 12 months. On an operational level, I look at how many people we actually have per store, which is system-wide and includes franchisees. In fact, in our system, people really can't tell the difference between a franchisee and a company owned store.

I also look at it as a sales success. There's a direct correlation between the successes of the people—that the turnover is low, that we've got good staff numbers for the restaurants—and the sales numbers and customer satisfaction. We can tie all of those together. You know, in our business we figure that it costs about $700 for every person we turn over. It costs us that in training, uniforms, etcetera. I was just telling somebody the other day; do you know that you would make $35,000 more in profit if you reduced your turnover by such and such an amount?

QUESTION: Are there other metrics you look at?

FIELDS: We do employee surveys twice a year online with an outside company. They have gotten better. Our financial incentives are tied to employee satisfaction. That's for all workers. Everybody. Organizational bonuses are directly linked to employee satisfaction as one of the measures we get graded on. If our employee satisfaction has not improved we lose a certain percentage of the bonus.

I did something this morning as a little bonus because we like to do some fun stuff in our office. I've got about 2,000 people in this office. So, we cooked breakfast for one of the floors. We had an omelet station, and everything. But what's so funny is that everyone was so excited about it. I mean, think about it, breakfast for one of the floors. The whole thing couldn't have cost me $500. But it got a lot of people pretty excited. Then somebody said, "Why don't you do this every day?" And I said, "You know what? If we did it every day, by the end of the week people would be complaining. It would raise the bar too high." So when you talk about satisfaction numbers, if all things remain steady and good, it should go up. But the fact is they don't, not very easily. Because we have low turnover, people start to expect more. They expect it especially because they know our goal is to satisfy our customers. So they think they should be satisfied, too. And they're right. They should. I mean, you can't say you're going to satisfy customers if you don't satisfy your employees. But it is funny. So the metrics, they'll improve one or two points a year. Last year they improved by seven points. But there's also a balance. If we had 100 percent satisfaction and we weren't making a profit, we'd all be out of a job.

CHAPTER 3

Dr. Victor Fung

GROUP CHAIRMAN OF THE LI & FUNG GROUP OF COMPANIES

One Big Company, One Big Family

Victor Fung presides over his family's group of companies—Li & Fung, Hong Kong's largest export trading company and an innovator in supply chain management—in a way that seamlessly blends hard-edged notions of economic performance and growth with softer notions of "heritage," "family values," and "loyalty."

A former professor at the Harvard Business School, Fung runs the company, founded in 1906 by his grandfather, with his brother, William. Fung credits what he calls the company's "open architecture"—its respect for local cultures in the more than 40 countries in which it operates—as a key factor in the company's global expansion over the past ten years.

In the post-9/11, post-Enron world of increased vigilance, skepticism, and corporate disenfranchisement, Li & Fung places a premium on loyalty that is measured, in part, by length of service. But even more importantly, Fung acknowledges that loyalty is not a one-way street. Loyalty must be from the employee to the company and from the company to the employee. As a result, working for Li & Fung, is more like becoming part of Fung's family than just taking a job. To make that work requires a very selective recruitment process.

At Li & Fung, once you're in, you're *in*. Traditional human resource departments are replaced by an emphasis on entrepreneurial spirit, backed by systems (financial, accounting, marketing) and structures robust enough to support that spirit. The bonus process is so transparent that managers set their own bonuses based on performance. There are no surprises. As much as possible, managers are given the same freedoms that any independent entrepreneur might have, right down to the notion that there is no cap on their upside earnings.

At Li & Fung, "family" members have the power to start their own businesses.

Fung is often heralded as an innovator who has transformed his company while steering it through the straits of economic and market shifts. In this interview, Fung explains his company's open architecture and how it has led to a decade's worth of stupendous growth.

QUESTION: Often, when two managers use the same management tools and techniques, one gets far better results than the other, with respect to managing, motivating, and leveraging human capital. Why is that?

FUNG: At the most basic level, it has something a lot of people call EQ (emotional intelligence quotient). If you and I both have the same set of tools, techniques, and so on, and we both have skills that are comparable, then if you have a better way of dealing with people and of making them feel comfortable, you will get better results.

QUESTION: So emotional intelligence is critical to being a talent innovator?

FUNG: Yes. People have different traits. In my view, it's one thing to have positive traits, but it is another *not* to have a lot of negative traits. People can turn against you or simply not follow your leadership, or even work against your goals. And you might not even know they are doing this if you have a lot of negative traits. That's a problem. People emphasize or even overemphasize the positive aspect of a good leader but they also must be aware that really good leaders have an absence of negative aspects.

QUESTION: How would you define some of those negative attributes?

FUNG: Well, the Chinese have a good way of doing it. You know, there are positive traits like trust, respect, and that sort of thing. You could be a very smart guy, really, but if people can detect that you're not really sincere or heartfelt—that you don't have a basic respect for people—then people will be turned off by you. I mean, you might do very well as a one-man entrepreneurial show, but if you want to be a big team leader, it's a different matter. You need positive traits and an absence of negative ones.

QUESTION: Your company is made up of people from all walks of life and from many different communities, backgrounds, and nationalities. Does what you are saying cut across these differences?

FUNG: Well, I think the fundamentals I just mentioned cut across all cultures.

QUESTION: How many nationalities do you have working at Li & Fung?

FUNG: We have people from over 40 countries working in our company, and while we obviously see ourselves as very much of a Hong Kong–based multinational, we are also global. My grandfather started the company in the southern part of China and we will always be very proud of our cultural heritage. But one thing we try very hard not to do within Li & Fung is to impose our area's culture on other people. Another thing we work hard on is what we call "open architecture," in terms of really working with people from different cultures. I think that's one of the things that has allowed us to really grow on a global basis the way we have done in the last ten years.

QUESTION: Could you describe what you mean by open architecture?

FUNG: Yes. It's really the idea of being proud of your own culture and respecting other people's cultures, and not necessarily demanding that people conform to a single culture. If I may say it, a lot of multinationals tend to come from a particular part of the world, and they tend to try to make the entire company everywhere around the globe adapt to that same cultural behavior. We don't want to do that. The last thing we want is for people to feel that we are fitting everyone into a Chinese culture. I say that even though we are

Chinese and we come from a Chinese heritage. What we do want, though, are things like family values. So, we respect long service. One of the things I try not to miss is to personally give out long-service awards.

QUESTION: That's a great idea. Why do you do it?

FUNG: We are in every sense a very entrepreneurial company and—I think—a strong meritocracy. We also have a huge respect for talent and performance. But we have not forgotten the fact that loyalty counts, too. I think the values we feel strongly about are sometimes rejected by other multinationals. I think we absolutely feel that family values are very important and should really be the basis of the company, and the thing that underlies the whole company. So loyalty is a very important aspect of what we are really all about.

QUESTION: In an entrepreneurial environment like Hong Kong, where people move around a lot, how do you make people understand that loyalty is a virtue?

FUNG: Well, it's really the way our value system works. And, to some extent, it's a process of self-selection. The people that don't feel high levels of loyalty aren't compatible with who we are as a company. So, chances are they won't be hired in the first instance. And, if they are hired, they won't stay with us very long, and so it's sort of a weeding out process that happens over time. On the other hand, the people who share our family values and place those values in high esteem remain with us.

QUESTION: How do family values work in practice?

FUNG: I'll give you an example. Whenever there is a conflict between work and any aspect of a person's family and personal life, I have no hesitation at all in telling people that family always comes first. I would never pressure anybody to put work before family, and I think that's very much appreciated by all our people. Our philosophy is very simple. If a person doesn't have a good home life and that person's family isn't strongly behind them, it is unlikely that the person could really perform at top potential inside the company. That's very clear. I think in a lot of so-called professional companies, there is an artificial separation between family life, personal life, and the company. We don't do that. We think it is very important that somebody in our company has a very strong and coherent family unit behind them.

QUESTION: How else does that work?

FUNG: I'll give you another example. We just celebrated our 100th birthday. One of the things we did when we came up with the celebration of the 100th anniversary was to say that while most companies would do a big celebration with a lot of external commotion, we would not do that. So we said no, no, no. Instead, our celebration was a totally internally oriented celebration. We don't want external publicity. Our focus was unabashedly internal, and not only were we focused on the staff members themselves, but also on the families. So in Hong Kong, for example, we had country celebrations. We kicked off with a country celebration in Hong Kong in which we took over Disneyland. We invited family members to spend a day with us at Disneyland. I can tell you it went over extremely well. And, truthfully, it actually bought us a huge amount of external publicity by word of mouth because of our family orientation. When you make a person's family feel good, the staff member feels good, the staff members talk, and we get a tremendous amount of positive word-of-mouth advertising in the community and beyond. And it all comes from within. From feeling the loyalty within. These good feelings often exude into our external PR. That's the way we do PR at Li & Fung. You never see Li & Fung corporate advertising. We don't do stuff like that. It's positive word of mouth that has to be built on good feelings. It's what our people say. As a result, I think we have a pretty reasonable reputation. Positive word of mouth comes from a real, internal strength, and that internal strength comes from our focus on family values. That's how it works.

QUESTION: That's a very different approach. For many multinationals, the leader's primary focus is on the financials.

FUNG: Yes. That's true. But it's our values that make us strong. We are a multinational in every sense of the word. I would say that our systems and our way of doing business—our business model is perhaps comparable to any multinational originating from any country in the world. But we have the additional strength of being a family company, and of being able to care about these values. And I think that's what our family orientation does. If I'm a professional manager looking for a strong performance over a five-year contract, then I'm going to do one set of things, right? But if my objective is to make sure that this company is passed on in a very strong way to my children and my grandchildren and to their children, I will look at things differently and have a different set of objectives from short-term objectives. I think people can see that. So the question is how do you actually use that set of values? How do you, in a sense, marry those values with all the techniques that we learned at Harvard Business School, in terms of systems, processes, and structures?

QUESTION: Do you have a set of metrics against which you hire people? Do you test them, for example, to see if they fit those values?

FUNG: We're beginning to do a little bit more testing just to see whether people have what we call negative biases or traits. Sometimes it doesn't come through in an interview because the person could be very well rehearsed and very slick. So I think we're doing a bit more testing. But most of the time, it's really about spending time with the person and really seeing the person in different settings. We do a lot of acquisitions and a lot of investing in companies. One golden rule I have had over the years is that I try not to really make a final decision to invest in a company until I've actually seen the entrepreneur in his natural habitat in the company. I know that if I spend some time there with him, I will have a much better feel for the culture of the company. That's important. If we take a guy out of his environment and start spending a lot of time in a hotel room or in conference rooms, it isn't the same. You've got to spend time in a person's own habitat to see who they really are.

QUESTION: Doesn't this put a huge set of demands on you as the leader?

FUNG: Well, I used to do it all myself. Now, our top management is my surrogate. We have much more of a group leadership style now. In addition, my brother is my partner and extremely active.

I say I used to do all that myself when the company was a little smaller. Now, of course, I'm not able to do that. So people I trust do it. The important point is we still do it. We still get to know people in their own habitats.

QUESTION: Your values are critical to your management and leadership style. Are they what makes your company unique?

FUNG: Well, I think they are certainly the key distinguishing factor. But the truth is, if you read our set of corporate values, 80% of them will read like any other company's. But what I'm doing now is emphasizing our differences. One is our commitment to family values. Another is that we still have a very strong entrepreneurial spirit. This is manifested at our company in the fact that while we are a reasonably large trading company, we do not act like a bureaucracy. In fact, we actually organize ourselves into small entrepreneurial units that are able to compete extremely well with small private businesses and with our competitors. You know how small trading companies operate. They are people who pick up their customers at their airport. They are people who know the first names of their customers and of their customers' wives. They know where their customers' children go to school. We feel those are the people we are competing with—small entrepreneurs. So we must organize ourselves in the same way they do. As a result, we have 170 different profit centers, each run by what we call a "Little John Wayne." Little John Waynes are the entrepreneurs within our company who run their own shows. They are real entrepreneurs.

QUESTION: How well does it work?

FUNG: It actually works very well for us. But what it means is that we have to recruit entrepreneurs. We have to recruit the type of person who—if they didn't work for us—would be running their own business. Those are the type of people we want. We don't want corporate types. We don't want people who can write good memos. We want entrepreneurs.

QUESTION: How do you keep a group of John Waynes, together, working as a team?

FUNG: First, we give them a lot of freedom and let them really operate as if they're running their own business. But we also give them totally centralized finance and IT functions. So they have autonomy, but they also have the support base of a large company.

QUESTION: So you create support and conditions for success and then let your entrepreneurs go out and do it?

FUNG: Yes, that's what we do. But I think you've got to think very hard about the type of environment you're creating. We are trying to create a *real* entrepreneurial environment—and I emphasize the word *real*. What I am saying is that we've got to take a person who basically says, "I don't want to work for a big company, I want to run my own business," and hire them. Now why would someone like that have a reason to stay in Li & Fung and continue to work with us? Those are questions we have to answer. So that's why we are organized in small, entrepreneurial units. That's why we have our Little John Waynes. But it's also the way we have developed our incentive system. You know, management by objectives, 360-degree evaluations, and all that, is strange to us. We basically look at the bottom line and share a percentage of the bottom line with each of our entrepreneur-managers at the end of every year. Our people can calculate their own bonuses. These are not things that depend on a boss's decision. It's their own entrepreneurial drive that moves us forward and they share in its proceeds. And one thing we always make sure of is that we never cap anybody's upside. We think that the worst thing that you could do is say to someone that you can only earn a bonus that's, say, equivalent to 50% of your annual salary. That's the worst thing you could do to anybody.

QUESTION: Why is that?

FUNG: Because we don't believe in capping our people's upside. We are either entrepreneurs or not. If we are entrepreneurs, then we must duplicate as much as we can the environment of the entrepreneur. And no entrepreneur ever says "this year my earnings will be constrained to be no more than 50% of my annual salary." Isn't that right? Independent entrepreneurs don't cap their upsides. Why should we? It's a unique system that you don't find in multinationals. By the way, we never lost anybody in the company at the senior management level because he said "I'm not getting enough pay."

QUESTION: That's a very different system.

FUNG: Yes. But we are screening for people who have a real entrepreneurial spirit. That's why our whole philosophy is different. And we really mean what we say. We foster an entrepreneurial spirit and we have systems and structures to support that.

QUESTION: Is this something other companies can do, or is it unique to your business and your business model?

FUNG: People don't think like we do. They have huge human resource departments and structures. They don't foster real entrepreneurship. Let me give you a little bit of history. We evolved our system. When we inherited the company, we were a very Chinese-family type of company in which at the end of every year, the patriarch would hand out red packets of bonuses to each employee. Nobody knew how it was determined, whether there was favoritism or whatever. I'm sure there wasn't that much favoritism, but the process was totally opaque. So my brother and I basically said that the old system didn't work too well, and we decided to get away from it. We moved 180 degrees the other way. Basically, we say, you set your bonus. You don't even have to depend on somebody else evaluating you. You tell me at the end what it is. It's based on all the numbers for the particular unit.

QUESTION: It sounds like what you're describing is more like a partnership with your employees.

FUNG: You might say that. It's in fact a partnership with a group of very active entrepreneurs. But the thing is, they stay with us and grow with us. Hence, loyalty is important. And I think it's also good that they feel part of a much bigger family. And this stretches around the world.

QUESTION: And do you find that this system works in all cultures?

FUNG: Absolutely, absolutely. People told us this will never work in Japan, but we're doing the same thing there. People respond.

QUESTION: Does that mean corporate culture can be stronger than the local culture in which someone is brought up.

FUNG: I would say so. We have a different model and we're quite transparent about it. I think a lot of people are aware of it. I think maybe it's not easy for other companies to adopt our model—our system—hook, line, and sinker. But aspects of the philosophy do make sense and other companies can adopt them.

QUESTION: In China, economic activity is so hot that attracting and retaining talent is a major issue. Have people looked at your model from the standpoint of retaining talent?

FUNG: Sure. People come to talk to us all the time. Our story is fairly well-known. And it's exactly the point that you just mentioned. If we have a world talent shortage, we don't want to compete like all the other multinationals are competing. If people are working on a scale and things like that, then maybe a slightly more lucrative or attractive offer would actually move them immediately. But what we offer is the opportunity, frankly, to do your own thing; be an entrepreneur and be with a group of people who have similar sets of values. And at the same time, if you really do well with the sweat of your brow, you're able to make a lot of money. I think that makes people feel good.

QUESTION: But will they need someone as unique as you to make it work?

FUNG: No, no, no. What I'm talking about is none of this inspirational fearless leader business. We have a culture and a large group of managers at the top who see that what we do works.

CHAPTER 4

Anne Ruddy

EXECUTIVE DIRECTOR, WORLDAtWORK

One Size Does Not Fit All

Anne Ruddy, President of WorldatWork, has impressive background credentials. She's a certified compensation professional, a chartered property casualty underwriter, and has extensive experience leading and managing large organizations at the highest level. But that description does not really do Ms. Ruddy justice. Most importantly, she is a talent innovator who uses her organization, WorldatWork, and its staff of 160, as a laboratory to increase knowledge and transfer ideas to its membership regarding human capital.

At WorldatWork, and previously as a senior executive at a number of large companies, including Travelers Insurance, Ms. Ruddy has been on a relentless hunt for talent. When she meets someone, her first instinct is often to ask herself, how can we work together? What can we do?

At WorldatWork, one of the most important not-for-profit associations of professionals in the field of total rewards, benefits, and work life, Ms. Ruddy's takes her lifelong passion for talent innovation directly to her members, many of whom come from the largest and most important companies in the world. At conferences, meetings, and in its publications, Ms. Ruddy not only helps her members learn, she also helps them to innovate. In this interview, Ms. Ruddy explains how one size does not fit all.

QUESTION: One of the talent-innovation issues for which you are known is total rewards, which links together employee compensation, benefits, rewards, and other forms of payments and recognition into a single package made up of a number of variable parts. How did the concept evolve?

RUDDY: Let me start with what I think is responsible for so many of today's changes in the workplace: Different people have different motivators. As our society changes, many of our organizations are also changing. As a result, people need to be looked at much more holistically than they were in the past. That includes the way they are rewarded and recognized. People want different things depending on their age, gender, racial background, culture, and country. That means it's essential for managers and business leaders to think beyond the narrow idea of salary or paycheck. Instead, they need to recognize people as individuals in order to get them to contribute as much as they're capable of contributing in a workplace. So, for me, the topic of rewards is really part of something bigger, the issue of employee engagement.

QUESTION: Why is it necessary to broaden the concept from rewards to engagement?

RUDDY: It comes from the fact that people in the workplace differ. It also comes from the fact that unlike, perhaps, in our parents' generation, the workplace isn't just in one country or in one city anymore. It's global. In fact, oftentimes the workplace isn't even a physical premise any longer. It's everywhere, thanks to electronics, telecommunications, computers, and networking. So I think those changes are what brought it about. I say that because if you look back in history, all the way back to the '30s and '40s, rewards was mostly about paying people and deciding, "gee, a paycheck is what I really need." This was particularly the case during the Roosevelt era—the whole issue then was to take care of people by giving them enough money to live on.

QUESTION: What came next in the way rewards evolved?

RUDDY: We needed to look at things like health care and understand that in exchange for the work people give us during their working lives, their lives after work also needed to be regarded as important. That's how the concept of pension arrived.

QUESTION: And then?

RUDDY: It all changed again as we watched a new generation of women emerge as a major part of the workforce. When that happened, we began to recognize that, yes, work was important, paychecks were important, health care was important, pensions were important, but what about this thing called *family?* How were people going to balance work and family together? Couple that with the way the whole world has changed and how much energy and effort it takes to keep somebody really engaged in the workplace and, in addition, to be able to afford to take care of their families. Now, add to that that the fact that you have two income-earning families trying to have children and support other dependents including large extended families. That's when the issue of work life balance emerged and became important, along with issues like dependent care and employee assistance.

QUESTION: When some people hear the term *total rewards* they think that there is some standardized formula that will work everywhere in the world. Is that a misapprehension?

RUDDY: That's definitely a misapprehension. Total rewards models are based on five major components. There is compensation, benefits, work life, performance and development, and career opportunities. The concept is that all of these elements are in play everywhere. It's the mix that varies. The mix of these components can vary by workforce, by industry, by culture. If, for example, you are in a culture outside of North America—Western Europe, perhaps—the concept of pension is essential. In fact, it's mandated by the government in some countries. It's something that is a very big piece of the overall pie. As a result, that component will look very different as a proportion of the total rewards of someone working in the US where pensions are viewed differently and the government is not so involved. In addition, that component will look different because in the US, compared with Europe, the turnover rate for most employees is high so there is no accumulation of seniority and no pension.

So the same five components will vary depending upon the work-force. What we see is that smart companies look at each of these components as different levers that they can pull. How exactly they pull them is dependent on the local environment.

QUESTION: Is it the aim of a total reward program to look at human capital from the strategic perspective and to reward people in ways that achieve a company's overall objectives?

RUDDY: Absolutely. Let's use the example of the dotcoms. In those days, when many startups didn't always have enough cash to pay people well, they still needed a lot of really smart people to build the business. To get there, companies used the concept of stock options. As a result, broad-based equity participation plans really took off during that era. It was out of necessity and it was due to the environment of the time. These programs were the only way organizations without much cash could attract and motivate people. And, for the generation that worked in those dotcom companies, many of whom were in their early twenties, they were willing to invest enormous amounts of time and energy in exchange for equity in order to help build those companies. As a result, owner-ship was a very powerful attractor during the dotcom era. During this period, companies that weren't dotcoms found themselves competing for the same IT talent. These other companies did not have ownership or equity plans and had to adjust their way of thinking to deal with the external forces of the time. They wouldn't have been able to attract the best talent, otherwise. So the non-dotcom companies developed programs of their own. It's very interesting to see how this has changed over the years. Trends begin somewhere and then they move along. When they do, companies change.

QUESTION: Does that mean there are half-lives for total rewards pack-ages? Do they have to be reevaluated periodically?

RUDDY: Yes and no. The fundamentals—the five major components—remain the same. They are sustainable in the long run. But good companies regularly look across their demographics, they look at their competitors and they say, "What does the workforce need now?" Smart companies do these things before the bleeding begins. They do them before their employees leave, before their top talent is taken by somebody else. Many other companies unfortunately wait until the bleeding is so serious that it's almost impossible to stop it. Sometimes they begin acting when it is too late.

QUESTION: In your experience working with talent innovators, how do they match a total rewards program to their organization's needs? Where do they start?

RUDDY: The real innovators start with their business strategies. They connect their total rewards program to the company and its goals. Human capital to me is just another major part of the balance sheet. You have your bricks and mortar, your technology, and you have everything else. But it's the intellectual capital and the human capital that creates a competitive difference between your company and your competitor's company. So, you cannot even begin to create a strategy to reward, recognize, attract, retain, and motivate your workforce if you don't know where your company is going. You need to understand what your opportunities are going to be—*not just in the current year*—but in the future, as the organization moves forward and tries to accomplish its goals. That's why I say that first and foremost, anyone who thinks about a rewards strategy has to start by asking what are the business' goals, where is it going, and why does it want to go where it wants to go? Then, you have to ask, what do I need to create a total reward plan in order to help make that happen?

QUESTION: What do you do next?

RUDDY: The next step is to look at the culture of the organization, at the jobs and the functions inside the organization. As you do that, you need to measure the talent that exists in your organization today in order to find the talent gaps you need to fill so that the organization can get where it needs to go.

QUESTION: That sounds like you need some well-developed metrics in order to make sure that your total rewards system is working and to recalibrate it if it isn't. What types of metrics do you see real talent innovators using?

RUDDY: The basic ones that almost everybody looks at are usually too elementary. They are metrics like, "What's our turnover rate? What's the average tenure of our employee population?" If those are the metrics, then I say, "Okay, tell me what they mean?" I always tell people, "If you're driving a car and the only thing you pay attention to is the speedometer, and you never look at any other gauge, then you're really going to regret it. You're going to regret it because if the temperature gauge goes into the red zone and you're just driving along, you're going to have a problem. And, if the gas gauge goes to empty, that's another indication that something's wrong." The idea that an organization can use a single metric to measure human capital is no less dangerous. But what's even worse is that when companies use a single metric, the one they choose is often wrong. So, I tell people to think about the whole dashboard.

Some of the innovative measures we've seen—and that we use—are measures like revenue per employee that we benchmark against virtually all of the associations that we work with. That's a simple metric. We also look at the cost of compensation as a share of the total rewards package—how much do does our workforce's pay cost as part of the entire employment deal? Then we take a look at something that I think measures return on human capital—which is a very interesting concept. We take the cost of all of our programs, whether they're salary or benefits, and calculate a metric based on the average dollar cost against revenue.

QUESTION: Can you explain that in a little more detail?

RUDDY: Yes. The way we get to a true ROI on our employees is to use this formula: Company revenue, minus operating expenses, minus the cost of compensation and benefits. We put those figures on the top line. Then, we divide that by the cost of all compensation and benefits programs.

If I look at our own organization, WorldatWork, the results are really interesting. For every dollar that we spent on compensation and benefits for our employees in 2005, they gave us back a dollar

and two cents. So, in essence, we had a positive return on investment. Now, that's a very sophisticated measure that a lot of companies don't think about. But when you use a metric like that you
can begin to ask, am I spending my money in the right places? Am
I getting—as a chief financial officer wants to know—a good return
on my investment? This metric ties directly to the company's strategy. If you believe that most organizations judge the success of
their business strategies by their revenue gross, then this metric tells
you if your compensation and benefits costs are behind, equal to,
or better than how you're growing your revenue.

To give you some other ideas about how we look at things, we
measure 14 different factors every year. We do that just to say,
"Okay, we're looking at the dashboard now. How's everything
running? Does anything look odd?" Some of those 14 factors are
compensation that cost a percentage of revenue. That's interesting
to look at. We look at something absolutely crazy that many people do not look at—income per total full time employee. The formula for that is revenue minus operating expense that gives you
what you're paying people divided by the number of employees.
The usefulness of that measurement is that it gives you a sense of
income per person on an annual basis. It's a very interesting little
formula for us. The whole point of these metrics is to quantify the
value of people.

QUESTION: A lot of people have said that you run your association as
a kind of laboratory to see how well the ideas work that you're
talking about with your members. Is that true?
RUDDY: Absolutely. When you are the association that works with
people who are rewards professionals, you better walk the talk. If
you don't, they'll find out pretty quickly. The most embarrassing
thing would be to hold meetings about total rewards and about
how to build packages that include flexibility and career opportunities and job enrichment and all of that, but not do it here. So
we take a lot of what we learn in this organization and we try it. We
try different things in a very safe environment in terms of experi-
ments. When you have a workforce like ours of 160 people, many
of whom are rewards professionals, you can be sure that they expect

to employ what we what we talk about with our members in our own organization.

QUESTION: You spent a lot of time thinking about globalization and the HR function. What have you learned?

RUDDY: It all goes back to some fundamental principles in rewards. You pay people to do work. All jobs have content. All jobs get valued and are worth something, no matter where you are in the world. All of these major premises exist everywhere. What needs to happen as you move around the globe, however, is to understand how things are different in each locality What is important? What are the values of the culture and society and what are the rules and regulations? What's considered acceptable and not acceptable? So I'm not sure exactly which company first used the word "glocal"—to mean merging what's global with what's local—but it is a good concept, and a true one.

When we go to Asia, whether it's to teach or conduct a conference or have a networking session, what you see is an emerging workforce that is becoming sophisticated and increasingly interested in US practices. "What do you do in the US?" they ask us all the time. "Tell us what you do because we want to do it too but we also want to make it better."

Europe has a much more mature social structure; a much more mature business and economic environment. You have many companies that have been established and have done business and have very complete infrastructures and long tenured people. So, it is a very different environment and you cannot simply say, "Here in America this happens, therefore it would be good for you to do this too." You have to understand where you are and what the needs are there. Is it about networking? Is it about education? Is it about understanding how to make changes to a workforce that's suddenly 30% female when five years ago it was 2%? How do you deal with that? The best companies, many of whom we work with, really do "glocalize" things as they move around the world.

QUESTION: As companies become more global, do you see them incorporating ideas from around the world?

RUDDY: There's more two-way exchange now than there ever was. But capital structures are so different between, say, the European and US markets. Even so, there will be changes. One reason for that is that shareholders are everywhere now. It's not just Americans owning American companies, or Europeans owning European companies. Companies are now owned by shareholders from around the world. They want to have a voice in how—*and how much*—people are paid. They want to know how CEOs, in particularly, are rewarded.

With respect to Asia, I think the degree to which there is a cross-fertilization of ideas depends on the country. There really are some big differences between countries, especially in emerging market countries like China versus developed market countries like Singapore. For example, at present I see a lot of Chinese companies struggling with things like motivation. How do you motivate, reward, and recognize somebody who has improved his or her performance? While the Chinese are focusing on issues like that, companies in Singapore and Hong Kong are very sophisticated and well-developed.

QUESTION: In some global companies, there are differences between the way people are motivated, rewarded and recognized, depending upon the country where they are based. Sometimes that creates tensions, even jealousy. Do you see those tensions within companies? How do talent innovators handle them if they occur?

RUDDY: In some countries, like Germany, companies are very heavily regulated and welfare benefits and a lot of labor practices are legislated into law. No single company can change that or affect it. So that's the environment in which some companies are going to have to operate. On the other hand, if a company's philosophy is that within each market people are going to be rewarded and recognized *appropriately,* and it still can't stop the grumbling, then the leaders have to go home and say to themselves, "we're still treating people right, wherever they are in this world, and that's okay." I say that because companies don't really have the option to legislate within the US all of the rules that French companies operate under with respect to vacations or pay. And if they did have that option, maybe even that wouldn't motivate people in the US anyway. Good companies look at the environments in which they operate, the people who are there, and the systems and metrics. And then they try to develop programs that work for individuals.

QUESTION: What about when you have a multinational team working together on a single development project and all of them are operating under different compensation and benefit systems and recognition systems?

RUDDY: When you establish global teams, you have to figure a formula that levels the playing field for everybody. If you have a participant from India, another from Mexico, and one from Canada, Spain, and the US, you've got to build a teaming concept on top of all those different rewards systems that say if you win, you win as a team, and you win big as a team.

QUESTION: So you develop the team, and it shares in some special things, like recognition or access to top management, and that helps it work together to succeed?

RUDDY: Yes. Most commonly we see organizations put together huge task teams to build something or to improve a process and never look at the rewards structure for the team as a *team*. That makes you say, "Wait a minute, if it isn't all about you anymore, if it's about the team, then why are you rewarding *individual* performance?" If your whole system is based on individual contributions, and yet you put somebody onto a special team and have taken off their billable hours—which is how they are rewarded and promoted—then how can you expect good team results? It just doesn't work that way.

QUESTION: You have your finger on the pulse of many important trends. How do you make certain your members are aware of these things?

RUDDY: Well, we use our conferences obviously. But we also do a lot more. We do a lot of blogging about trends we're picking up. Every day on our Web site we update news about what's happening that affects people in our field. We're constantly posting information and ideas from the U.S., Europe and Asia, because we really care what's happened in markets like China today because that will affect us all tomorrow. We also try on a weekly basis, to provide our members with new information. It's all electronic. And then we have two other publications that we use—our monthly magazine and our quarterly journal. In those publications we look at case studies and at emerging issues. For example, we examined GlaxoSmithKlein's resilience program. They have a very good resilience program for their workforce. We've highlighted it. What we try to do is shed light on the best practices that are out there. We think it's our obligation to know what's out there and to make sure our members have access to best practices and the most current information that's out there.

QUESTION: You're a membership organization and not a publicly-traded company. Is there a difference between the way public and private companies should think about talent?

RUDDY: Smart organizations and companies of all kinds say, "You know what? Publicly traded or otherwise, we have to maximize the investment return on the human part of our capital. It's the one part of our capital that cannot be duplicated." Everything companies do can be duplicated—except for their people. Yes, there are patents and things like that. And Starbucks does have good coffee. But somebody can invent a new system and have better coffee. But what someone else can't do is replace the human side of making coffee. That is totally proprietary. It is what they're really in the business of building. So my point is that talent innovators understand that if they have to choose between having really, really smart people doing great things, on the one hand, and investing, in a technology, on the other, they choose people. They understand that people make all the difference. *All the difference.* They also understand that making sure you keep those people who are critical to their success is a lot easier than going out into the market and trying to find new people, train them, mother them, and get them ready to really be productive—which probably takes a year from the date of their hire.

QUESTION: You are described as a talent innovator. What does that description mean to you?

RUDDY: First, I am on a relentless hunt for talent. Always. I think talent innovators have to be relentless about it. I am always meeting people and looking at them and thinking how could I use them in my organization someday? Most people think, "Do I have a job for you now?" That's wrong. I never think that way. I think, "Could I use you someday?" I can't tell how many times I've watched someone in my career and said, "You know someday we're going to work together," and it's happened. So, I think first, talent innovators have to be relentless about finding talented people. Just relentless. They can never stop hunting.

Second, I think great talent innovators have this ability to be able to look at the individual and really *know* what that person needs to be successful. Now that doesn't mean that in an organization of 100,000 people you can know what *everyone* wants and needs and also understand what's going to motivate them. Even so, talent innovators understand what people in their organizations need in order to really be committed. In my case, I have eight direct reports and every single one of them is different. And, while my standards never change, my style will. That's hugely important because each person has an individual makeup that requires you to figure out a formula and know what will work for them. In organizations, that creates an environment of respect for one another and for the diversity of talent. As I said, none of my direct reports is treated the same by me, financially or in their programs, because they're all so different. Yet they all bring something to the organization that I would never be able to bring by myself.

Third, I think talent innovators never think about what do I need to get the job done today? They're always looking for people, and at the people within their organizations, who are bigger than the organization is *at present*. They are looking for people who can pull the organization toward them as opposed to watching the organization grow. Let me give you and example. Before I joined World at Work, I had a number of opportunities that I was looking at. People would say to me, "I really want you. I really need you." The CEO would say, "I'm a $50 million company and in five years I want to be $500 million." And I would say, "I'm just the person to do that for you." And they would say, "Great." And I would say, "And here's what I need for compensation . . ." Then they say, "Whoa..!" What they would generally do would be to hire somebody who, from a rewards point of view, was going to get them to $70 million, not to $500 million. That's shortsighted, but understandable. And then, when they didn't make it to $500 million, they couldn't figure out why. But there's one final point: If you want to have talent innovation spread throughout the organization, the CEO must embrace it.

CHAPTER 5

Dr. Richard Boyatzis

PROFESSOR, WEATHERHEAD SCHOOL OF
MANAGEMENT, CASE WESTERN
RESERVE UNIVERSITY

Positive Change Only Happens
In Positive Environments

Of all the management theorists, few bring as much to the table as Richard Boyatzis, a professor at the Weatherhead School of Management at Case Western Reserve University. Boyatzis, whose field is organizational behavior and psychology, is one of the world's foremost professors of leadership and organizational change. Among Boyatzis' contributions are the concepts of emotional intelligence, resonant leadership, and his theories of organization change. Some of these concepts have been popularized by other writers, but Boyatzis' contributions are foundational.

Among Boyatzis insights is the view that there are "positive and negative emotional attractors" that influence the way people in organizations behave.

As the following interview shows, within organizations, achieving positive, lasting change rarely happens when the environment is filled with negative emotions. Fear of failure (a negative emotional attractor) may focus the mind, but it won't change behavior.

The reason fear and other negative emotions don't lead to positive change is that these emotional attractors close people down. In the face of fear, for example, people become defensive and resistant to change. In organizations where negative emotions predominate, people withhold information and rarely take chances. When fear predominates, creativity dwindles, individual initiative diminishes, and risk taking wanes. Corporate cultures can turn toxic.

Positive emotions, on the other hand, like those associated with praise, have the effect of opening people up. When they are open, they are receptive to guidance, new ideas, and new ways of thought. When the atmosphere is positive, people are more likely to take risks.

From a talent management perspective, organizations have emotional lives. Some organizations are upbeat, others are down. And, according to Boyatzis, the emotional life of an organization has a real and immediate impact on the bottom line.

QUESTION: Let's begin with a very simple question. What's your definition of talent?

BOYATZIS: By talent I include a person's competencies, their values and philosophy, their motives and traits, their style, interests, and their career life-stage or cycle. Thirty-seven years ago, when I did the first full competency model, those of us who were doing this kind of work focused a lot on motives and style. Since then, I have developed a more holistic theory of personality which has these things in it plus the physiological—the effects of stress, for example. But the important issue to keep in mind is that every one of these levels I just mentioned affects all of the other levels. This means that that we all have a lot going on at once. This is true for all individuals. But it is also true for couples—or dyads—families, teams, organizations, and so on. There are a lot of forces at work.

QUESTION: You mentioned competencies. What do you mean by that?

BOYATZIS: If you ask, what is the full range of a person's competencies then we are basically saying there are three clusters. There's the emotional, there's the social, and there's the cognitive. And you can further split this into self-awareness and self-management, social awareness and relationship management, and so on. Cognitive usually splits into two specific competency systems, thinking, and pattern recognition. Right now one of my graduate students is doing a thesis on what we're calling *cognitive agility* that may become a very important competency as well. These three arenas of competencies are central. At the individual level these competencies are sets of behaviors.

QUESTION: Are companies good at hiring and assessing talent and competencies? How about with regard to promotions?

BOYATZIS: No. The problem is that when you say, "I want to assess this person on his or her competencies"—his or her values, interests, style—you're talking about investing a huge amount of time and effort in the process. And, while people could do it for promotional reasons, they usually don't. So you have this huge problem. But there's something else going on too. Most of the time companies can't afford to hire people who are *already* good managers because they have to hire engineers, marketers, journalists, and so on. They have to hire people with technical specialties. So my contention is that management is one of those arenas that you could and should develop.

Now, once we move away from what I call the human resource set of challenges, and that's mostly hiring and promoting, you have the development challenges. Now, with regard to the development challenges, there are different ways to cut it, but I think it involves not just helping people develop their abilities, but it also helps them with their motivation to use those abilities.

QUESTION: Given that, what does it mean to be a talent innovator?

BOYATZIS: I'm a former CEO of a consulting firm, so let me start with a framework. The reason we need leaders and managers is to coordinate the efforts of others and to use capital in an organization to achieve the organization's objectives and mission. When you take that general concept, you realize that the responsibility of leaders is to utilize and create capital. There are a lot of ways to describe that. But the ones I like the best focus on financial, physical, intellectual, human, and social capital.

Now, I think we would all agree that if executives spent all their money on current performance it would be irresponsible. Organizations have to be concerned with the future. So, we would have to think that the job of an executive is to get current performance *and* long-term sustainable performance. To do that requires using capital now but also investing it in the future. This applies to human capital, too. The problem is that most of the time when people think about managing talent they immediately go to, how do I motivate people? How do I get the maximum performance from people? That frames the problem in a very short-term context.

QUESTION: It is also a very narrow context, right?

BOYATZIS: Yes. In fact, it's hardly ever seen in more than a single year context. As a result, almost everybody who is trying to manage talent is actually liquidating it.

QUESTION: Liquidating talent? That sounds pretty drastic. What do you mean by that?

BOYATZIS: What I mean is that they are expending most of their organization's human capital on current performance. Let me give you an example. One of my doctoral students is trying to come up with what I call a human resource profit and loss statement and a human resource balance sheet. The problem with existing measures like the balanced scorecard is that while they are moving in the right direction, they get it wrong because they look at almost everything in terms of financial measures. Human capital shouldn't be measured in financial terms. It should be measured differently, in human capital terms. My point is that we should approach the management of talent with the notion that you should manage human capital so it is greater at the end of the year than it was at the beginning of the year because you're investing in it.

QUESTION: How do you know that the value of your human capital has increased?

BOYATZIS: That's where you get into measurement issues and it's obviously one of the reasons why everybody puts things in financial terms. They think it's easier or more accurate to measure money than human capital. But Enron proved to us that it isn't. In fact, if more frequent measurements help, how did Enron happen, because the company was audited frequently? In my view, the issue is creativity in measurement. Right now, we've got two measures that people in consulting use and some academics use. The first is what we call a *climate* measure. This measures what it's like to work at a company. The second is a 360-degree competency measure or skills measure.

QUESTION: Many companies already do 360-degree evaluations. Are you talking about standard 360s where people up and down in the organization are asked about an individual's performance?

BOYATZIS: Yes. But I also mean something more, too. I mean a 360 that is typically a questionnaire in which the person answering is asked to describe an individual. What I'm talking about is a questionnaire that asks the respondent to describe how frequently a person demonstrates a series of behaviors. Usually it is either how frequently or how characteristic of an individual those behaviors are. You typically ask the person to fill it out, the boss to fill it out, and three to five peers, three to five subordinates, etc. But what we do in our programs is also to ask the spouse or partner to fill it out. We ask adult friends, siblings, and even classmates because our notion is that you shouldn't only look at work. People have multiple selves, so to speak.

Most of the time, 360s contain self assessment sections. What we do is take that out. Self assessments may be useful for feedback and for development, but they are not really helpful because of what we call delusional issues—men tend to be overestimators and women are underestimators of their strengths. So we take that out.

So in our frameworks, the 360 is a consensus view from a whole bunch of people anywhere from 8 to, well, I had one student collect data from 67 people! So it's a consensus view on the frequency of a person's *behavior*. Now, if you have information about frequency of behaviors on a cross-section of managers, executives, and professionals in an organization you've got a pretty interesting view regarding the quality of the human capital and you also understand what everybody in an organization is actually *doing*. And, if you do a composite of these 360s, you're getting something that may look similar to a corporate-culture climate study. In fact, what you're doing is taking the average measure of competencies and behavioral habits, inside the organization. That really tells you something.

Now, if research like this is done regularly in organizations, you really have a chance to understand that organization's competencies. And, by doing that you can begin to predict the organization's effectiveness. So, doing 360s the way I'm describing them teaches you a lot.

QUESTION: What does it teach you?

BOYATZIS: Well, it helps you understand things like whether an organization has a culture or climate of high-conformity among its employees. High conformity doesn't really help an organization very much unless it's in a high reliability type of business like running nuclear power plants. In most other types of organizations high conformity is bad. The 360s I'm describing pick that up. The cultural climate these 360s try to measure might be called *what it's like to work here*. It's a one-time snapshot of the company and its culture.

QUESTION: What are some other types of performance a talent innovator would try to measure with regard to an organization?

BOYATZIS: Clarity, for one. By that I mean, do people understand what they're supposed to be doing and why? Are standards high? Are rewards and recognition high? Do people understand them? Is there good team spirit? These are the kinds of things you are looking at with regard to clarity.

There are a number of very well-researched climate instruments. There are, of course, hundreds of other instruments that aren't very well-researched. Nonetheless, it is common practice for organizations with more than a few hundred people to do both 360s and climate surveys. And yet they don't do the extra step of aggregating the results once a year and saying "Okay, here are our measures as of January 1, plus or minus three months." And if you did that every January 1, plus or minus three months, wouldn't you have a pretty good status report on the condition of your human assets? In terms of talent, the competencies would speak about demonstrated abilities and the climate instruments would tap into how motivated people are, how committed they are, how much conformity there is, how much clarity, and so on. The measures I'm talking about tell you a lot about the state of an organization and the condition of its talent.

QUESTION: Let's talk about how leadership and management and their effect on talent. You developed the concept of the resonant leader. What do you mean by that term?

BOYATZIS: A resonant leader is a person who establishes leadership relationships with the people around him where everybody feels in tune with each other. Resonant leaders tend to set a positive emotional tone overall, a sense of hope, that tends to be compassionate. They set up an environment where people care about each other and there tends to be a high degree of authenticity. Resonant leaders help the process of change move back and forth between what individuals need to be doing and what the team or organization needs. In sports, when you have a resonant leader, one of the things you notice is that the team improves as they get individuals improving.

QUESTION: But why the term *resonant* leader?

BOYATZIS: When I coauthored the book *Resonant Leadership* the reason we used that word was that we discovered in our research that in many organizations, dissonance is the organization's default setting. This relates in part to stress. It is our contention that the cumulative effect of chronic stress is that people become more dissonant with themselves, their bodies, their families, their workplace. They lose touch and then they eventually make bad decisions, and become ineffective. They narrow their view.

My research from the 1970s until about 2000 indicates that if you really look at the data it consistently says that 50% of people in management and leadership positions are detracting from an organization's value. Another 20 to 30% in management and leadership positions are neither adding nor subtracting value. This is a rather shocking discovery and means that 70 to 80% of an organization's people in management or leadership jobs aren't adding any value. You can take these people out of the organization and it would probably function more effectively. The fact is that the people who are adding the most value are only the top 5% or so. In a really high performing organization like GE of the 1980s, it might be as high as 10%. But the research indicates it's never more than that.

Now, let's loop back and ask ourselves, why does this happen? Why do so few people add value? In my view, there are a number of reasons. First, most people are promoted into management positions or seek management positions for the wrong reasons. They seek those positions for social status and compensation. These people actually don't know what else to do and in many cases they're bored. This means they're going into the new position but they don't really want to become a manager. They'd actually like to stay doing what they do. But somebody says to them by now you should be head of this group or that group or even CEO of the company. The fact is that there is a big difference between individual contributions and what you do as a manager or leader.

QUESTION: Sometimes the people who are the best individual contributors—scientists, engineers, software experts, pharmaceutical researchers, journalists—are promoted and become very poor managers. What can be done about that?

BOYATZIS: Sometimes organizations have what they call the "professional track." They recognize someone who is a real contributor, like a journalist, and reward that person but don't make the person a manager. But the problem is, it doesn't always work.

Research and development organizations have done it better than others. Universities have in some ways done it the best because seldom do you find anyone at a large research university who thinks that the dean or even the president has more status or power than a tenured full professor.

But let's go back to the real issue—the leap between an individual contributor and becoming a manager or leader. It is a huge leap in terms of the nature of the role and the competencies involved. And, as I mentioned, a lot of people have pursued becoming a manager or leader for the wrong reasons, from an organizational point of view.

Now, in the research that underpins the book, *Resonant Leadership*, my coauthor and I went out on a limb and said that an awful lot of leaders and managers have the requisite competencies *but then choose not to use them*. It's like someone staying in a management or leadership position and not liking it, and over time using less and less of his or her ability. Now, what is happening here is actually the effect of chronic stress—which I mentioned—combined with a lot of physiological stuff that results in closing down the mind, narrowing the view. When this kind of thing happens, people disengage. It happens most frequently when you are in the presence of a dissonant leader. It creates a toxic situation in the organization. It actually has a sclerotic effect on the organization. It hardens the arteries. The organization becomes less adaptive, less resilient. The effect of this kind of stress within the organization is that there is actually a physiological response among individuals. Their Sympathetic Nervous Systems change which means they're literally getting poisoned by their organizational environments.

QUESTION: Are you saying that if I work in a business where my focus ought to be on my customers, in the presence of a toxic or dissonant leader, I will lose my focus or even shut down?

BOYATZIS: Yes. You'll be second guessing yourself. Constantly asking yourself, am I doing the right thing?

QUESTION: And the customer becomes less and less important?

BOYATZIS: Exactly. What happens is that a dissonant leader refocuses everyone on a narrower and narrow spectrum of performance. Most common, of course, is that this type of leader makes everyone focus almost entirely on the financials.

Now, obviously, you have to manage the financials. But not to the exclusion of everything else.

QUESTION: How does all this relate to talent?

BOYATZIS: If a person is in a leadership or management position and they are dissonant, they have a toxic effect that is contagious. This has been documented a lot. Toxicity can be an unbelievably fast contagion that literally brings everybody down.

Now, what happens is that there are people who think they can motivate a workforce by using threats or a sense of urgency or by scaring them, which is absolutely ridiculous. When you do that you get short-term compliance-oriented behavior. But do people work to their fullest? No. Do they innovate? No. Do they think about their jobs on Saturday— which is the ultimate test of how committed the workforce is? No. So if your workforce says, "It's 5:30, that's it, I'm going home, I don't care about my job," then they've compartmentalized away their jobs from their lives, which is not psychologically or organizationally healthy.

QUESTION: Why do people stay in situations where there is a dissonant or toxic leader?

BOYATZIS: Our employment arrangements with any organization are not "we're committed to you for life." It's not marriage; it's more like free agency. People can choose to leave any day. So if you stop and you take that perspective then you start to ask, why do people stay? The answer is the development issue. We've seen this on survey after survey since the mid-eighties. The number one reason why people want to stay at an organization is their belief that they can learn and grow in the organization. I mean there's the issue of fair pay, but for most managers and technical professionals fair pay is not the issue. In fact, people do not always go to the company or organization that offers them the most money. What that means is that people want to have a chance to grow and develop. That's primary in their mind. People think of themselves as an asset. And they want to keep increasing the value of their asset. That's how people handle bad bosses. They say to themselves—when they go home and pour themselves a drink—that they don't have to stay. But they also ask themselves, "What's staying worth to me?" Most of the time people in that type of situation end up sorting it out and deciding that it's better for them to stay and weather a bad boss as long as they can learn and develop.

QUESTION: So what does positive change look like?

BOYATZIS: I asked some of my students to study what's worked with regard to sustained change, and what hasn't worked. I asked them to use concepts from intentional change theory and complexity theory for their analysis. I told them they could use any additional theories they wanted to use. What they came up with is that every case of sustained desirable change requires some type of a vision or shared vision. It doesn't matter whether it's a couple, a marriage, or a community. The problem is that when you have as a major focus what I call a negative emotional attractor, it will inhibit your ability to create sustained desirable change. You may get revenge, but if the emotional attractor is negative, you'll wind up with a pyrrhic victory. To get sustained desirable change you need a positive emotional attractor.

QUESTION: What does a positive attractor look like?

BOYATZIS: I'll give you a very simple example. I ate at a Michelin two-star restaurant in Barcelona recently and I actually asked them for copies of the menu because it had a statement from the owner on it. It contained his vision, which was to invite people to join with him in a playful experience. It said he had a lot of fun in the kitchen and he wanted to share it. See, the owner's working on a shared vision. He's of course also working on shared other things, but he's doing some exploring and it's all part of the positive emotional attractor. This is part of the complexity theory concept. Through specific neurological arousal a positive emotional attractor enables you to be cognitively open. And because you are emotionally more at peace you not only can see things and can handle them cognitively, but you're also emotionally disposed towards trying. That's very important.

QUESTION: What about individual choice?

BOYATZIS: Choice is always important and the basis for desirable change. Choice is critical even in those cases were you have an accident—9/11 happens, for example. Or, a distant relative that you didn't really know dies and leaves you a huge amount of money. Accidents happen but you choose how you handle the consequence. So if we're talking about competencies, for example, we're also talking about a person choosing to develop or exercise their competencies. The fact is that sustainable change is self-directed change. Organizations are always changing, evolving, and moving in and out of equilibrium. Toxic people can always come in and shake up everything. But real, desirable, and sustainable change begins with a positive vision, and it requires choice.

CHAPTER 6

Robert Joy

FORMER SENIOR VICE PRESIDENT, HUMAN
RESOURCES, COLGATE-PALMOLIVE

PROFESSOR, EXECUTIVE MASTERS IN
HUMAN RESOURCE LEADERSHIP
PROGRAM, RUTGERS UNIVERSITY

Leadership Preparation: Practical, Local, and Fast
Don't Worry About Getting It Perfect

For 11 years, Robert Joy was responsible for human resources at Colgate-Palmolive, the $13.8 billion, global consumer products company. Joy's day-to-day challenge was to develop Colgate-Palmolive's leadership and talent in 208 countries. Colgate-Palmolive employs about 36,000 people worldwide.

In a highly competitive, fast-moving industry, Joy's operating principle was that the company could not afford to lose any talent in the organization, anywhere, any time. Joy's mission was to develop the company's next two to three generations of leaders.

To develop those leaders, Joy had to ask and answer a number of important questions: How do you drive accountability down to the local levels while maintaining corporatewide quality and standards? How do you distinguish between high performers and high-potential employees? How do you identify and introduce your next generation of "stars" into the larger organization? How do you educate, grow, and incent your best people?

What tools, beyond financial incentives, can you create to make people feel "special?" How do you make sure you retain your best people?

At Colgate-Palmolive, the commitment to talent retention took place at the company's highest levels. At the request of Colgate-Palmolive CEO Reuben Mark, currently the company's Chairman of the Board, Joy established a retention hotline. Whenever a high-potential employee signaled they were leaving, Joy and the COO were to be notified within 24 hours. Within a day, they were to present the employee with a counteroffer.

The corporate leadership development programs Joy developed are now widely perceived to be among the world's best. At the time of this interview, Joy was transitioning out of his role at Colgate-Palmolive in order to teach part-time in the Executive Masters in Human Resource Leadership program at Rutgers University.

QUESTION: You're moving from Senior VP of Human Resources at Colgate-Palmolive, one of the world's largest and best-performing consumer goods company, to teach part-time in the Executive Masters Program at Rutgers University, and at Colgate in its Organizational Development Program. What was your role at Colgate?

JOY: Basically, I managed the entire human resources function globally, and reported directly to the CEO. From very early on, I felt the key for us at Colgate was to focus on having the best talent. The distinction that I may have made, versus some of my peers, was that I really believed that you had to have the best talent globally. I also strongly believed that you can't afford to lose that talent at any level in the organization, anywhere.

QUESTION: Anywhere? How many countries are you in?

JOY: We're in 208 altogether. We have about 25% of our people in the United States, 75% are outside. We are a truly global organization and when I took over, we decided that I was going to manage the human resources process globally. We weren't going to have 208 different processes. At first, a lot of people objected to that. A lot of people thought that I was getting a little heavy-handed. But the reality is that you cannot make talent management work unless you have a global process and everybody's aligned around the same key factors. What I did with our business was simply point out that human resources is no different from global advertising or the global supply chain.

QUESTION: How else did you redefine the human resources function at Colgate?

JOY: Human resources can be perceived as a transactional, administrative organization. Or, it can be perceived as a value-added organization. When I took on the function, I thought we really had an opportunity to drive the most important aspect of what Colgate is all about—capability through its people.

QUESTION: What are the key success factors a person needs to transform human resources into something more pro-active, meaningful, and talent-oriented?

JOY: First of all, if you don't have a CEO like Reuben Mark, forget it. You have to have somebody who's committed to developing leadership in an organization. Reuben is passionate about leadership. I think if you don't have a CEO who's committed, you just can't get it done. And what does the CEO want from the human resources, anyway? In my view, the CEO wants human resources to simplify the notion of talent development, talent innovation, and talent management. The CEO wants human resources to put a process around these things. And, he wants to be able to measure it.

But the problem is that a lot of human resources people don't do that. As a result, the function sometimes comes across as a bureaucratic, paper-driven process that goes into a black hole somewhere.

QUESTION: What about the actual human resources office itself? How did you build up the capability there?

JOY: You have to have people who really understand the global part of the organization. I took some of my human resources people who were actually division people and had worked in the field. That's who I put in charge of talent management and development.

QUESTION: Why?

JOY: I wasn't so worried about the technical aspects of talent management. What I was really trying to do was build credibility. You can't get anything done in an organization unless you have credibility. But the only way you get credibility is to have people who understand the business, understand the business model, and understand the culture. One key to being an effective human resources leader is to understand your business culture and your business model. You have to do that before you do anything. If you understand your business model, and you understand your culture, then you have a map that tells you how you should proceed in the organization to get things done. And if you try to go against that, you're going to have a higher chance of rejection than if you use those things to get things done effectively.

QUESTION: What were the points around which you aligned human resources globally?

JOY: We were aligned around identifying high-potential and high-performing people early in their careers and giving them challenging assignments. We were aligned around making them feel special and making sure that they got constant feedback. We did this not only in terms of performance, but in terms of where they may go over the next two assignments.

QUESTION: How did you make sure all the component pieces of the talent management system were coordinated?

JOY: Early in my tenure—I was in my role for 11 years—there was some resistance from the human resources people as to what I was trying to do, more so than from line managers. The human resources people were more interested in the mechanics of human resources than in its strategic role. Because of their orientation, I had to undertake an educational process with my own people that was in some ways more challenging than what I had to do with the line. But for me, the key was just to be open and honest and passionate about what I was doing. I also had to give my people constant feedback.

QUESTION: How about aligning around your underlying principles?

JOY: Absolutely. I said very early that this would not work unless it was owned by the line and I really believed that. Human resources plays a critical role at Colgate and if you were to ask people at the company who was one of the most influential people with regard to career moves, my name would come up. That's not the case at a lot of companies. But my influence was really in conjunction with my role with line managers and with my ability to influence them and get them to make things real.

QUESTION: At Colgate, you really focused a lot on retention. Can you describe what you did?

JOY: In a lot of companies, human resources looks at the top 300 jobs and focuses on them. I thought that approach was not very efficient in terms of the overall focus on talent management. So, we completely refocused what we were doing.

You see, I believe passionately that you have to have line ownership of everything you do. Fortunately, as I said, my Chairman and CEO, Reuben Mark, was very supportive. So was the COO. Together, we said that one of human resources' main goals was to focus on building the next two to three generations of leaders at Colgate.

QUESTION: Which means focusing on more than the top 300 jobs?

JOY: Yes. The first thing that we wanted to do was establish some accountability for talent development. The way we did that was consistent with our overall corporate philosophy that you can't afford to lose talent at any level in the organization. We defined our high potentials and our high performers and they became the focus of our talent management program. I believe that both of those groups are critical to your organization, not just the high potentials, but the high performers as well. We also defined that group into three categories: local, regional, and global.

QUESTION: What's the difference between a high performer and a high-potential person?

JOY: A high performer is different from a high potential in two ways. High performers may not be upwardly mobile within the organization, but they perform at an outstanding level. The second difference is that a high performer may have specialist skills, such as being the best tax guy in the world, or the best treasury person in the world, or a fantastic engineer, or a fantastic IT person. These people may not necessarily have the capability of moving into a general management role.

We wouldn't exclude that person from moving into a general management role. But primarily, from the standpoint of internal motivation and performance, we wanted to focus on those people and not just the ones that are going up the ladder and could potentially make it all the way to senior levels.

QUESTION: Would a high-potential person also be a high performer?

JOY: Absolutely. Both groups have to perform.

QUESTION: So the difference is that the high-potential candidate would have more organizational mobility and perhaps more potential to assume general management roles?

JOY: Right. And in talking to a high-potential person, I would define the local, regional, and global focus. But what I also did with a high potential was to talk about the next two positions within a 3- to 5-year time frame. Early on, you also do the same thing with high performers. The point is, if you had somebody who was one of the best sales people you could possibly have, why would you want to lose that person?

My philosophy is that the person is critical to the organization. But the individual might say, "Look, I love doing this, and I've got an account that's bigger than most of the other ones out there. So, I don't want to move. I want to stay right here. I love this thing." And so at that point, we would say, "That's great. We need you, we love you, stay where you are," and we probably do some other things to make sure we retain that talent. That's how the distinction between high potentials and high performers works.

QUESTION: Colgate is a very big company. How did you actually find the high potentials?

JOY: I was asked when I took on my role to come up with a process to define high-potential people. What I said was, "Let's not get hung up on this to the point where we become bureaucratic and lose focus on what we're trying to do. So, what we did at a local level was have the local general manager and the local functional experts get involved. What we did was have the general manager and the marketing director at a subcompany—Brazil, for example—identify in their view all the high potentials and high performers. Then that list would be submitted to the division president and the division marketing person. In this case it was the vice president of marketing for Latin America, and the division president for Latin America. They would vet those lists coming in from each of the subs, and they would forward that list to me. Then I would sit down with a group of senior line people—the COO, the global marketing vice president, and I—and we would vet the list further. Then we would send the list back down, and it would then become the list. There would be no question about who was on the list or what functions were on the list. If we were talking about finance, then we'd use the same process except that on our level, it would be the CFO instead of the global marketing vice president, along with me and the COO.

QUESTION: How did you do your assessments?

JOY: We indicated that high-potential people had to be able to move at least two positions up in the organization within a 3- to 5- year period, and that they had to be either a number-one or number-two performer. Then, we added pieces onto that in terms of mobility and a career tracking piece. But we wanted to start simple.

What gets in the way of talent management a lot of times is that we try to make things too complex. So what happens is people say, "Well, I don't know. This guy looks fantastic, but he's only been with us a year and I don't know how far he can go." And I would say, "Don't worry about it. All I want you to do is to judge whether or not that individual can go up two positions in three years." And if he can, and he's performing at a number-one or -two level, let's put the person on the list. And if they fall off, they fall off. And this is what I mean when I said accountability because I think the key to this is to have a process that has accountability from the line.

QUESTION: How does accountability work in practice?

JOY: With all local high potentials, accountability was with the local general manager and the functional head. To go back to the marketing example, the general manager was responsible for all high potentials in his or her particular company, and then the functional expert would be responsible for all high potentials within their function.

That's how you have accountability. Now, in addition, we put into our incentive plans that we had to retain at a minimum of 90% of our high potentials and high performers or the line people lost some of their bonus.

QUESTION: A 90% retention rate? Isn't that a pretty steep ladder to climb in order to get a full bonus?

JOY: We made high retention rates part of the long-term plan for senior people. Retention was basically in there twice for senior people. It was in their long-term plan and it was also in their short-term plan. That's how much we valued it.

QUESTION: Did you do that for accountability reasons?

JOY: Absolutely. That's how we did it locally. Now let me explain how we did it regionally and globally.

As soon as one of those next two moves was outside of your area, so if the next move for somebody in the Brazilian sub was to a division job or a corporate job, they would then become a regional high potential, with accountability shifting to the division president, and the divisional functional person.

And if you could no longer handle someone, in terms of a regional job, and one of that person's next two jobs was global, then accountability for that high potential person rested with the COO, myself, and the functional head, like the global marketing vice president, or the CFO, or another global leader. That was the way accountability worked for our high potentials and high performers, and it was also how you were paid. If you messed up, it was pretty evident in your paycheck.

QUESTION: What did you actually do to achieve high rates of retention?

JOY: One of the big reasons you lose high potentials or high performers is because they don't feel special. So, without necessarily saying, "You're a high potential," or, "You're a high performer," we did the following. Every person that was designated a high performer or a high potential was put on some type of a retention plan.

If it was a local plan, in one of the developing parts of the world, like China or Brazil, then the retention plan would focus on cash because that's probably what drew the person to us at the beginning of their career. The plan would be that if you stayed with us for three years, at the end of that period you would receive a sum of money. Those payments—we designed the plan globally—could range from between 50% of the individual's salary to 100% of his or her salary. You didn't have to get approval from global to pay someone that money as long as you followed the plan's design. All you needed was your division president's approval and your general manager's approval. The point is, everybody who was a high potential had to be on some form of a retention plan.

QUESTION: If you want high retention rates, how much of it is due to money and how much is due to job satisfaction and pride in what you do?

JOY: Early in people's careers, it's probably fifty-fifty. As you get into the organization after three or four years, it becomes about 80% related to your affiliation with the organization and to your satisfaction with the type of challenge you receive in your job.

QUESTION: Is it important to design jobs that help a person take pride in what they're doing?

JOY: That's a piece of it. What we did was to integrate everything and align everything. You have to establish your accountability and you have to have everything working right in your incentive system. But then you have to do a number of other things, too. One is you have to make high potential people and high performing people feel special.

To make people feel special, we did a variety of things. For example, every time a division president, a functional person, or somebody from global visited a sub, they would do two things. First, they would make sure high potentials or high performers got a chance to present in front of them in a meeting, such as a budget meeting. Second, we would have a lunch or a breakfast meeting strictly for high potentials and high performers. As a result, high potentials and high performers would get exposure to very senior people in the organization.

Now, you might not think that has much power. But, I will tell you, outside the United States, when a product manager sits down with a COO or division president, or even with me, it counts.

In my case, when I would travel to a sub, I would meet individually with high potentials every time. I would meet at least ten high potentials or high performers on each of those visits. I would see them individually and also in group sessions. By doing that you immediately make them feel special, like part of the family.

Another thing we did was to say, "Okay, let's give them some exposure." What we did was to give them an opportunity to travel outside their sub. They did it either on a business review or on a swap assignment for three months. On swap assignments, they didn't have to make a commitment to stay in another country for a long period of time. They just swapped jobs for a while. For example, we'd swap two high potentials, one from Venezuela, the other from Brazil, for a few months.

We did something else too in order to get them exposure. We would bring them to New York, our headquarters, as part of a global program. We had two sessions a year, each with about 25 to 30 people. They would come to New York on a Friday and we'd do an Outward Bound experience with them over the weekend. The following Monday through Friday, we would give them exposure to every area of Colgate globally. They would have exposure to every senior manager and every function globally. They would really get to understand the company and they would be seen.

QUESTION: That seems like a very significant commitment to your high-potential and high-performing people. Did you have your CEO's support?

JOY: Absolutely. In fact, when we would bring in these people, we would give them a project to work on that they would present to our CEO, Reuben Mark. They would do it at the end of the week. Other members of the senior management team would be there. And then, at the end of all that, Reuben Mark would host a dinner or a lunch for the people we brought in to conclude the program. When the high potential and high performers left, they would be on cloud nine. Talk about feeling special!

QUESTION: Would you say that was one of the differentiating factors with regard to Colgate's leadership culture?

JOY: Absolutely. If you really look at the *Harvard Business Review* of February 2005, Ram Charan, the consultant and writer, mentioned Colgate's way of leadership preparation as unique and probably better than anybody else's that he had seen. The reason for that was that my whole approach was to try to make leadership development practical. I tried to simplify it and make it understandable to everyone in the company. I also tried to change the human resources mission to help improve people's ability to deliver business results.

QUESTION: How do you make certain that moving people up is not just being done to reward someone's favorite? How do you make certain the right people are being elevated?

JOY: The way to do that is to make every move in the organization from a direct report to a general manager and up, requiring the approval of the COO, myself, and the functional head. Now, you might say that's bureaucracy. It's really not. We pledged to make decisions within a 2- to 3-week time frame. But the line made all the recommendations.

QUESTION: How did you know that the program worked?

JOY: To make this thing work, you take an existing form; you don't add new ones to the line. People have so little time. They have increased spans of control and there's so much information that's out there they have to pay attention to. So I didn't want to add a lot of new steps. All we did was add a section to the budget reviews. Every general manager had to take 30 minutes and report on their high potentials and high performers. They had to talk about comp and their ratios of high potentials to high performers. They had to talk about any issues that might be bubbling, in terms of retention.

QUESTION: What were the other elements in the program?

JOY: We did something that came directly from the CEO. It really sent a message throughout the company that said we were serious about retaining talent. Reuben Mark said to me, "If you really believe that we can't afford to lose talent then we need to put in a notification system." At first I had no idea what he was talking about. Then I understood. His idea was that if a high potential planned to leave Colgate, both the COO and myself must be notified within 24 hours. And, within 24 hours of our notification, we had to present a counteroffer to the sub to present to the high potential before they left.

You can talk about how important people are, but when you have a hotline that people have to call immediately and say, "I've lost a high potential," that's not an easy call to make. Secondly, if you have to get a new job lined up—or something else—back to the person, fully approved, within 24 hours, that's not easy either.

QUESTION: That's an amazing turnaround for a company that size. What have been the results?

JOY: Well, the first result has been that everybody says, "Hey, they're really serious about this stuff." The second result is that we have a way to cut through all the bureaucracy.

QUESTION: Colgate is an incredible human resources story. What advice would you give a CEO or head of human resources at another company that wanted to accomplish some of the things you did at Colgate?

JOY: I would say, don't worry about getting it perfect. Get commitment, and then start. Make sure you do what you're doing within the context of your business model. And, if it's not perfect, don't worry about it. You can change things as you go and you can adjust. I don't think you ever have a perfect product launch, and human resources is no different. Once you get buy-in, commitment, and line ownership of the process, you can figure out the rest as you go.

CHAPTER 7

Joel I. Klein

CHANCELLOR OF THE NEW YORK CITY DEPARTMENT OF EDUCATION

Set Big Goals, Give People Freedom, Hold Them Accountable

At first blush, Joel I. Klein, Chancellor of the New York City Department of Education, was an unusual choice to head the largest school system in the United States. Klein, a lawyer, spent most of his career practicing law either privately or in the United States Justice Department, where he prosecuted a major antitrust case against Microsoft. But Klein never ran a school, let alone a school system with 1,450 schools, 1.1 million students, 139,000 employees, and a budget of about $15 billion. As a manager, he was Chairman and CEO of Bertlesmann AG, one of the world's largest media companies, for about a year. Klein was appointed Chancellor in 2002.

Though he had never run a school system, Klein brought passion to the job as well as a lifelong interest in education and a long history of community involvement in education-related projects. As a student, Klein took leave from law school to take education courses and teach math to sixth graders in a New York public school.

What Klein brings to the job is a fresh perspective, a close working relationship with the Mayor of New York, who appointed him, and a background as a lawyer known for a keen intellect and propensity to win cases. As a lawyer, Klein brings the ability to fight for reforms. He also brings an ability to go head-to-head with unions, city government, teachers, and parents. In some organizations, changes will not occur without a fight.

Under Klein, New York's schools have made improvements in student scores on standardized tests and on dropout rates. He has given his principals more autonomy, involved parents more deeply in the running of the schools, and created incentives for teachers. He is not afraid to innovate.

Even so, as Klein freely admits, a great deal needs to be done to fix New York City's public schools. Klein understands that repairing the city's schools cannot occur overnight. As the following interview shows, sometimes the best perspective for a change maker is to arrive without a lot of preconceptions. Though he lacks in-depth experience in the education field, Klein's perspective has been broadened by years of experience in other realms.

QUESTION: You came in here from a very different kind of background than one might have expected for an education position. What were some of the obstacles that you encountered from the point of view of talent and people issues?

KLEIN: There were multiple levels. The first challenge for me as an outsider was to be able to assemble a team at the highest level. When I became the head of the antitrust division at the Justice Department, it was a cakewalk for me to figure out what my team was. But here I didn't know the world, so there were enormous challenges. And it has taken me a while. I think now I have the best senior team that anyone has ever assembled in government. I've brought in, over the course of the years, some extraordinary talent. But that was number one. Number two, fundamentally—and this is the greatest challenge in education—the whole human resource equation was run in the wrong way. The word "talent" is not a word you were allowed to use.

QUESTION: Really?

KLEIN: It was not a merit-based system; it is a longevity-based system. And it is premised on the notion that we reward people pretty much for staying, not for how they perform, and not for quality and not for merit. The second thing was that our human resource division was fundamentally preoccupied with one thing, which is the musical chairs version of human resource allocation. Let's say, every school needs X teachers. From the central human resources function, the idea was that we've got to get them a teacher. Good teacher, bad teacher, really knows math, doesn't know math, none of that mattered. The whole nature of the challenge was that you don't have anything remotely like an intelligent human resource approach. And that, to this day, remains a significant piece of the challenge.

The second part of that was there also seemed to be no particular urgency in dealing with the kind of things that you would find, for example, at AT&T or Microsoft. The first year I was here, something like 12% of the people, new hires—which was more than 1,000 people—didn't get their paychecks. It's not as if their landlord told them, "That's okay, we'll defer your rent for a month." It just seemed there was no urgency about that. It felt like they were saying, "They're dependent on us. We've got a lot of people who need what we're offering here. We'll get around to them. So what?" At almost every level there was, in my view, irrationality about the human resource equation. And it was very hard to attract talent.

For example, we have a massive IT system here. But you can only pay certain levels in the government, so we have to use a lot of IT consultants. And it would be much cheaper in the end, and much more efficient, if I can actually hire somebody at a higher price instead of bringing in all the consultants. I could go on about the challenges for a year.

QUESTION: What contributed to this problem?

KLEIN: It's a combination of inertia and a civil service/trade union mentality. And the transformation of education will require moving from a civil service/trade union mentality to a professional union mentality, where merit is rewarded and differential challenges are remunerated differently. People think I make this stuff up. I'll give you the simplest example and I can give you this example a thousand ways until Sunday.

At a $50,000 salary, I can get so many physical education teachers and far fewer math teachers. It's just a simple supply/demand intersection. Now, if I pay all new teachers $50,000, I am inevitably going to be short of math teachers. But, if I have to raise everybody's starting salary to $100,000 to attract enough math teachers, I'm going to break the bank. Any place but here presumably, they would say, "We need to pay great IT people two times more than what we need to pay salespeople or what have you." Because the whole structure here is based on the civil service/trade union mentality, it is very tough to change. We've been changing that over the last five years, but incentives are still misaligned.

Let's say, if I put $500 million to a pay raise, a vast amount of that money goes all across the board, so everyone gets 10%. Now, after five to seven years, almost nobody leaves the system because you've got a pension lock-in effect and it's still a defined benefit pension. So if I give you $500 million, almost $400 million of that money is being absorbed by people who are committed to stay in the system. And, by and large, they're going to roll that up into a pension so it has a multiplier effect. So if I give a 10% raise across the board, and you're making $80,000, you get $8,000. But the people I'm trying to attract at the front end only get $4,000. Again, rational systems would never work that way.

QUESTION: What are you doing about this? You are a strong advocate of pay-for-performance.

KLEIN: At multiple levels, you do several things. First of all, we started to do differential pay. So to recruit a math, science, or special education teacher, I pay them $15,000 more if they'll come and make a three-year commitment to me. That's for people who are already teaching; it's not for new hires. Second, we created a position called Lead Teachers. If I think someone is a great teacher, I send him or her to a high-needs community such as Harlem or the Bronx. He and another colleague go together. It's fundamentally a 50% teacher, 50% coach/mentor arrangement. And they each get an additional $10,000.

So now people who are teaching at traditionally higher performing, often middle class schools, are more willing to go to the hard and challenging schools. We've completely eliminated through hard negotiation this involuntary transfer system we've had. Each year, between 2,500 to 3,000 teachers at the end of the school year, show up at schools and say, "I have a seniority right to a position in the school." If the principal said, "We don't particularly want you," they say, "It doesn't matter." So 3,000 people are moving around like that. We've totally eliminated that practice. And we now have an open market in teaching.

But I'd be the first to tell you, I think unless and until you're willing to put a lot more pay differential to attract people who are highly qualified to go to high-needs schools, if you fund it through merit pay and hardship pay, you're not going to be able to get it done. With school principals, we've actually created a fundamental change and we're probably leading the nation in this. Our principals' base salary is $125,000 to $150,000—again based on seniority. In addition, if I say to you, "I think you're terrific. Go to this school. It needs a turnaround. You give me a three-year commitment and I'll give you $25,000 more a year. And then you can get another $25,000 based on this accountability system we've created in which our schools get better grades." And this is like a real bonus system.

So if, in fact, your school makes real progress in the course of a year based on a system that we've articulated (fundamentally, it's based on student performance, and particularly on student gains) you can make another $25,000. That's an additional $50,000 a year, which in this world is massive. Remember, this is not a hedge fund.

That $50,000 also gets rolled up into your pension. So this has real long-term benefit to it. And what we've done working with Mercer, we completely recast the HR system to a service center, which you'd think we'd already have. Now there are HR specialists who are assigned to schools to help the schools locate the talent they need. Not just the teachers. This is one of the things I didn't know until I got here, now it's like second nature to me. But the phrase, "A teacher is a teacher is a teacher," is a kind of employment view, but it's not the real view. Everybody knows the difference in teachers is monumental. Al Shanker, former head of the teacher's union, said, "Some are spectacular, some are good, some are terrible." It's like anything else.

QUESTION: It's hard to believe that a system could so badly undervalue its most important asset.

KLEIN: In our world, they talk about teachers as an undifferentiated mass. And everything that we're about is to try to professionalize the ranks of teaching. Treat them as professionals, and differentiate based on merit, on hardship assignment, and all the things that rational economic systems and rational corporate people do.

QUESTION: How difficult is it to find quality teachers today in this environment, especially coming to the New York City school system?

KLEIN: In my tenure, we've given teachers a 43% raise. That's over six and a half to seven years, but that's a lot. What you just asked has to be parsed. For example, I get very high-quality teachers to teach at certain schools, traditionally high-performing schools. If I have a vacancy at one of my really "high-performing, middle class, upper-middle class schools," I can get 200 to 300 qualified applicants. So finding talented teachers for those schools is not a problem.

QUESTION: Really?

KLEIN: Oh sure. But the problem is in schools that have the greatest challenges—high-poverty kids, schools that have the most discipline problems—each year I have to send 10, 12, 15 new people. It's like musical chairs. That's why when people say "the pay problem," the pay problem has to be addressed in a rational and intelligent way, which is through differentiation. The second thing: It's a profession in which the principle portion of your pay is something that in the private sector people no longer get, which is a long-term payout on pension and extraordinary health benefits.

So if you could monetize that piece, and use it at the front end, and say move to a defined contribution plan, it would attract even more people. Because when I'm 25, the prospect of a defined benefit pension 30 years from now is much less powerful of a motivator in today's world than it might have been 50 years ago coming out of the Great Depression, Second World War, and so forth. There are a lot of things we could do, but it would all be premised on the notion of differentiation and putting your limited monies against a challenge that can't be seen as "It's hard to get teachers." It's just a certain place at certain times and certain conditions. For example, it's harder to get math teachers than it is to get physical education teachers.

QUESTION: You've instituted a program in which you offer subsidies for housing for teachers who are willing to relocate to New York. Has the housing allowance been a success?

KLEIN: That's the $15,000. It's called a housing allowance, but it's really a signing bonus. We've recruited several hundred people that way. But, let's be candid. If I said to you, you're going to a school in the Bronx, a really high-needs neighborhood, and if your students make, let's just say, more than a year's worth of progress in a single year, I'll give you $5,000, $8,000, $10,000 in additional pay. Or you can stay in the school you're in, where I've got plenty of teachers. But the $8,000 is available in the high-needs school. A lot of people are going to say, "$8,000, that's a lot, it could be a 15% hike in my pay and that's real dollars." That's the kind of system I'd like to see. It's the kind of system we now have with principals. That $15,000 extra bucks is mega in my world.

QUESTION: So much of this is about pay, and rightly so. But, what about other motivational factors?

KLEIN: The same thing applies. In fact, you put your finger on something critical. People basically work for two things— monetary and nonmonetary compensation. What's the nonmonetary? The working conditions, their excitement about their job, and feeling part of a successful enterprise. And one of the things we need to do is to both rearrange the monetary, and then increase the nonmonetary. So those schools I'm telling you about that are highly stable, that have several hundred people apply for every vacancy, in those schools, it's all aligned. The mix of monetary and nonmonetary is working.

In other schools with massive turnover, with teachers who in many instances couldn't get a job anyplace else, and so end up in those schools, you feel like you're part of a negative spiral. So the nonmonetary compensation is not good. You feel like you're in an unhappy, bad, unsuccessful situation. And I can't compensate. If I could compensate, I would change the mix and over time, I'd get more talent. Talent mentors talent. Talent supports talent. And I would create a positive feedback loop. We're doing it way more than most school districts in the United States. But, it's an enormous challenge.

The other thing that is indispensable to our work; the unit that matters, is the school. Everybody talks about the school district, but I've had discussions with people who run, whether it's a branch bank or Barnes and Noble, where the unit in public education that matters is the school. That's where you send your kids to get an education. And if the school is good, you're fine.

So when people tell me New York has a crummy school system, I say, "Some of my schools are spectacular and some of my schools are terrible." You've got to differentiate. Once you realize the unit that matters is the school, leadership is critical. So of all those nonmonetary compensation factors that we were talking about, leadership is key to that. Do you feel like you've joined something?

I've got a school in the Bronx called Bronx Lab. This is being run by a young kid who was in Teach for America, went up to Harvard, and got a joint degree in education and in business. He goes up to the Bronx and opens up a school in one of the toughest communities with all sorts of challenges. You want to know the irony, he was 29 or 30 years old when he started, and many principals told me that it insulted them that I thought a 29-year-old could be a principal. Because in our world you've got to be 40. But he's up there, he recruits people and he tells them, "Here's the deal. You're going to change the lives of people. We're going to get a 90% graduation rate for African American and Latino kids in a city that has overall a 40% or 45% rate. So we're going to double it. And we're going to be legendary."

QUESTION: There will be a movie.

KLEIN: Exactly. That's what he tells them. And he also tells them, "On the other hand, we don't play by the traditional rules. You don't come here at 9 and leave at 3. I don't want to hear that you're not willing to teach this. We are in this together." He creates an entirely different compact that is culture-based not rule-based. With that in mind, we invested $70 million that I raised privately with the Mayor to create a leadership program.

QUESTION: Is that the Leadership Academy that you started in 2003?

KLEIN: Yes. I put on the board of that everyone from Jack Welch to Dick Parsons (Time Warner Chairman) to Sy Sternberg (New York Life Chairman) at New York Life. I was trying to do what a rational organization would do: Recruit, train, and support a new generation of leaders. Like this young man from Harvard, I send those people to high-needs schools and they deal effectively with the nonmonetary side. They make teachers feel like they're a part of it. There's a sense of a shared vision. There's a sense of real mutual commitment. There's shared responsibilities. It's not dictatorial and it's not rule-based.

QUESTION: It sounds very promising. It's just that it must hit up against the reality of the day-to-day issues, the drugs, and the drop-out rate and the violent situations that inevitably come up. How do you stop these folks who come in with such enthusiasm from getting cynical and burned out?

KLEIN: That's the intervention that works. I told you about the school, the Bronx Lab. The school used to be one of the worst places to go to. There were all sorts of gangs and all sorts of problems. We broke up the 3,000-person school and created six 500 person schools. They're all the same kids, but there aren't drugs, and there aren't guns. And you know why? Because those kids are now engaged in their education. You can turn this around, but you won't turn it around if you keep doing what you've been doing.

When Sternberg and these guys go there, they create a compact with the kids. I'm not going to say there's never anybody there with drugs or a weapon or anything. But the whole safety of schools has turned around 180 degrees. They created a compact with the kids. We'll invest in your learning, if you'll invest in your learning. That is very different from a lot of schools that basically say "these kids can't learn." You set low expectations, almost always you'll hit them.

QUESTION: How does the principal empowerment concept fit into that story? Would a principal like that have been able to do what he wanted to do without having the liberties and having the empowerment?

KLEIN: I've had principals even before empowerment who were able to do such things simply by their power of leadership, their strength of conviction. However, what we have done, and again this is unique in New York—we've given our principals enormous budgetary discretion and decision making.

QUESTION: They're like CEOs of their own small companies.

KLEIN: Someone once asked me, "What do I think the most important change (Mayor) Mike Bloomberg has made in public education?" I said, "Transforming the principalship from an agent of the bureaucracy in the building to the CEO of the building." It's an entirely different role. As a result of that, though, it attracts a different person, because they don't want to be cookie-cutter, and they're excited about it. And second of all, for the first time we've seen real differentiation experimentation.

What I did in the last two years was dismantle $230 million worth of bureaucracy. I took that money and I gave it to 1,400 schools, on average $165,000 per school. And then I set up a dozen organizations—some private, some public—and I said to people, in this empowerment thing, "You now have $165,000. Here are these dozen organizations, they range in price from $30,000 to about $80,000. You pick whichever one you want." It was a kind of "hire your own bureaucracy." Only instead of you working for the bureaucracy, the bureaucracy will now work for you, and it has to compete for your business. It's been enormously powerful. And again, you can't go anywhere else where this is happening.

QUESTION: Give me an example of that.

KLEIN: It used to be I had a regional superintendent, and then for every regional superintendent, I had ten local superintendents, and the ten locals had ten schools. Fundamentally, those people were top down supervisory on the schools. Now I just say to the schools, "You can hire Fordham. We have a private group we call New

Visions. I created four things inside the school system. They're called Learning Support Organizations and they are highly differentiated by former superintendents. They all put a price tag on their services. We worked with McKinsey. We developed a model. They all came up with, "Here are my services." We had this massive meeting in one of these hotels and they all presented. It was like a fair. Then we put out all this literature, and then people did follow-ups, small groups, the whole thing.

So instead of having this bureaucracy where they basically can tell you, "You don't have enough teachers, hire one more teacher." When you respond, "No, I've got plenty of teachers. What I really need is a community group." In the past, the supervisor would say, "No, no. You'll hire a teacher." If that was your rating agent, you'd hire the teacher, let me tell you right now. So we eliminated that.

Then these people choose. They're very different. The people compete for the business. So next year, or the year after, we'll have another round of open market. New providers will come in. Schools that are currently with X, if they're satisfied, they'll keep X. If they're not satisfied, they can choose Y or Z or A or B.

QUESTION: So these principals are unshackled in terms of making decisions for their individual schools.

KLEIN: The notion of empowering principals has two affects. One, it unleashes dynamism and two, it attracts a different breed of cat. For example, I would actually at some point in my life love to be a principal. I think it's very exciting. But if you said to me that I was going to be a principal and I had zero budgetary discretion and somebody outside of my building would tell me when I had to do this, and when I had to do that, I wouldn't do it.

If you said to me, "You're a principal. I'll hold you accountable. You better get results. If not I'm going to fire you," but, you decide how you want to launch this ship, that to me is an entirely different bargain. As a result of this work, every principal in the city now has signed a performance agreement, tied to our accountability system, which says that if you get F's and D's two years in a row, we terminate you. And if your school gets F's and D's four years in a row, we close the school. We can accelerate that, but that's a big change in the way things have been done.

QUESTION: Do most of them get A's and B's now?
KLEIN: No, no. Right now, this is our first year in the system. I would say probably somewhere around 60% will get an A and B. And probably about 15% will get D and F. These are real numbers.

QUESTION: What do you have to do to get an F?
KLEIN: Basically, make no student progress, either compared to your peer group, which are similar schools that have the same challenges, or compared to the rest of the city. Also, fundamentally, no absolute performance improvement. So it's both progress and absolute improvement compared to similar schools in the entire city. We also have a survey process. We give parent, student, and teacher surveys and that becomes part of the grade. And the whole thing gets rolled up into 100%. We crunch the numbers, do the algorithm, and then provide scores. In about three weeks we'll announce for the first time, the entire city, all of our 1,450 schools, which are A's, which are B's, which are C's, which are D's, and which are F's.

QUESTION: It's about accountability.
KLEIN: It's not only accountability but to create further energy for reform. I mean, in some respects, we're bringing the house down on ourselves. But, that's important because it's a little like everybody says in polls, "I don't like the Congress, but I like my congressperson." They also say in polls, "I don't like the school system, but I like my school."

This is going to become a very powerful means of transformation. The only other person I think who did it was Jeb Bush when he was governor of Florida. He put an A–F system in place. And actually if you look at their results, it was quite effective.

QUESTION: I was just curious about the entrenched opposition or people who are going to get their backs up about this. You have the teachers with tenure who have been around a long time.

Change is not usually their favorite word. And then you have the Teacher's Union. How are you addressing that?

KLEIN: In a couple of ways. I talked to a lot of people who did transformations in companies. Change is often resisted in any organization. That's the nature. To some degree that was what was so painful for AT&T, after having run a phone monopoly, and the Baby Bells, and how they eventually had to migrate into competitive enemies. That's very hard—to go from a rate of return organization to an organization that has to have a profit in order to stay in business and could lose its customers to a competitor. So there are a couple of ways you address this.

First of all, you oftentimes have to lead change. It will encounter resistance. But as people see its impact, like with this empowerment program, they like it. Even though they didn't like it conceptually, they like it. And to some degree sometimes you have to move the system. That's what leadership is about. Then people will adjust to it. In all of these instances, if a couple of things happen, it will work. One thing is that people start to feel more successful. Our school system this year was rated the number one urban school system in the country, and won the $1 million Broad Prize for Urban Education. People are very proud of that. That's given us some wind to our back.

Second of all, when they see the changes, if the changes are effective, if they feel like they're going to help them succeed, then at least some of them start to become adopters. And, in any organization, you'll have three groups of people. You have early adopters, who actually get it and are excited about it; you'll have the large middle that is waiting to figure out which direction things are going in; and then you'll have your resisters, who are very, very noisy. Those are the people who are in the newspaper and you can read about them all the time.

But what you're fighting over is heart and mind share of that vast middle. If the things work, if they find their work day more congenial, they'll go along. It's the same kind of process with the union. It's tough negotiating. They want more money; we want things in exchange, and we've been able to do that. The Mayor, as I said, put in a 43% pay increase that enabled us to, in effect, purchase certain kinds of reforms that we felt were necessary.

QUESTION: Any examples of these kinds of responses?

KLEIN: Two recent experiences, one on empowerment. Last year, we had 320 empowerment schools, and the head of the union said publicly, "In 90% of them, the teachers are happier." That helps in a big way. Then this year we went through a massive restructuring. We took out almost $200 million out this year, and about $50 million last year. We completely redesigned a system and eliminated this bureaucracy, and went through all I've discussed with you. And the head of the union said it was the smoothest school opening she's ever seen.

That's the process. We made some mistakes that cost us some. You'll have some people in any organization who will continue to resist because they liked it the old way, or they don't like what you're doing or whatever. But, there's a process, and it's a dynamic process and it doesn't happen overnight. What it's about at its core is transforming a compliance-driven, excuse-based culture into an accountability-based performance-driven culture. I said when I started this job that it would take a minimum of two terms, which is in effect, eight years. And I think it will probably take more than that.

We're well along in this thing right now.

QUESTION: I think you've been quoted as saying you'd like to go beyond this term.

KLEIN: I would love to because I want to make sure that the arc we're on continues. At some point, I want it to be a system transformation, not tied to an individual mayor. Although of course, it never would have happened without this mayor. But that will depend on the next mayor, and what he or she wants.

QUESTION: Can you talk about that Leadership Academy?

KLEIN: Sure. There's been a kind of hierarchical structure to which people would select principals. Typically, they would go from teachers, then after about a minimum of eight, nine, ten years, they become an assistant principal for five years, and then a principal. So it's a very rigid structure.

My theory was, if we're going to succeed at a turnaround, you've got to have great leaders. What I wanted to do is start to look through the system for a talent that actually didn't want to follow the traditional pathways, either because they found that it was too much who you knew, or too long to get there, or what have you. So I went out with the Mayor and in three years, we raised $70 million. We put in place what we call An Aspiring Principal Program. That was our major program. We had some other leadership training we did for existing principals.

I brought in a guy who had actually done part of the turnaround at Southwest Bell. He was a turnaround guy who had done a lot of work with Noel Tichy. I brought him in and married him, and it was a shotgun marriage, to the person I thought was the best academic principal trainer in the city. She was the dean, he was the CEO.

Then they went out and started really recruiting. It's an attractive opportunity for people, because we pay them with this 14-month combination of what we call principal boot camp and apprenticeship/mentorship with one of our best principals. It's a very intense program that we have designed. We generally start with about 90 people.

In the course of the year, about 10 or 15 invariably drop out. But out of the 70 or 75 that remain, almost all of them become principals, some become assistant principals. I would say overwhelmingly they're doing work that's good or better.

It's been very, very powerful because when you think about a systems change, you always think about tipping points. Everything we've talked about is "When does it tip?" I've always believed that this system will tip when you have at least half the principals aligned with the vision we're talking about here. And these principals, in no small measure because of the nature of the training, the way they were selected, and what their own vision is, these principals were heavily aligned with the vision that I've been articulating: performance-based high expectations.

QUESTION: Are you close to that 50% mark?

KLEIN: I think we are pretty close. If I were to candidly assess, I would say probably that where we're going is the right place to go. The whole notion of empowerment has been so exciting to a lot of the people who have felt constrained and tied like the Lilliputians tying down Gulliver. That's the image that permeates.

When I got here, a principal couldn't hire her own assistant principal. The superintendent had to pick the assistant principal. This is your number two person, right? So I changed the rule, and I said the principal picked hers. The first thing that happened is their union sued me because they also represent the assistant principals. And the second thing that happened is a number of my superintendents *ignored* me. So I held a meeting and I said, "Look, I put this out. I said it and I meant it. What's going on?"

A number of people very candidly said, "Well, we know you meant it, Chancellor. But you don't understand something, these people wouldn't know how to pick an assistant principal." I said, "Let me tell you, if they don't know how to pick an assistant principal, I've got a different assignment for you. You better get me another principal." I said, "You bring me another principal who cannot pick an assistant principal, then we're going to find another superintendent." And that was the discussion that changed the whole thing. But that's the level of infantilism and top-down, marionette-like control of the people that has been in the system. I think a lot of the principals are now worried about accountability because they know I'm serious about it. They know I'll terminate people. But, they're excited about the opportunity, about empowerment, about discretion. That's how I think we're going to tip this system.

QUESTION: There's a mentoring aspect to the Leadership Academy. Tell me about that.

KLEIN: You start with a summer intensive, which is really extraordinary, and then when the school year starts, the classroom type work, which is all problem solving and modeling, that piece recedes to a day a week and an evening a week. And then I assign you to a great principal and you work in his or her school for the school year. They mentor you and give you assignments, they coach you. Then they report to us on what they think your progress is.

So if you're talking about 70 or 80 people, I've got 1,400 schools so I've easily got four or five times that many people who could be effective mentors. It works very well. That mentor stays with them. Now I'm a principal and almost invariably, I wouldn't say 100%, but almost invariably, if you were my mentor, you become one of my first three go-to people when I need advice or a recommendation. So it's a very powerful program.

I'm a big believer. I'm less enamored of these classroom sessions that are pandemic in public education. Some of them can be okay. But a lot of them are fundamentally talking heads or group listening. I believe people make real progress—and certainly in my life as a lawyer I made real progress when I was mentored by Justice Powell on the Supreme Court. It's transformative. When several of my former law partners, who were brilliant Supreme Court advocates, watched me, they let me watch them, they moot courted me, and they critiqued me. And that's where I think growth and learning come from, much, much more so than I do in terms of sitting in a classroom.

QUESTION: This all sounds very corporate. Was there a model you had in mind when you took the job? For example, David Stern in the NBA, instead of using say the NFL or Major League Baseball as his model said, "Disney is my model. That's what I see." Was there any thinking like that?

KLEIN: First of all, the closest thing that I thought of as a model at that time was what was happening in San Diego. Also, there was a guy I knew from the Clinton administration who was not a traditional educator, Alan Berson, and I looked at a lot of what he was doing. But, by and large, my model is effective organizational theory, which I spent a lot of time thinking about and studying. People say it will work in business, but it won't work in education. It's about organizational theory. They want to figure out how to strengthen their human resources. If I don't effectively deploy, recruit, retain, or support talent, I don't move the needle. So it's about organizational theory. It's not a question of a business model, or an NBA model; it's a question of, are you going to be able to use the resources you have to deploy the talent you need to make sure you get the best?

Supposedly one of Bill Gates' "Aha!" moments in life, they say, was when he was sitting in an airplane, and he finally figured out who was Microsoft's greatest competitor. You know who it was? Goldman Sachs. Because Gates understands at its core that what he's competing for is human capital. So if you don't understand that, then you can't understand organizational theory. Everybody said his greatest competitor was Apple, but he got it. And that's fundamentally, I think, the way you have to think about any organizational challenge: Mayor Bloomberg, who did it at Bloomberg LLP, gets it instinctively.

But let me tell you, I have this graph, I use it all the time. In any transformative effort (he draws a classic four-cornered chart) boldness of ideas, and then quality of execution are the keys. I jokingly like to say—the people are way up here (he points to the top left grid). The worst thing in the world is very bold ideas poorly executed. Because you get all of the noise and none of the impact. Obviously, you are shooting for this quadrant: transformation (top right grid).

A lot of people, they're on the blogs, they're at the think tanks, they're at the universities, they have very bold ideas. But if you don't do this piece, the execution, you're going to end up up here (in the upper left quadrant). And so everything we're talking about is to move the horizontal access in that direction, to make sure that you get the execution. You can't get execution without people. That's what the game is all about here. That's why it's about organizational theory. It's not about business or nonprofit. It's that if you want to maximize your chances of improving the results—in my case results mean significantly different graduation rates; that's the ultimate result, along with much better reading and math performance as interim results. If you want to do that, you need transformative ideas very well executed. This execution piece is, in the end, a human resource piece at its core.

QUESTION: You mentioned your team early on. In order to get that execution, you can't do it all by yourself. You're talking about a massive system here. Do you have a core team of lieutenants who are out there?

KLEIN: I absolutely do. And this is something I'm enormously proud of. I've attracted talent both from within the system and from outside the system. So I have got people that I think you could put up in terms of a team against any of the great teams that are out there.

I recently brought in a guy who was a very distinguished Columbia law professor who designed the accountability system. He had worked for the Legal Defense Fund, was first in his class at Stamford Law School, and had clerked for John Stevens on the Supreme Court.

Another guy who clerked for Justice O'Connor went to work for Edison. He spent ten years as the president of Edison, which is developing a legitimate for-profit model about education. He's a brilliant guy who I happened to work with in the Clinton White House. I've got a chief operating officer who came to me actually through John Doerr and Kleiner Perkins. She was working with them. She graduated from Stanford Business School. She's one of the most effective operators I've seen. I've got a guy who's been in the school system now for 40 years who is always the leader at the empowerment and the autonomy efforts. And he's now become a phenomenal leader.

I've got another woman who has been part of the system 30 to 35 years who is known to be one of the best educational pedagogues. She knows the art form of education. I've assembled that group. But now it's become an enormously powerful and a very well-integrated and effective team.

QUESTION: And they're in it for the long-term? You're not losing people?

KLEIN: In the course of this thing, in any given year you might lose a person. But these are people who will be here for the duration. I mean, the team has really jelled. What I said at the beginning, it was just hard, I didn't know the world. It's just the same kind of dynamic. As we became successful, as I became more confident about what I needed, it created a positive feedback loop. More people wanted to come, and more people wanted to come because more people who were terrific were coming.

QUESTION: The most eyebrow-raising thing I've read that you've talked about is paying the students. And I'm not sure we're getting the whole story on that. So I thought I'd ask you and you could explain your ideas.

KLEIN: Here's my idea. I think the word "education innovation" is an oxymoron. Because if you try ten things, two or three may be powerful. Others won't. What we have worked on and what most people in education work on is the supply side, the provision of the service. It can have a demand-side effect because a well provided service can attract good people. But what we were trying to look at is the demand side, how do we motivate students? And particularly students who grew up in high-poverty communities and often dysfunctional families.

As background on this, there's a guy who does this work with me. I'll tell you how I met him. His name is Roland Fryer. He grew up in the streets. His cousins were all running drugs in Florida. This has all been written up in the *New York Times Magazine*. It's amazing. His father was convicted of rape when he was 12. He had no mother. So this kid understands the streets. He went on and became this great economics professor at Harvard.

He always tells the story about going to schools in high-poverty neighborhoods, saying to kids in school, "If you do well in school, you could move out of this neighborhood, you could live in a fancy house. Drive a big car. Go to all the concerts you want." And a kid said, "Yeah, I know that." And Roland says, "Well, why are you dropping out or failing?" The kid says, "That's not me."

So the question is for a kid to grow up in an entirely different environment, and for whom the American dream or success or deferred gratification that the tough work of education requires doesn't resonate, the question is, can you motivate them? You can simply say, "Well, we can preach to them." But the truth of the matter is that it hasn't been effective.

What Roland Fryer said was, "Let's see if we can work with tangible incentives." Now, will this be very successful? I don't know. But I'll tell you one thing, if you talk to the schools, and you talk to kids, they're excited about it.

QUESTION: What's the status?

KLEIN: We've rolled it out in about 70 schools and 70 control groups at two grades. I think it's fourth and seventh grades. Now we're starting to administer the exams, and we'll see about the performance. We'll have a baseline. We'll compare it to kids outside the school.

But I don't want to oversell it in the following sense. It really is innovation.

And again, when I was in the Justice Department I spent so much time thinking about innovation, and disintermediating technologies, and all the other things. And will this, in fact, prove very powerful? The answer is, we don't know yet. But, that's no reason not to try it.

QUESTION: So this is all brand new?

KLEIN: It's literally being rolled out this year.

QUESTION: And the funding?

KLEIN: We raised private funds. It is all private money from everybody from the Eli Broad Foundation to other donors. We have a whole program going well beyond the school base. We have it for adults. It's called Conditional Cash Transfer based on the model the World Bank uses. I think the city must have raised about $55 million to $60 million to do this. Our piece is probably about $5 million. Don't hold me to the number, just on the school-based incentives. My prediction, whatever it's worth, is that this will have immeasurable impact on student performance.

QUESTION: What about the metrics in all this?

KLEIN: The way I measure it is every year now we test kids from grade three to grade eight, standardized tests in math and English language arts. Soon we'll be adding science and social studies. What I look at is year-to-year gain. I roll it up across the school. Let's just say in your school, the average third grader was 2.5, which means about a half a point below proficient. In my school, the average third grader is 2.47. And we each have at least 100 kids.

Let's say in your school the next year, in the fourth grade, those same kids go from 2.5 to 2.9; in my school, they go from 2.47 to 2.4. That's how I compare it. And believe you me, that shows the impact of the school. That's the power of teaching and learning. That example may be a little extreme, but you'll get big differentials like that. And that's the way we'll measure it.

QUESTION: If we use the corporate metaphor a little bit more, the consumers here are your students *and* the parents. The parents from where I come from are always very involved with all this. How do they fit into all of this restructuring?

KLEIN: We actually did a survey. We got 250,000 parents responding. You get a much better sense of where people are. You know, in any transformative effort, as I said, there are resisters, including some parents who resist. Those people inevitably are able to attract a fair amount of media attention. Parents fit in, in my view, in several ways. The most important way goes back to the whole motivation piece of this. The most important thing a parent can do is to make sure the kid is motivated about education. That's the principle thing. The second thing a parent can and should do is get involved at the school. That's critical, because we need parents, both in the sense of sending a powerful message to their kid. And second, we need the support and then the help and the input.

So what we did first thing, one of our major reforms, we put a parent coordinator in each of our 1,400 schools. It was about a $70 million initiative. And that person's function is not just to answer questions and solve problems, but also to attract parents. So some of them put in place, for example, dual-language programs for parents and kids to help train them, because we've got a lot of immigrants.

The third role for parents is part of a system we have, both at the school district level and at the entire level, where there are parent representatives and leaders who get elected and will have an effect on recommendations, on policy, which in some areas it's mandated that they actually approve. In the end, what often happens is people have their own opinions and views. For example, we take the view that there shouldn't be cell phones in the schools. Some parents disagree with that. So that becomes an issue.

And a lot of times what you will read is somebody saying, "He's not listening to us." It's not that we're not listening; we legitimately disagree. And in the end, part of my job, and ultimately the Mayor's job, is to make the tough calls. We're held accountable.

QUESTION: Whenever your tenure comes to an end in this job, how will you measure if it's been a success?

KLEIN: You'll see very different graduation rates. You'll see a school system with different reading and math scores, which you already see. You'll see a school system fundamentally operating on the basis of performance, on the basis of rewarding excellence. You'll be able to absorb the culture. And when you see that, you'll create the organizational dynamics. I think we're getting there and I've never been more optimistic. That's the way you'll know it. The results are the thing that matters.

When I took this job—let me just give you one metric. The state didn't keep its graduation rates until two years ago. But, let's just use their graduation rates. The city had a somewhat different metric. But two years ago, we had a 44% four-year graduation rate and the state had approximately 80%. In the last two years, we moved it up by six points, and the state has come down two points. And in a five-year graduation rate, we went up ten points, and the state went up about four.

So if you look at the two of them, over two years it's about a ten-point closure. If, in the next two, three, four years we can continue that four-year, five-year closure so that the City of New York, which is a high-poverty, heavily immigrant, high-minority city, could actually have the same graduation rate as the state, in the next four, five, six years, that would be mega. No large, complex, urban setting ever would match that. So that's the pathway that I want us on. And if we continue three points a year in four years, and a lot more in five, that's a lot.

QUESTION: The attrition rate of teachers as well has been an issue.

KLEIN: But that's going down. Again, it goes back to the same principle for everything we talked about. The attrition rate of teachers in high-need schools is very different from the attrition rate of teachers in high-performing schools. You will see we're getting many more people applying for jobs in the city. And you'll see our attrition rates go down. But in the end, the metric that matters in my work is the outcomes for students. Probably the best proxy for that is what we call a Regents Diploma in the state of New York. You've got to pass five exams to get the course credits. And if that isn't changing and changing significantly, then we haven't accomplished what we need to accomplish and what we set out to accomplish.

QUESTION: How do you feel about the changes to the HR function, and how they've progressed through Project Home Run and other initiatives? More importantly, what do you see as your expectations for them in order to be part of this execution and to fulfill the vision.

KLEIN: Because of the work that Mercer and others in Project Home Run did, we fundamentally retooled this organization's HR function. We reconceptualized it. We said, "What's our number one concern?" Our number one concern is getting high-quality teachers into our kids' classrooms. You couldn't have had this discussion when I got here.

Our number two concern is we've got to make sure we service our employees, which is an important HR function—medical care, healthcare, etc. And number three: We've got to support the senior leadership team and develop it. So they reorganized the whole HR function. Now we have a service center for our employees, which they love, with all the metrics that a real world organization would have. How many calls do you get? How long did you keep them on the phone? All the kind of things that professionals in this field tell you are indispensable. When I got here, this was unimaginable. So we did that.

Then we took our people who were looking at the teacher role and recruiting the teachers, guidance counselors, and all of that. We're training them. We're developing competencies. And we're saying, "here's your dozen schools. Now, your job is not just to get them a warm body. Your job is to get them a qualified senior math teacher who can mentor their qualified people." So you have what's called an HR, not a compliance, function. And that's been terrific. We're starting to try to mature the third piece of it.

But, this was so different from when I got here. It took us three years of work on Project Home Run, again with a lot of Eli Broad money, a lot of Dell money, a lot of Microsoft, Gates Foundation money. I think we must have put together $8 million to $10 million to pull this thing off. But, if you go to at 65 Court St. in Brooklyn now, which I used to never go over to, because it just depressed me so much; it looks like an HR program. It's just run differently.

CHAPTER 8

John Tyson

CHAIRMAN, TYSON FOODS

The TAO of Management:
Talent, Alignment, and Optimization

Under John Tyson's leadership, Tyson Foods, Inc. has become one of the 100 largest companies in the United States, employing approximately 104,000 workers at more than 300 facilities in the United States and throughout the world. Tyson Foods, Inc. is the world's largest processor and marketer of chicken, beef, and pork, and is the largest exporter of beef from the United States. Chances are you've eaten some of Tyson's products. The company is a major supplier of meat and chicken to McDonald's, KFC, and many other restaurant chains.

Tyson has a firm grasp of the demographic changes affecting his business. The company's talent bench strength initiative, Talent, Alignment, and Optimization (TAO), focuses on younger employees, the so-called "Millennials," and also on its more seasoned managers. Tyson understands that retaining the Millennials is essential to the future of the business. He also understands that it requires acknowledging that Millennials operate under a different set of imperatives than their predecessors. Whereas previous generations stayed on a career path for 30 years, the Millennials require variety and change.

Tyson is willing to accommodate these differences by providing experience paths, as opposed to career paths, for managers. Tyson is also willing to let employees "zigzag" throughout the company, allowing them to gain well-informed perspectives regarding how their actions impact the roles of others.

As this interview shows, "culture" at Tyson is not just about a single point of focus, like innovation; nor is it simply a descriptor of the company's personality or environment. According to Tyson, culture is a bigger concept and is about the lives—and sometimes life*styles*—of the company's individual employees.

QUESTION: Do you spend a lot of time thinking about your company's talent?

TYSON: It's something that's very important to me. So, I stay aware of it. As Chairman, I don't stay involved on a day-to-day basis, but the organization knows that the issue of talent is critical, and we've done a good job instilling that in the people's minds.

QUESTION: What's talent's role?

TYSON: In the country—the United States—we're running out of people. It's demographics. That means if we're not out there competing for talent and taking care of our talent and creating an environment for people to succeed—what I call both professionally and personally—then what you might have to work with may not give your company a chance to succeed.

QUESTION: Does developing talent include leadership development?

TYSON: Leadership development is really important, but there's one component I think we need to talk about. That is, the younger generation. They don't get that much play. But they have a different set of expectations and view of what their needs are. In some way, they kind of want to know what their life's going to look like. I mean they're not going to put their head down like maybe I did or my parents did, and work and show up every day and hope that things work out okay. They need to be developed all the time. That means you have to take care of them differently.

QUESTION: So they're less likely to follow a set path than their parents did. Why do you think younger people are like that?

TYSON: I think there are two reasons. One is that most of them growing up had so many different options of things to do. When I grew up I really just had sports. But when kids grow up today, they can play sports, they can do video games, computer, TV, they have lots of choices. So, it's not necessarily that they want to go to the next rung immediately, but they do want to be continuously stimulated.

QUESTION: Some would say overstimulated.

TYSON: Well, different types of stimulation, I'd say. They don't want to feel like they're caught in a rut. How many young people do we know that are successful and manage like a hedgehog, but they still have to be in a good little rock and roll band, playing rock and roll shows on Friday and Saturday night once or twice a month?

I think we've done a good job of letting people know it's okay to have a bunch of different interests. That you don't have to stay laser focused. But I also think society's done a good job showing people that you do need to be pretty good at one thing if you want to make a lot of money.

Now, some young people go after their interests sequentially and some of them do it in parallel. Michael Jordan played great basketball, but now he's a good owner of a clothing line and a tennis shoe line. That's pretty sequential.

And then you look at guys that go into one of the traditional lines like finance and they crossover into politics and come out a politician, and then go back into finance. You know, the Goldman Sachs trail to the treasury and to the Federal Reserve, and things like that. But, I think the crowd that's 25 to 35 years old—and even maybe a little bit older—they just don't want to get bored. That's not how they were raised. They need stimulation.

QUESTION: What motivates them to be like that?

TYSON: They saw their moms and dads get on a career trail and stay on it for 30 years. They also saw that it didn't quite work out and that their moms and dads were frustrated. And they also saw their moms and dads being happier when they were off work, you know, having a little barbecue on the weekends, than when they were working. There may be other reasons, too. But what I'm seeing in the younger generation is that they don't necessarily need a new title and more money. But what they do want is to be moved every two years so they can touch different things. They want their interest levels kept high. And, by doing that, they realize you're making them more valuable and that you're training them.

QUESTION: Is that how you're training them?

TYSON: Well, I think that's a little bit different than what we were trying to do, which is, training which was not necessarily career-path oriented, but it was experience-oriented. Training as a generalist, you could say.

And out of the experience you found a career path that was probably not direct, but was kind of a zigzag path towards whatever your final destination was. And then by having an experience factor available to you, you were a better contributor to the overall company. So, therefore, somebody may have still been headed to a career where they stayed inside their whole, like in quality assurance or QA as we call it.

But, if they were in QA and then they zigzagged over and actually ran some operations, and then they zigzagged over, and maybe did some research and development, and then zigzagged back over into QA, and then finished up in QA, by understanding how to run a plant, by understanding how to develop a product, they would have an appreciation of more things. They could then say, "I'm in charge of QA and I understand the consequences of my QA people shutting down the line. I understand the consequences if they don't shut it down."

They would also understand the consequences of what it takes to develop a product. And they could also explain to the people in R&D because they've been in operations and in QA that, yeah, it sounds like a great product coming out of R&D, but because they've been over here, this is why it may not work. And they could say if you did this, this is why it would work.

QUESTION: So, what kind of people should be generalist and do the zigzagging versus what kind of people are just better off being specialists?

TYSON: I would say the specialists are your real technical people. When I say "technical people," I mean people doing feed formulas in our business.

QUESTION: Feed formulas?

TYSON: Yeah. You know, like software writers or something in some other industry. They're people that have to design machines or something like that. They're the ones that have a real technical skill or specialty and a real technical need. It's not to say they couldn't step out of that and go on to be a generalist. But it's where they are. But there are some specialties within every industry that you just have to have. Every industry has to have its mad scientists, so to say.

QUESTION: I agree with that, but aren't there some jobs at Tyson Foods like line managing or managing a plan or doing something that's very process intensive? And, if so, doesn't it take a long time for someone to really understand how to be efficient within the context of that job?

TYSON: I think a smart person can pick it up assuming they have good people skills.

QUESTION: What do you mean by "good people skills?"

TYSON: The ability to clearly communicate to those folks who may not have the same understanding or ability; if you have to speak to somebody on an eighth grade level to know how to immediately change the words, your demeanor, and your conversation to communicate with a person on that level.

QUESTION: I see.

TYSON: And you can also flip that around. Somebody that you have to say, you know, this is a technical question. These are technical issues we've got here. How do you ask the driving, penetrating question in order to clarify something? So, the ability to, you know, to change clothes, so to say, depending on which audience you're working with on the operational side.

Of course, you get over into the corporation and you're out in the field on the sell side and these nuances change. They go from whether you're trying to sell the product, whether you're trying to explain to somebody why it costs so much, to being the purchasing agent and explaining the cost structure and why something costs so much, to being an animal expert.

So, that's how I would answer "people skills." You don't have to be an expert, but you have to be able to have enough language to help people understand maybe the complexity in some of the areas of our business.

QUESTION: I assume you also need to have the right people around you to help you out?

TYSON: That's right. If you don't have the technical skills you have to make sure you bring the person with you who has them if somebody wants that kind of detail. If you have somebody on the other side of the fence that's a customer, or you need to explain something, then you just go get some bright, technical people that are able to affect language changes and communicate. You have to make sure you have the people who speak the same language, and then hopefully they can translate it back into a middle-of-the-road language, which is what I like to call it.

QUESTION: Tell me about Talent, Alignment, and Optimization (TAO). Isn't that Tyson's corporatewide leadership development and talent management system? It's three years old now, isn't it?

TYSON: Yes, and there've been some modifications to TAO. You know, our management team's refined it, but it's an ongoing process of people having to identify who's coming up behind them, what are they working with, working on, and then we still have the job of trying to understand everybody's talent levels, and what their needs are, so we know where people are and where they're moving to in the company.

So we did a formalized TAO every six months, now it's gone to every 12 months. But it's part of the ongoing management team's review of people and part of their regular set of activities. It keeps them thinking about talent development, who's behind you, what are your needs now and in the future, and what do the people who work for you need to become better at their jobs. That's all part of management's responsibility.

QUESTION: How have your managers embraced TAO?

TYSON: I would tell you that about half of our managers have embraced it. It was such a change in the company. And about half of them still think, you know, "Why should we spend any time developing people? Why should we waste any money on people?"

So, you know, the person that works the hardest wins. But you also know that the person that works the hardest may be scamming the system. Yeah, they got the right numbers, but they're really not your best manager for the future. That's what TAO is supposed to focus on.

I would tell you that for a big company like ours to make an adjustment like this is probably a five- to ten-year commitment.

QUESTION: When you say an adjustment, aren't you really talking about a major cultural overhaul?

TYSON: I would say it this way: I could sit down and learn another language, but it would probably take me five to ten years before it became second nature. The first two or three years, you know, I can think about it, and it becomes mechanical. But as we go into the fifth or sixth year—and on into the tenth year—it gradually becomes second nature. So, when the switch comes on, you know, you're not thinking about it. The new language is second nature.

QUESTION: Why is it important for you to create a system like TAO within Tyson Foods?

TYSON: My belief is that we have to have opportunities for young people coming out of the college system to come here and stay. I mean, we're in small-town U.S.A., and if we can't show our bright, young people all the good things that our company offers them, and give them a career, then we would be spending a lot of time and effort and money to train them for three or four or five years, and somebody else in another industry would come in and offer them 30% more pay for a different job in their company. Somebody else would say, "You know, Tyson did a good job of training you. Here's 30% more money. Come on over here to my company." So we had to give our people a reason to stay.

The problem was that people at our company couldn't say, "Well, golly, you know, I've got five years invested at Tyson. If I stay another three or four years, this is where I'm headed. This is where the opportunities will be for my family." People couldn't say that. Instead, all they could say was, "I'm stuck. And, I'm stuck in this deal, stuck in this particular specialty, then I need to be paid 30% more for that specialty."

QUESTION: Have you seen benefits from the program?

TYSON: Yeah. I think what drove it home for me was the fact that by the nature of our industry and the price points we get to pay for talent in our industry, we had to do some different things to attract people and attract great people. To do that, they had to realize, they're going to get their hands on big issues sooner and quicker. They have to realize they're going to be actively involved in the company sooner and quicker. They need to know they have the ability to get themselves into a position to be in a real management job by maybe age 35 or 40, instead of maybe age 45 or 50. And they have to know when they get there, they're adding value.

QUESTION: Have you noticed a difference in the three years you've had the TAO system up-and-running?

TYSON: We've got a lot of young people that we are very excited about joining us. You know, it's going a little slower than we planned because of cost-cutting measures. But the organization has enough information now to know the benefit of the program, and what a modified version will look like. The pieces we'll carry on will be the best parts of the program. There were parts, when we started, that began to look like a government bureaucracy. We're going to try to eliminate those pieces.

QUESTION: Which ones were those?

TYSON: The paperwork everybody had to fill out. Some of that was to try to track things. What I mean is that some of the nomination processes for people to get into our leadership and development programs began to look like full-blown college applications. We're cutting that back. It just became a little too burdensome. Too bureaucratic. So, I think where we're headed is that we're going to have what I call people nominating folks. Now, maybe, there'll be a few managers that'll nominate their favorite pets who are not necessarily the best potential. But in a company as big as ours, you would assume that. So, I think we're going to have enough discipline to nominate the best potential talent.

And in the end, anyway, the best potential talent always comes forth. Those who were nominated by being somebody's favorite pet will finally expose themselves because they're not strong enough and don't have enough talent for the program.

QUESTION: Do you still maintain a mentoring program?
TYSON: Yeah, it's ongoing.

QUESTION: How strong is your bench-strength right now?
TYSON: There are places where it's stronger than others. We still have some work to do. We've probably got pretty good numbers at what I call the top end of the middle-level. And we've got to roll some of those into the bottom end of the upper-level. But I would tell you that the biggest challenge is when you move people from the top of the middle-bench into the bottom of the upper-bench. You see, there're a lot of people who feel like they still got a lot of running room, when they're at the upper-end of the middle part of it. The hardest thing, I think, is to let people know that we're getting ready to move you to the bottom of the upper bench. That's because when you move to the bottom of the upper bench, expectations go up, but the number of opportunities go down, and the competition level goes up. A lot of people who want to move there won't acknowledge those three things.

QUESTION: Have people failed because they haven't acknowledged all three of those things?
TYSON: Well, they didn't add those three things up to then match them to what it takes to compete.

QUESTION: Do you think that Tyson Foods, as a whole, is an innovative company?

TYSON: Well, I think the real question is, where do you drive your innovation? There's a tendency in our business, the food business, to think that innovation is product-based only. You know, things like convenience, performance, taste, and delivery. But in that realm, I doubt we're very good. I'm just not sure how much more you can innovate with regard to food products.

See, we've taken those products apart and put them in about every shape that you can get them in and it's really a combination now of flavors to enhance the food. I mean, in our business a chicken breast is a chicken breast. I don't know how much more you can innovate with that.

But what you can do is take and add a whole range of flavors from hot to mild to neutral. You can call it Italian, Mexican, Chinese, or whatever. But a chicken breast is still a chicken breast.

QUESTION: I understand that McDonald's hired away one of the top chefs from an expensive hotel chain and made him head of new product development. He came up with the chicken wrap which has been a real success.

TYSON: Well, I would disagree. Wrap-type products have been around for 15 or 20 years. They are not innovative. What was innovative was figuring out how to make wraps in McDonald's existing kitchens as they are currently organized, with the current work staff and the current ingredient base. He also figured out, "How do I turn it into another product for a different meal location?" You have to remember, the wrap already existed on the breakfast menu in the breakfast burrito. I always wondered why McDonald's doesn't allow them to make the breakfast burrito for lunch or for dinner. But, they stop that at 10:30 in the morning. So what the chef did was take that tortilla that's sitting there already, with the lettuce that was going into the salads, and combine it with some tomatoes and chicken and some other stuff. So what he's really doing—his innovation—is reassembling ingredients that are already there and doing it in existing kitchens. He figured out how to use the current system to deliver a current set of ingredients that already existed within the system and make it into a new product. That's what he was really clever about.

QUESTION: So you agree that's a form of innovation?

TYSON: Absolutely, because you're taking something that exists already and making it new. You're doing it by not adding anything to the system. You're just reorganizing the same things into different alternatives at different times during the day.

But, regarding food, people think you create great, new products whereas to me innovation comes from using a common set of ingredients. And, there was nothing new with the ingredients.

QUESTION: Are there other types of innovation in your industry?

TYSON: Yes. There is a lot of innovation in our industry in how you organize things differently, both inside the manufacturing system—like automating some set of activities—and also how you innovate in your delivery systems, like your transportation and distribution systems. There're innovations in those areas.

QUESTION: Given that second definition of innovation—process, logistics—how good of a job is Tyson doing at that?

TYSON: We're very good at it. We spend a lot of time and effort on it. If we can take some jobs that are difficult, and automate them and let people manage the equipment, then we've done some things within our facilities to make it more efficient. By doing that we're addressing the safety issue, too.

QUESTION: What about spreading innovation through the workforce?

TYSON: That's a good point. People either have shared experiences or different experiences from which to learn. Let me give you an example. You take a sales guy, let's say, and somebody in R&D, and you let them work in a plant together for 6 or 12 months. Well, they go into the plant and they say, "You know, this is what the customer wants. This is why the customer wants it. Have you thought about doing this?"

The flip side of that is you take somebody out of operations and you put them over in QA or over in R&D, or over in sales, and they're able to say, "Look, I understand you would like to do that, but you have to remember, I worked in the plant for four years, and what you're asking us to do is not going to cost our customer and/or the organization three cents a pound to produce. It's going to be 20 cents a pound to produce. You can't go promise that customer, "Oh, yeah, we can do that and it's only going to cost you three cents more," because it doesn't. Having somebody who's been there, been on the line, and been in that experience, gives them a lot more realistic understanding of the complexity of the task.

QUESTION: So, you are innovating with your talent by having them do different jobs?

TYSON: I mean, it's not breakthrough innovation, but it's innovation that lets you keep solving your customer's needs without making your processes so complex people can't run them or understand them.

QUESTION: I understand you believe religious faith ought to be part of your business practices. Why?

TYSON: Well, because we want everybody to be able to live their whole lives at work. I mean, by way of analogy, today we say it's okay for people to bring their sexual orientation to work. Ten, 15 years ago, you weren't supposed to bring your sexual orientation to work. You kept it elsewhere. Ten to 15 years ago, you actually weren't supposed to bring *yourself* to work. You couldn't have long hair, if you were a man, you couldn't have an earring, you couldn't have pink hair. All of those things have now been given permission to be part of the workplace.

From that point of view, the last remaining component of a lot of people is their faith, whether it's the Muslim faith, Buddhist faith, or Jewish faith. Or whether it's the Christian faith, or whether it's those folks who think everybody's religious faith is stupid. So, to me, it's really just part of bringing the whole person into the work place.

You know, in most places people already do that. Culturally, if you think about it, look at how the different faiths, particularly the Buddhist and the Muslim faiths, have become really incorporated into their people's ongoing lifestyles. Muslims, particularly in the Middle East, arrange their work day and create places where they have prayer rooms. They blend it into their day-to-day activities.

Besides, there are laws here in the United States whereby you can't make people work on Saturday, for example, because it's some people's Sabbath. So, how do you create the environment where you acknowledge that for a majority of folks, there is something of a higher power for them, whatever they choose to call it.

QUESTION: What effect does it have on the culture of the company to embrace faith?

TYSON: I think it just creates an environment of permission to be your whole self. So, if you are maybe a gay Catholic, you're now able to be all parts of yourself at work.

QUESTION: You've always been a strong proponent of diversity. Do you feel it's part of being a talent innovator?

TYSON: I think if you give people permission to be themselves, you get a chance to diffuse the tension, because then you've said to everybody, "You have to respect everybody. You have to acknowledge that we're different, and you have to treat everybody with respect."

Let's go back to when we used to hide the gay/lesbian side of the equation. There was a lot of attention because those of us that would be friends with gays would get ridiculed by the folks who were not willing to acknowledge. Now that it's out in the open more, there's more of an understanding and accommodation and respect, and you don't get the little remarks as much as maybe you used to.

So, that's why I think the acknowledgment is important, of giving people the permission to live their faith, so people with like interests can associate. They can accommodate. They can integrate with each other, have greater respect for each other's differences, acknowledge each other's differences, try to understand each other's differences, and then maybe out of that we get a better dialogue.

To get to the point, along the way, somewhere, senior management realized, they can no longer stick their heads in the sand and say they're not to going acknowledge gays and lesbians in the workplace. And they realized they could no longer ignore the fact that there're blacks and Hispanics in the workplace, or that there are men and women. So, along those lines, we all realized we can no longer ignore that the faith component is another one of those components.

I think once you start acknowledging differences, then you have a chance to talk about the differences. I mean, remember a while ago how we got so excited out on the West Coast with all those articles in the *Wall Street Journal* about how people could bring their pets to work? And how they could ride their bicycle to work? Well, the whole theme of those articles was, cool people get to be their whole selves. So, if I can bring my dog and my bicycle to work, why can't I bring my faith to work?

QUESTION: And it has a positive benefit for the company?

TYSON: I think it has for the company and society in general. On the things that we can control, you know, we're going to be in good shape. The things that we can't control, you know, corn prices going to $4.00 a bushel and higher, a cow getting sick, bird flu— on these things you know, we'll be better able to respond than any of our competition that's out there. But these types of dynamics are basically beyond our control. All we can do is react to them. You know, you just have to hope you're a half a step quicker than your competition.

CHAPTER 9

Tom Kelley

CHIEF EXECUTIVE OFFICER, IDEO

To Build a Culture of Innovation,
Do it Side-by-Side

Tom Kelley's company, IDEO, sells only one product: innovation. With his brother, David, Kelley is credited with creating more than 3000 innovations, from the iconic and transformational "mouse" for Apple Computer, to the more mundane Swiffer Sweeper for Proctor & Gamble. Kelley is the author of two books on innovation—*The Ten Faces of Innovation* and *The Art of Innovation.*

After 30 years of moving ideas from inception into the marketplace, Kelley, who is IDEO's CEO, has learned a thing or two about how innovation works—and how it doesn't.

Innovation begins with people. That means companies have to hire the right people—those with depth and reach. They have to hire people who know not only how to work as individuals but also how to form, build, and join teams. Sufficient flexibility to work alone or on teams is important because Kelley thinks the spark of innovation is ignited at the individual level while long-term success is the responsibility of the group. In Kelley's view, once an idea is hatched, it takes a team to figure out how to make it into a product. Teams figure out how to build a product so it won't break, how to sell it, how to talk about it in the right way, and how to get it into the right hands. Leading a talented group of inno-vators requires knowing how to manage individuals and teams.

IDEO is often called upon to help companies—and countries—build more innovation into their cultures. Can it be done? Yes, if you stand side-by-side with your client. Innovation isn't necessarily conveyed through books, training programs, courses, or drills. Instead, it's more like a skill you grasp by watching other people doing it, in real time.

In the interview that follows, Kelley discusses the points at which talent, ideas, and corporate cultural intersect.

QUESTION: IDEO is a fascinating company. It has been very success-ful and has also won numerous awards for its innovation and prod-uct designs. How did you start it?

KELLEY: IDEO was started in 1978. But I didn't really have any role in the founding of it. That's a popular misconception. My brother David started it. I didn't join him full-time for several years. I mean I was working here part-time during business school. But when I joined, there were already 20 people here. Today, there are 500. So, I was here for the growth days of the business.

QUESTION: Did you enjoy it more as a smaller firm or now that is a bigger firm?

KELLEY: Well, there are really wonderful things about a small firm. And there's this kind of magical size that I'm sure others have talked to you about at around 40 or 50 people. When a firm is that size it really feels like a family in the best sense of the word. You know everybody in the firm. You know most of their stories. You know their significant others. You know where they went to school, what they like and dislike, and stuff like that. I confess that I miss that part of being a small firm.

But ultimately—and I know this sounds corny in a business context—we aspire to change the world. Maybe that's just from being an idealist in the 1960s. But if you want to do something like that, then size is quite a good thing.

QUESTION: Why is it good?

KELLEY: Because then you get to work on bigger projects. You know, we've been approached recently by three different countries. And they came and said, "Can you help us increase the strength of the innovation brand of our country?" You don't get that opportunity as a 20-person firm.

The size of the firm I joined was really fun. But we also have aspirations that have moved us beyond products and beyond the services we provide. We'd like to work on sustainability, for example. We'd also like to work on K–12 education. We'd like to work on surveying markets in developing countries. These are long lead-time items. And you need size to accomplish them.

QUESTION: So you need size for growth?

KELLEY: Yes. And, you have to invest pretty significantly to have a chance to sit at the table and talk about those topics. A 20-person firm basically couldn't afford to do that for the most part because you're just trying to feed the hungry mouths. So there are a lot of aspects about being larger that I love.

QUESTION: You talk about changing the world. How does that affect the talent that you are trying to recruit into the firm?

KELLEY: Well, this is a place that's not for everybody. The biggest single piece of managing a group like ours is that there's not a lot of supervision. It's not like you have somebody here who's telling you what to do. I mean, we're mentoring a lot and we're helping people find their place within the firm and, hopefully, within the world. But our firm is not like a franchise operation where you come in and you don't really have to think about what you're going to do at work because you're going to be told what to do as soon as you get there. There are no instruction sets here. And we don't have a lot of rules. So, I think hiring the right people is a gigantic part of making things work. It's like that little Hollywood phrase I mentioned in my book: Good directing is 90% casting. If you get the right people, wow! The right people take care of a lot of things. And so we invest a lot in finding the right people.

QUESTION: Your business is innovation. So, what kind of attributes do you look for in the right person?

KELLEY: Well, there's a whole list of things and a lot of it varies by discipline. You know, like back when we were hiring mostly engineers, we were looking for a certain kind of engineer. We were looking for people who weren't purely math-based engineers. They better be darned good at math, though, of course, but we're looking for people that took bicycles apart as a kid and that still like to do that kind of stuff. But that's very narrow. That's very discipline-specific. In a broader sense, we're looking for collaborators. We're looking for people—and this is a concept we have across the firm—who are T-shaped.

QUESTION: What do you mean by T-shaped?

KELLEY: It's about having that depth. That's the vertical part of the T. Having something that you are world-class at. But beyond being that, you have to have something in your background that demonstrates that you are interested in other stuff and that you have respect for people in other worlds.

We live in a very technology-based culture in the Silicon Valley. I mean, the firm is spread around the world but I work here at Palo Alto. And there are plenty of people in Silicon Valley that are I-shaped, right? They are extremely good engineers, but in their own words they would say, "Well, I don't really suffer fools gladly," by which they mean they have trouble speaking to nonengineers.

I think that it's good that we have such people in the world, because a lot of those people win Nobel Prizes and things like that. But we've found we don't really have room for it at IDEO because ultimately everything worth doing is done in groups. It's not solo efforts.

The thing is, if any organization is going to distinguish itself, it's not going to be for having the best of a certain category of persons. If somebody were to stand up and say, "We have the smartest engineers in the world." Well, first, that's a hard claim to make. Two, it's hard to sustain, right?

But if you say, "Look, we don't have to have the best engineer in the world. We just need the absolutely top-in-their class, 90th percentile and above engineers."

Once you're in the 90th percentile and above, then what you're looking for is an interesting mix of an engineer and a human factor specialist and maybe an economist and a designer or somebody with a business and marketing background and stuff like that. So, you try to have the best mix of skills that might be unusual or maybe even unique in the world. And that's where you have a chance to be distinctive because you found this inner section of talents that other people maybe haven't found exactly in that same combination before.

QUESTION: How do you get those different kinds of people to talk in the same language?

KELLEY: Well, to be fair, our biggest single answer goes back to what we said before. We don't get them to speak in that language. We screen for people who already speak in those languages. Having said so, if we spot somebody who's an I-shaped person before they get in, then they don't get in.

QUESTION: How do you screen them to figure out if they have that T-part capability?

KELLEY: I wish I had some super-clever thing like we did a brain scan on them or something like that. But, no, I think it's brute force. We make them talk to at least a dozen people before they get in. And that would include some people from all those other disciplines. And usually the truth comes out, you know? By the way, we notice MBAs fall into this category. Certain types of people are really good at maintaining their game face for a one-hour interview, right? But when you're talking to 12 people, the real you is going to come out. That's one approach we do, and that one's brute force.

There's this other thing we do and this is not in all cases. This is more of an experiment we've been doing for the last two years. The way it works is that we'll bring people in for a day and actually have them do something. We'll come up with a nonclient topic. The most recent one I saw was "How might we make the Palo Alto campus more sustainable? Greener than it currently is." It's already pretty green. But, we bring in a group of people and we have them work on it. The group of candidates works side-by-side with IDEO people. But it is exactly like the work that they will be doing when they come to IDEO, if they come to IDEO. And so, sure, you're looking for bright people. But if you find the kind of person tries to draw too much attention to themselves? Guess what? We're not looking for that person.

So there's this Zen challenge to it, which is try to draw attention to yourself by not drawing attention to yourself. You know what I mean? Like you have to not just be the superstar. You have to be the superstar collaborator.

By the way, when we bring people in for the day, to make it work, you have to be "on" all day. You know, you have to be collaborating, you have to be ideating, you got to be communicating your ideas and sketching things out, and it takes mental energy. It takes physical energy, too. We've had multiple people at the end of that day say, "You know what? If this is what you guys do, I don't think I can do this every day."

QUESTION: To use a sports analogy. It's like when a basketball star realizes that he will be more successful as an individual when he helps the team pull together to accomplish things.

KELLEY: That's not necessarily an analogy I would have used, but when you use it, it sounds right to me.

QUESTION: I'm trying to get at your Zen-like dichotomy of the individual and the group.

KELLEY: Well, bringing people in and having them work on projects is a process, a tool, maybe even a trick—if you want to call it that—for finding the right person with the right qualities for our organization. We've found that to be quite effective.

QUESTION: It sounds like a very effective means of determining who's a fit, along with some sort of initial screening. Together it seems you have developed a very good triangulation process for finding the right candidates. Has it worked?

KELLEY: It has worked for us. You know I had a consulting career before I came here and I lived overseas and interacted with a lot of people. When I was consulting, I half-expected the people I worked with to be gods because of the projects they undertook and the rates they charged. But I actually found them to be pretty regular.

Then, when I came to IDEO, it was different. The people here really were extraordinary—and I don't make any claim to objectivity here. I've now been here for 20 years and I still feel that way.

QUESTION: What kind of attrition rate do you have?

KELLEY: It is pretty low. Just as an example of that, when we were getting started in the late 1970s, early 1980s, my brother hired the first four employees—four design engineers. And they're all still here.

QUESTION: That says a lot about the culture that you have created.

KELLEY: IDEO is a special place to work. And when we lose people, it tends not to be to the clients. It tends not to be to other companies. It's people leaving to pursue some life goal. The most common reasons are when people leave to start their own company or to go back to school for something. These are two quite common reasons for a departure.

QUESTION: Let me ask you something fundamental to your business and your talent model. Do individuals or do groups innovate?

KELLEY: You can always trace sparks to individuals. But if you want to trace anything you can call a success, it goes back to our groups. This is a problem I have with the inventor community. I've now gotten out of that role, but over the years, I've gotten thousands of calls from inventors and they've come up with an idea and they think it's done. They think it's like, "Wow, look! There it is! It's done!" Their concept is that that they've done 90% of the work but the reality is that they've usually done one percent of the work, and if the other 99% is not done well, they're going to have created something with zero value.

So, you see, it's the team of people who figure out how to make the product, how to sell it, how to make sure it doesn't break, how to introduce it in the right way, how to get it into distribution. The group does lots and lots of things that are highly collaborative.

QUESTION: How do you help companies develop more innovative culture?

KELLEY: Well, we certainly aspire to do that. And, I think we've done that. And, there are two answers to how we go about it. One is, as Tom Peters would say, about 30 seconds after I pass the reception desk, I get a sense of what a company is about. You can read a corporate culture pretty quickly. We, and every other human on the planet, have some intuitive sense of that right away.

Having said that, we also have a thing we call the innovation audit where we go through and try to systematically look at innovation in a company. Where are the gaps? What is their culture of innovation like? We also have a group that deals directly with culture.

But often we're not trying to take on the whole culture issue all at once. One of the things we do is just agree to work side-by-side with the client in a way that senior executives of the client organization believe will affect culture in the long run.

QUESTION: Have you been able to affect a company's culture?

KELLEY: Sure. I'll give you a specific example. About ten years ago we started working with Samsung. At the time, it was not one of the world's greatest brands. Today, it's absolutely world-class, according to global brand surveys and values. In 2005, the global brand called Samsung passed the global brand called Sony. Now, I always thought of Sony as number one in the world of consumer electronics. Now, we didn't tell them how to change their culture. We cohabited with them. We opened an office in Palo Alto, a separate building, but on our campus, and we stocked it with a bunch of their people and a bunch of our people and we worked side-by-side for three years. Then they rotated people through that building from Seoul.

So what Samsung was doing was modeling good behavior. They watched how we collaborate between the engineering team and the design team, for example, which they were not previously doing. Now, I don't want you to think that IDEO takes credit for this rise. We don't. But I think that little piece Samsung did with IDEO was part and parcel of the changes that happened at their company in the last decade.

When you look at these programs, you can spot them almost without failure. You can say, "Does this aspect of our work and this program tend to support or tend to hinder a cultural innovation?"

So I don't try to take credit for the rise of Samsung, but I would say that the three years we worked together in the IDEO Samsung office has tended to support the changes happening at Samsung, as opposed to tending to hinder them.

QUESTION: Is there a process for converting the individual inventor into a team-based innovator?

KELLEY: Partly. Here's where you get the payoff in having a strong culture, right? Because these are smart people or they'd never get in the door. I mean we have people who are still inventors. But when you come in, during your first week at IDEO, you'll get invited to a brainstorming session. And so you watch in a brainstorming session the way people are selfless, the way they generally listen and then build on the ideas of others. You see the way they don't try to hang onto credit for an idea. You hear the way they jump in and throw out another idea and even in your first week, you know you are part of a team that is doing real brainstorming work.

And, if you're smart and aware and stuff like that, you start to notice that what you just participated in is the cultural norm. So, either you start to act a little more that way yourself or maybe eventually you say, "You know, this is not really for me."

QUESTION: So when a company like Samsung is actually working side-by-side with IDEO, and they're seeing all these great new things, what sort of transformation do they go through?

KELLEY: So here's what we will typically do if we're trying to change a company's culture. We'll do a pilot project. We'll find some manageable approach to it. And, like in all client work, there are a million things to work on at once. What we'll do is pick some small, discrete thing. Not a big problem, not something that's going to take eight months to wrestle to the ground, and we'll work on it together. We like to take something that you can work on that will take between three days to six weeks.

So let's say it's the end of six weeks and we've come up with some great ideas. I mean, we haven't implemented them all, but we've come up with something that everybody around the table believes will be successful. And, the feeling is, "Yeah, we're going to do this, right?" And everyone agrees. Then, with everybody in the room, you say, "Okay, let's be mindful of this process. Was that fun for you?" And then everyone says, "Yeah, yeah, yeah, it was fun." And, then we ask: "Anybody think we came out with a good result?" And they answer "Yeah, yeah, it was a good result." And then the key question that we try to bring home is: "What would keep us from doing it this way every time?"

Now, that's a really a big question. So, someone says, "Well, project managers only have authorization to spend $180 and we spent $500 on that piece of the problem." And you suddenly get into these rules under which they are operating and they're kind of trivial. But they are the rules under which everybody's playing, right? And if you have senior managers in the room when you ask this question, when they hear the answers they frequently say, "Oh, that rule? Oh, no, you don't have to pay attention to that rule." So you break down their resistance first by having a good experience that also happens to be fun, and by acknowledging that the fun process was not playing around.

QUESTION: They don't expect work to be fun?

KELLEY: Right. What I get upset about sometimes is people think that because we're having fun, we're just fooling around at IDEO. No, we aren't fooling around! We're having as much fun as we can, but we're trying to deliver, if possible, a billion dollars worth of value at the bottom line, right?

Now, if the person is unreasonable I'll just take my bat and ball and go home. There are plenty of clients around so I don't have to work with any that are completely resistant to a new concept.

But if they're reasonable they'll see it. They'll say, "Hey, wait, this was fun and we had a really good business result. Sign me up. I'd like to do that again."

QUESTION: Does that change the culture?

KELLEY: Well, you've won them over. So now what you're doing is in their repertoire of ways to behave. They've still got those old behavior patterns around and available to them. But if they manage their own teams, or they get transferred to another department, they might say, "Hey, let's try this out. I did this really successful project that you might have heard about. Let's try using it on our problem in this new department." And it spreads.

QUESTION: Do they really take what they've learned to a new group or department?

KELLEY: Well, this is the nature of our transformation work. This is sometimes the discussion. We had an Asian client several years ago who put it in the context of the net and the fish. The fish is the new product or service or solution that you come up with. The net is how you do it. And the client said to us, "I don't just want a new fish, I also want a new net." His comment was apt. In the transformation portion of the work we do, it's more about the net than about the fish.

QUESTION: How else have you been able to change cultures?

KELLEY: We used these same processes on a Kraft Foods, Safeway Stores project. In it, we got Kraft together with a very important part of its distribution chain, which is Safeway, one of the largest supermarket chains. It was too good to be true. We actually doubled sales of a product. We even got these people who hadn't been getting along especially well to get up on the stage with their arms around each other and receive an industry award—the CPG Award for Innovation and Creativity from the Grocery Marketing Association.

Since then, the person we worked with at Kraft, Ron Volte, has done this program on his own with Target and Albertsons, a big retailer and supermarket chain. He's even been off doing the same program in the UK with big retailers there.

But here's my point. He's now doing it without us in the room! And, you know what? No one at IDEO is mad about that. It's a big success story because it's not that we just delivered the fish. And it was a pretty big fish that first time. We also delivered the net. And, it was really fun. So it's fun to talk to Ron Volte and hear about his successes. He's also having more fun and he's getting tremendous impact from his work.

QUESTION: Do you think of this as developing his leadership capacity?

KELLEY: Yes. But I want to make sure you know I'm not overstating anything. It's not like he was in the doghouse before we began. What we did was add a little push. But that little push made a big difference. It expanded his role, it gave him new tools to work with, and it got him out traveling the world. He's having success after success after success using these new tools with his retailers. And we're not talking about just the relationship. We're talking about hard financial results that have resulted from applying these techniques.

QUESTION: How much depends upon the company itself making sure that the underlying rules and systems support the kind of action Ron undertook with you?

KELLEY: You need support. People like Volte are able to cajole support out of the people around them. But, of course you need cooperation along the way. If everybody tries to thwart you, transformation is really hard.

QUESTION: Which is more important to focus on, rules and systems or culture?

KELLEY: I don't know. I mean it's certainly important if you have an idea to have it in an environment that's friendly. That allows you to look at it as an experiment. So we did our first project with Safeway and we viewed it as an experiment. Nobody knew what would happen. We knew things were not as good as they could be. But nobody knew exactly what would happen. But all of this represented a very small investment from Kraft's standpoint. So, it was worth trying. And we had a big success. So, the question is, should we try to do it again? I mean, the management team could have said, "Look, you got lucky, that could never happen again." And that would have been it. But Ron Volte convinced management to give it another try. So, you need a supportive environment. Even so, personal effort is still required.

Look, it's not like this innovation stuff just happens. You've got to have individuals and small groups pushing it and saying, "Okay, I'm super busy today and I'm still going to find time to push this a little bit farther."

QUESTION: You need people who are pushing innovation even though they are also doing their day jobs?

KELLEY: Right.

QUESTION: What kind of skills do the Ron Voltes of the world need to convince people to experiment with a new process?

KELLEY: It's just enlightened self-interest. I mean, there's always going to be the urgent stuff around. But look what it did for Ron. He'd be doing exactly what he was doing ten years ago. And, you know, I'm sure he'd get a good cost of living increase and all that kind of stuff. But by looking beyond today and saying, "Look, if this idea is real, this could be good, big!" It's giving people a chance to be a part of something new. And, it enhances your personal brand in the organization and in the world.

QUESTION: How do you convince somebody who is really focused on their day job that all of the creative things you're talking about are true?

KELLEY: I'm not avoiding the question, but I don't have to convince anybody. If I'm in a company, I just go around searching until I find somebody who's willing to try what I'm talking about. Then, I'll go around and I'll find somebody else. I'll keep asking everybody at their desks around me until somebody says, "Yeah, I'll go out to lunch with you and talk about it."

QUESTION: So, you need to be good at finding people who would be receptive to new ideas in the first place.

KELLEY: Yes. Yes.

QUESTION: Okay. And that person has to be able to sell it?

KELLEY: Of course. But you know, even the stick-in-the-mud people who don't want to change anything like success. So, what's hard is when the first three projects are failures and you have to rally everyone again. But if you can hold out, if you can keep at it until you get to your first success, then people would be stupid not to at least listen to you.

QUESTION: Suppose Ron talks somebody into working on a project a second or third time and it ends up being a failure. What then?

KELLEY: Well, then you got to decide whether it was a failure or a mistake? Failure has learning attached. You learn something that will allow you to move forward. When it's a mistake, it doesn't work out and it doesn't yield any insight either.

Early in my career, I sold against IBM. And IBM was the best mainframe maker in the world. And they had that little bootleg project in Boca Raton, Florida called the PC. And everybody mocked that project within IBM.

Well, thank God for IBM. They took the risk because when the mainframes started to disappear, they had a business. For IBM, at the time, the PC was just a little side bet.

QUESTION: You talked about going into companies and brainstorming and having people really get behind it. How do you go from ideas to execution?

KELLEY: We have a process of where we understand, observe, visualize, evaluate, refine, and implement, but never mind that. Lots of companies have a lot of ideas and they have trouble sorting through them.

Let me give you a couple of data points. You may have come across a software company in Rhode Island with a name like Rite Solutions. They used this technique that a few companies are using now—an internal stock market. In it, you give each employee 10,000 virtual dollars and have them invest in the different ideas that are out there. Rite Solutions had an example of an idea proposed by one of their admin people that the CEOs did not like. The CEOs didn't think the idea had value. But the stock of that idea was so popular that they said, "Look, I got to give this a second look." And they implemented it. They created a new piece of software that they say cost them only $20,000 to make. Now, this is a small company. It cost $20,000 but they've made over a million dollars in royalty revenues from one of the big toy companies. That's a kind of open source innovation technique for getting ideas from everywhere. In this case you're tapping into the idea base, the opinions of your employee base.

QUESTION: What do you think about ideas like IBM's Innovation Jam where anybody can put forth new ideas?

KELLEY: I think it is kind of a key success factor for companies that want to be innovative. They have to be able to tap into the ideas that exist anywhere in the organization. I disagree with people who say talent is centralized. Frank Gehry, the architect, had a job washing airplanes in Southern California. He said if somebody had been nice to him and taught him how to fly, he might have been content washing airplanes. Who knew he was to become the greatest living architect? He was washing airplanes. Do you think if they asked Frank Gehry, he might have had a creative idea or two that might have surprised the CEO of the aviation firm? I think he might have.

QUESTION: But how many of those ideas spread around the organization are going to make it to market?

KELLEY: How many good ideas do you need to make an idea market? Look, you don't need to introduce very many new successful products or services a year to be a super successful company. Look at Apple Computer. I think they're considered number one or two of the most innovative companies in the world. It's not like they're introducing 100 new products a year.

QUESTION: Is knowing where to focus the real skill?

KELLEY: Right. That's where you use the prototyping part. You do the rough prototypes, the quick prototypes that get you more feedback so you can show it to more people. Then, as you show the prototypes to 50 people and all 50 people say, "And what is it again?" You know you've got enough of a negative reaction to say, "Okay, I guess it's not going to be this one?"

QUESTION: So you're asking a wide cross-section of the talent within the organization to get involved?

KELLEY: Yes. But we shouldn't regret the death of some of those ideas along the way. That's a natural part of the process that gets you to the successful product that you actually introduce.

Google does this and you could say they can do it because they have this luxury of one really, really, really, successful offering, which is called search. But this thing where they say, "You know, a lot of the things we've tried haven't worked." Okay. So what? A lot of people would still like to be working at Google and have Google stock. So, what I'm saying is that the culture has to expect some ideas not to work. You really only need a hit once in a while.

QUESTION: What about 3M? It's considered to have a very innovative company culture. They invented Post-It Notes. What about them?

KELLEY: It is the quintessential innovation story. But I saw a presenter from 3M talk about innovation and he said, "Look, I hate that Post-It Note story." And I said, "Huh? What do you mean you hate the Post-It Note story?" He said, "Well, it's obviously a giant success. But have you ever thought of the process of that story? The process of the story is Art Frye, the inventor, sitting around, and he has a flash of insight."

QUESTION: What's wrong with that?

KELLEY: Because it says it occurs to Art Frye that the world needs something and so he makes it. The 3M presenter said, "Well, that's good if you're Art Frye on the day that the insight happens. But my job is *repeatability*. I need a continuous stream of innovations. I can't go tell my people, 'Look, go sit under apple trees and seek enlightenment.'" The point is that you need a culture and talent that churns out innovations. The problem with Post-It Notes is it is not a repeatable process.

Even so, with Post-It Notes in a small way, or the Internet in a big, big, big way, the creators couldn't imagine all the applications people would find for their products. I love an invention that has secondary or tertiary applications beyond what anyone originally imagined.

QUESTION: What companies come to mind that have cultures of innovation?

KELLEY: Well, you know, just based on where I am and my life experience, it's hard not to think of Apple pretty early on. And Google, as we talked about, is right up there. I love the kind of *joie de vive* around Virgin. It certainly seems like they're doing some stuff right, and they keep bringing freshness to new markets to the things they are doing. The jury is still out, but I'm curious about GE's efforts in this area. They've been a buttoned-up culture but very successful. Now they're nurturing cultural innovation. Also, in my personal experience, Proctor & Gamble. I think it's the biggest single innovation turnaround story. They've always been solid. But they've become palpably different in the last five years under A. G. Lafley.

QUESTION: What has changed their culture?

KELLEY: Well, I don't know all the reasons. I think it would be a great case study for somebody to work on. It's partly the CEO. It's partly the kind of change from the previous CEO to him. It's partly he hired a lot of really good people, or promoted them. And it's partly permission. One of the things Lafley has done, which I think is a big deal, is to try to shift people's mindset from being problem solvers to being solution finders. That shift is much more than semantics. We helped them come up with the idea of printing on Pringles. We thought you could sell more Pringles if you printed trivia questions and things like that on the chips. It's a really fun idea and it came out of a brainstorm we did with them. Printing on a chip is difficult. So they didn't take a problem-solving approach. They took a solution-finding approach. They found some obscure bakery in Italy. They enhanced the process a bit and their sales went up 14%.

QUESTION: Proctor & Gamble changed its culture. What are some of the characteristics of an idea-friendly culture?

KELLEY: Here's where you start. When you bring something into the boss's office, everybody's looking to see what's going to happen. Are they going to like kick you out of the office because the idea was too rough? People are interested in how the boss reacts and word runs through the grapevine very quickly and people self-edit. Or, they don't bring ideas forward, or they only bring ideas forward after they've polished them a lot. That kind of kills the idea-friendly environment and that can kill the company.

CHAPTER 10

Simon F. Cooper

PRESIDENT, CHIEF OPERATING OFFICER
THE RITZ-CARLTON HOTEL COMPANY, LLC

Values-Based Hiring:
Ladies and Gentlemen Serving Ladies and Gentlemen

Longtime hospitality industry veteran Simon F. Cooper took over as President and COO of The Ritz-Carlton Hotel Company, LLC in 2001. A two-time winner of the Malcolm Baldrige National Quality Award, Ritz-Carlton operates its luxury brand in 21 countries around the world. By 2009, it expects to grow from 72 hotels to 95, and to have expanded into the lifestyle residence market, with 60 residences and clubs. Ritz-Carlton is a brand of Marriot International.

The Ritz-Carlton currently has 38,000 employees around the world. By Cooper's own estimation, two-thirds of these employees have jobs that may prove repetitious, relatively lowly paid, and not particularly rewarding on any given day. And yet Ritz-Carlton has one of the lowest turnover rates in the industry.

How does Ritz-Carlton find the right people, train them to do the right things, recognize and reward them, and—in the end—retain them? In Cooper's view, there is only one answer to these questions: *culture.* Culture keeps the company functioning at high levels, while keeping it profitable and enabling it to win awards. Cooper explains that the Ritz-Carlton culture is about the relentless and unremitting desire to deliver world-class service.

Culture starts with the hiring process. The company hires for empathy and values likely to deliver a truly great guest experience. Next comes training, which is relentless and unremitting. Recognition, when it comes, is personal, often in the form of handwritten notes.

In this interview, Cooper gives examples of the kind of service that distinguishes Ritz-Carlton hotels from other hotels. He also provides insight into talent acquisition and retention on how to integrate employees directly into the guest experience.

QUESTION: When you took over as president of Ritz-Carlton in early 2001, you were inheriting a company with a stellar reputation for quality and performance. Have you changed anything dramatically in your tenure?

COOPER: I don't think anything has changed dramatically. Both my predecessor and I were well aware that the success of our business is going to be based upon the talent that we hire. Whether it is the talent operating a hotel or talent that we hire to develop a new hotel, either way it's about the talent. One of the realities that I've encountered is that we're much more global than we were. By 2008, we'll have more employees outside of the U.S. than we have in the U.S.

QUESTION: How many properties are we talking about?

COOPER: We're talking about 72 hotels right now. But we're going to be at 95 by 2009. There are also going to be about 60 residences and clubs. One of the major differences over the last six years is that we've initiated a very strong lifestyle product development, both in terms of products we have open today, and in terms of ones we have under construction. So it's not just about overnight lodging in luxury hotels; it's about if you liked your stay here, why don't you buy a fractional interest in the club next door. And if you really like that, why don't you buy one of the residences. We actually have as many residences and clubs under construction as we have hotels. We plan to have more than 60 clubs and residences by 2009 as well, which is up from five clubs and 15 residences today.

QUESTION: Marriott International took over Ritz-Carlton in 1999. Given what one assumes are different corporate cultures, how have you handled that in terms of talent evaluation and hiring?

COOPER: One of the key things that one must have for any branded service product to be really successful is an operating culture. You could probably be successful if you've got a product that nobody else has, if you have a monopoly or a route or a location that nobody else has. But by and large over time, to be successful in any kind of service industry you've got to have a great culture. And we've seen so many examples of when you had a poor culture and what it did to the company and how the leadership lost trust. Eastern Airlines was a great example of that.

Marriott has been smart enough to figure out that we're a luxury brand owned by Marriott, not the luxury brand of Marriott. What we try to do is make sure that behind the scenes, we leverage all of the Marriott size and benefits, be it insurance, be it employee benefits, or such things. But on the stage, we execute as Ritz-Carlton. We try to nurture that culture. And that's a very important piece of what we do.

QUESTION: What is the culture of Ritz-Carlton?

COOPER: The culture is an absolutely unrelenting desire to deliver world-class service wherever it happens to be, whichever department it happens to be. One of the things that we try to do is to marry-up our guest engagement with our employee engagement. And when I say we marry it up, we always are searching for and finding the evidence that a great employee culture results in a great guest experience. And a great employee culture, we believe, comes from our ladies and gentlemen, as we call all our employees, being fully engaged in the business of Ritz-Carlton.

QUESTION: How do you determine that they are fully engaged?

COOPER: We have a number of key questions in our employee opinion survey, which we get about an 80% response on. There are a few key questions that get over 90% response, such as "I understand the mission of Ritz-Carlton. I understand my role in the organization." We have about 38,000 employees around the world right now and I would guess that at least two-thirds of them are in jobs that are very repetitive, not particularly rewarding, and relatively lowly paid. But, nevertheless, we have a key question in our employee opinion survey that marries a question to our guests. The last question on our guest survey is "I cannot imagine a world without Ritz-Carlton." And for the employees, "I couldn't imagine working anywhere else other than Ritz-Carlton." On the guest side we get about 54% positive response and on the employee side we get higher than that. Those are the true bellwether questions that indicate whether we own the heart and mind of either the guest or the employee. And we marry these two up in our culture.

QUESTION: You described the type of job that would seem to be exactly the kind that would turn people off, leave you with a high attrition rate, and keep you scrambling for new hires. How do you get them on board?

COOPER: It's about execution. As a two-time Malcolm Baldridge Award winner, we have a responsibility to pass on what we've learned and it's all about execution. When I'm asked to speak to corporations about this, the first thing I always do is remind them that just because we have fancy hotels and you spend a lot of money when you stay with us, don't think for a second that we're not pulling our employees, our ladies and gentlemen, from exactly the same pool as you are. And I also make the point that at least 60% of them are doing relatively repetitive, low paying, and boring jobs.

We have our corporate credo and we publish this so everyone can see it, but at the end of the day, you have to execute it. We have visitors here at our corporate offices all the time and they say, "My goodness, you're giving me all your secrets." Well, actually we haven't, because the secret is execution, not just the words. It's that you stuck your neck out and said, "This is what we stand for." Especially with new hires coming in, if you are cleaning rooms or washing dishes, the values may be a little less important initially, but eventually we'll suck you in.

QUESTION: But with that execution there still needs to be a set of, say, rewards?

COOPER: Recognition. We don't use rewards. I hate the word. [laughter] It's part of the culture. In our culture, I hope that every single lady and gentleman does the right thing, not because they think they're going to get a reward. But, hopefully, they'll get recognition. We recognize people.

QUESTION: How is recognition different than reward?

COOPER: I remember once, I ran another hotel company and the service was atrocious. During the Olympics in Atlanta, I put in a sort of an Olympics thing whereby if you did something great you got the bronze, and then you got silver, and eventually gold. People got these medals to wear that indicated the award. It was really a very manufactured way to try and improve and recognize the people that were our best. It actually worked for a while. But it's not structural. It was just purely programmatic. And one of my competitors later told me, "It was great, I could go to your hotel and find all the best employees." [laughter]

But, when I took over here, we actually had a culture that was imbedded with the idea you did the right thing no matter what. And critical for us is recognition. We do a lot of recognition.

QUESTION: For example?

COOPER: Most of my Sunday afternoons I spend writing personal cards. So if I get a letter or an e-mail from a guest, or I get a copy of one that went to a hotel, as long as employees are mentioned, they'll get a card from me. We do what we call Wow! Stories on Mondays and Fridays during our morning lineup meeting. And everybody who's mentioned in those will get a card from me. At the hotel level, there are Employees of the Quarter. You try to make sure you recognize employees from the heart of the house, as well as employees from the front of the house. There's also a lot of training. Training, in many ways, is recognition.

QUESTION: How so?

COOPER: Training is critical. I'm sure we spend more hours training than most competitors. For example, our lineup every day is 15 minutes, and every single lady and gentleman around the world is going to go through lineup on a daily basis.

QUESTION: What is the lineup?

COOPER: Lineup is when the department gets together in the morning before they go out on their shift. We had one here at five past nine in the morning in the head office. Basically the message that's communicated is exactly the same around the world. We use it to communicate new initiatives. We use it to communicate great Wow! Stories, as we call them. So somebody who did something great in Dubai gets recognized by their peers around the world. We use it to communicate new openings.

QUESTION: And that's by e-mail?

COOPER: It goes out by e-mail and then it's printed at the hotel. What happens is we send out a standard message for the day. It will contain one of the service values or one of the credos, or one of the gold standards. So they'll have a template for the day, and then the individual hotel adds on what they want. I was at our hotel in Half Moon Bay two days ago. They listed all the VIP's who were coming in that day, all the things that were happening in catering, etc. And then each department will add its bit. Housekeeping, for example, noted that it was going to be a big turnover that day. So they'll be talking about how they get through the day. As soon as the room is clean, give it to the front office. Because when there's a big turnover, you want to get the clean rooms available as quickly as you possibly can because people are waiting in the lobby. So each department will then do it for itself. And each Wow! Story from around the world is on the sheet. You could do something wonderful in Bali and it will pop up in every single hotel around the world the next morning.

QUESTION: Given that in the hotel business, your lowest paid employees are usually the customer-facing employees, one would presume that they would say, "It's great to get a pat on the back but I'd really enjoy a little bonus attached to this." How do you address that?

COOPER: Well, we really don't address it. All I can say is that our turnover is low compared to the rest of the industry. We're down into the teens, and it's been getting lower over the last 10 to 15 years.

Now, I won't tell you for a second that a doorman in San Juan isn't motivated by tips. I'm not trying to say there aren't those departments where you could say the congeniality of the service may be partly related to the rewards they're going to get. There are no two ways about it. But the bulk of the hotel doesn't have that opportunity.

A lot of this is about our selection, training, and culture. There's no doubt that you can get really good service in a lot of places, a lot of restaurants you eat in. There are certainly individuals who are only motivated by one thing, which is the reward. "What am I going to be able to put in my pocket at the end of the day? And I'll smile until the cows come home to do it." But, that isn't the bulk of the hotel.

The kind of things that create the Wow! Stories, that create the guest engagement, are when you get great service from people you didn't expect to get it from. You might get it from loss prevention. Why the hell should the loss prevention office give you great service? Or from a room attendant. You expected something from the bellman or the waiters because they're getting compensated for it. But it's when the lady or gentleman who just happened to be walking by turns the experience into a Wow! Story, that you know the culture is working.

QUESTION: Is there a Wow! Story that resonates with you?

COOPER: There are lots of them. The Wow! Story of the year was in Dubai where a couple checked in and the wife was in a wheelchair. The room attendant heard her husband say to someone, "We had a wonderful day, but I'm so disappointed. I can't take my wife down to the beach." So that night, the room attendant went and got a couple of people in the maintenance department and they built a wooden walkway for going out to the beach. Food and Beverage heard about it and they decided to put up a tent for the sunset and served dinner to the couple out there.

QUESTION: That is a good one.

COOPER: And there are little ones. I did a session for DHL executives and I brought three employees from Orlando to the meeting. When we do sessions on leadership, I lock them up with employees at the end of it. Because we can tell you everything, but if it isn't executed and people don't believe it, it's not worth the paper it's written on. One of the ladies I brought along was working in room service and delivered a sandwich to a meeting planner who was stuffing bottles with messages, a cute item she was going to hand out at her meeting. She had a whole room full of these bottles and our room attendant said, "When do you need this by?" The guest replied that it had to be done by the next morning. Our room service person figured the guest was going to be up all night if she didn't do something about it. So she spoke to her supervisor, got two of her friends who were working in the hotel. The three of them went up and helped stuff bottles and they finished in two hours.

I might have offered to send in some tea or offer something to eat later on. I might not have made the automatic leap to say, "You know what, why don't I get a couple of other employees to come here and help."

QUESTION: What in the hiring process do you look for that would get you that type of person?

COOPER: Empathy. When somebody asks me about the qualities we're looking for and wants to know the most important, empathy is the outcome I'm looking for. And if you pin me down and say, "Okay, if that's the outcome you're looking for, what's the input to create that?" I like Tennyson's *Self-Reverence*. Tennyson had this expression that to be a great leader you needed "self-reverence, self-knowledge, and self-control—these three alone lead to power." Self-reverence means you like yourself. You're comfortable with who you are. And it's amazing. When you think about people who didn't work out, they were not comfortable with themselves. They haven't come to terms with who they are. And if you haven't come to terms with whom you are, and if you don't like yourself, you can't empathize. You don't have the ability or the time to put yourself in other people's shoes; you're still trying to figure out your own shoes.

Self-knowledge is knowing what you're good at, which is partly what we try to do during the hiring process. We like it when people come in and say, "You know what, don't put me on details, that's not me." It's all about square pegs and round holes.

QUESTION: So once you make the bet on somebody, then the training begins. How much training does the average Ritz-Carlton employee get?

COOPER: When you join, you have two days of nothing but training about Ritz-Carlton. You haven't started in your department. You do two days of orientation, which includes meals and restaurants and training in meeting rooms. You're treated like a guest. So you get a little bit of the context.

QUESTION: And that's from the highest level of hire down?

COOPER: Everybody. I went through it. And keep in mind that in order to get hired, you've already gone through a huge number of interviews. Sitting in that first training meeting of say, three or four hundred people, you've got only 2% of those who applied. We only hire 2 to 3% of the applications we receive. There follows an eight-day process that encompasses: These are the values of Ritz-Carlton to these are the things we're going to do in our department. We examine how to create a mission statement around our department and then how are we going to execute that mission? We go over all the processes and procedures. So it's a very intensive, very energizing eight days. We tell people, for example, that we like profit. Profit is in our mission. We absolutely believe profit is good, and we want you to believe profit is good. It creates new hotels and new opportunities for you and for others. It also includes conversations like, "You are going to have a bad day. Let's discuss that now and talk about how we're going to handle it." We make a point of telling people at their orientation meeting "And by the way, if you didn't like what you heard today, say so now. Don't hang around. We think you've got the talent, but you may not have liked what you heard. That's fine, no problem. Tell us now."

QUESTION: And training is ongoing after that?

COOPER: Absolutely, nonstop. We have about 174 hours per employee a year. And that's not counting the 15 minutes that's automatic every single day for every employee. You add that up over 200 days. It's a fair amount. That's 50 hours right there.

QUESTION: What about the metrics? How do you measure the impact of your training?

COOPER: We've upped everything on the customer side. When I joined, we had basic satisfaction surveys seeking customer satisfaction on the more practical issues. They didn't get into customer loyalty, which was the next stage. You dig for the loyalty factors. "Would you recommend Ritz-Carlton to somebody else?" We added more about how you felt about your stay and how you felt about recommending the hotel.

And loyalty is good, but loyalty isn't the end of it. You could be loyal to an airline because you happen to be in their frequent flyer program. Customer engagement is what we're trying to get at. So there are 11 questions regarding customer engagement. And as I said earlier, the last one is, "I cannot imagine a world without Ritz-Carlton." That's a tough damn question. Customer engagement really measures the hearts and minds. But we still carry on with the basic customer satisfaction measures because we need to know how the fitness club ranked, how room service did. So there are lots of metrics that are very practical.

QUESTION: How do you gauge the importance of the responses?

COOPER: We focus on what are the responses that really make a difference? So we weight the responses. If you checked the top box on question X, you're more likely to be an engaged guest. If you take resorts, for example, the number one question was, "Did you have a sense of well-being?" That question, if it gets a five on a scale of one to five, is the highest metric in terms of customer engagement.

Interestingly, cleanliness is number two. This is very interesting and important for us because we keep reminding everybody that while engaging guests and creating unique experiences that lead to that sense of well-being is key, you don't get there if everything else isn't perfect. So that's why I love that cleanliness is number two. When you're talking to housekeeping or room service or the front desk, you can talk about how the platform of your hotel has to be absolutely spotless. Everything has to work; your systems, your check in. If they don't work, you're not ever going to get to an engaged guest.

QUESTION: The alarm clock isn't shut off by housekeeping and it goes off at 4 a.m.

COOPER: Absolutely. It's very practical measurements of customer satisfaction. We used to count the 4 and 5 boxes; we now only measure 5, the top box. So all of our general managers are incentivized on the top box, on the assumption that if you checked 4, you didn't think it was a 5. We want people walking out thinking something was a 5, not a 4. If we do 4 and 5, we're running about 94–95%, which is another problem. Because if you're running 94–95% in customer sat, it's just so steady there, you're not really looking at the underlying issues. That's one of the reasons we go for top box only.

QUESTION: How about metrics for your employees?

COOPER: On the employee side, you have pretty much the same thing. Our Employee Opinion Survey is two parts. One is very practical, more about your pay and your benefits and your supervisor, etc. "I know what's going on, I understand the mission." Then you have 12 questions that are employee engagement questions. Gallup does our work for us at the moment and the Employee Engagement Questionnaire has some great questions. There are critical questions in there that are key indicators as to whether an employee is going to be long-term or not.

QUESTION: Such as?

COOPER: "I have a best friend at work."

QUESTION: Really?

COOPER: That's my favorite question. It's a very high indicator of a long-term career and a long-term engaged employee. "I have a best friend at work."

QUESTION: Why do you think that is?

COOPER: Because it means that you've established friendships where you are. And you look at an employee entering Ritz-Carlton, we don't expect to get them fully engaged probably for a year or a year and a half. We're going to move them from "I've got all the tools and training I need to do my job" to a higher level of commitment. And then you move up the hierarchy and you begin to get the emotional engagement which is when you capture their heart and their mind. And when you get right to the top of the questionnaire, there is that statement, which is "I couldn't imagine a career outside of Ritz-Carlton."

But that one question, "I have a best friend at work," is intriguing because it's highly correlated to long-term engagement for an employee.

QUESTION: How important is it for your people, specifically the rank and file, to feel there's a pathway upwards?

COOPER: It's very important. You have to look at it two ways. A lot of satisfaction comes from feeling they have a career. But more importantly, it probably comes from feeling they're recognized. A lot of our least paid employees, their mother tongue will probably not be English or the language of the country in which the property is located. Either they may be imported labor, if you're talking about the Middle East, or they may be immigrant labor. So a lot of that is a reality. And they probably have fewer expectations about their career opportunities.

QUESTION: They're just happy to have a job?

COOPER: It's that but more. "If I can work in the best possible place where I'm going to wash dishes superbly or clean rooms superbly, but I'm very well recognized, then I am satisfied. I've got a great work environment, I've got a wonderful boss, I work for a wonderful company, I'm proud to do what I do." A lot of the studies around compensation, for example, show that when you look at line employees, their priority in compensation is actually equity. They want to know they're getting as good as, if not better than, the hotel down the street. Whereas the minute you move into leaders, it's about absolute money. "What am I getting?" It's not whether I'm equitable to the leader down the street. I've got a career and it's absolute money, absolute compensation.

If you treat someone equitably from a compensation point of view, and then provide an environment that respects them as an individual, you'll see the impact. At one of my leadership sessions, I brought in one of our employees from Ghana and I asked him in front of the group, "What happened to you? When you joined Ritz-Carlton how did things change for you? And he basically said, "I think I always had it in me, and they just pulled it out of me." So part of it is about the environment that you get plopped in. If we can put somebody in an environment where they have tremendous self-respect, long-term opportunity, and long-term security because they're going to do a good job, they're going to raise their kids to do better than they are. They themselves are probably resigned to the fact that they're not going to be doctors or lawyers, but they're wonderful human beings.

QUESTION: The Ritz motto is "We are Ladies and Gentlemen serving Ladies and Gentlemen." What does that signify?

COOPER: One of the things I say when people ask me that is "Our ladies and gentlemen may not have the same wealth, may not have the same education, may not have the same knowledge as our guests, but they have the same values." That's what I focus on.

QUESTION: As you become a more global company, how do these issues translate to other countries? One would think that expectations for a luxury hotel in Europe or the Middle East or the Far East would be very different.

COOPER: It's no different than Singapore Airlines versus an American carrier. Internationally, levels of service are probably higher in Asia, and the expectations are higher.

QUESTION: Is it more difficult to find and keep talent?

COOPER: No. It's amazing. Even in Tokyo where we opened in 2007, it is not that difficult. We're fortunate being in the luxury end of the business. If you're a mechanic, would you rather work on a

Volkswagen or a Bentley? We get the people and our challenge is to retain them. In fact, I would argue that one of biggest challenges is the growth of competition in our segment, because there are so many new luxury chains opening up. It has been the growth segment of the industry. A lot of investment, whether it's Middle East money, whether it's Asian money; a lot of money is going into luxury hotels. It feels like there's a new luxury chain popping up every month. Ten years ago, there were three chains. Now there are about 20. So it's a challenge to try and keep leaders.

QUESTION: Talk about that. Are you thinking of changing the way you compensate people?

COOPER: No, I don't think so. We're going to compensate fairly. We're in the business of making money, so we're not going to overcompensate. Somebody running a two-store chain, or having an independent hotel, will always have to pay more money than we do. We try to find long-term career opportunities. We try to find people who want that, who fundamentally believe that even though they got a great offer, and a nice title, it's not going to get them the career goals that they want.

One of the encouraging things about our international growth is that we've got a very good cadre of international leaders. And we're creating much more opportunity for them. Because, to be frank, coming to the U.S. today is not as easy as it was, both in terms of work visas and other issues. Obviously, from some countries, it is very difficult, especially countries that we might typically be looking to hire people from.

In our hotels on the Gulf, we try to find leaders from Muslim countries for obvious reasons. Whether it's Malaysia or Indonesia or Morocco or Tunisia, these people are more comfortable in those settings and they have the language skills we want. We've also got a lot of Indians, Nepalese, Sri Lankans, and Pakistanis. So if you want to work for Ritz-Carlton now, we've got a lot more opportunities.

QUESTION: How do you respond to this increased competition for talent in the luxury market?

COOPER: You have to be really fast on your feet. You have to have really good leaders. Good leaders tend to know when their people are getting targeted. In some ways, it's a rock and a hard place because I say to all of my direct reports, "I hope you're getting a phone call (from the competition) every three months. Because if you're not, you're not as good as I thought you were. [laughter] On the other hand, I want you to hang up." I had one executive come in the other day, and he said, "You're terrible." I said, "What have I done now?" He said, "I just hung up on the second best job in the world." I said, "Oh yeah, what's the first?" He said, "The one I've got." [laughter]

The amount of activity at the luxury end is astounding and where do you think they go to find talent? They go to the biggest player.

QUESTION: One of the things global companies are facing is hiring for tomorrow's needs today but not overhiring. How do you address that?

COOPER: That's a very big deal because by definition, you've got some redundancy, and that's a tricky thing, because redundancy is expensive. And any time you say, "How do I improve the margins?" you look at the redundant positions. With that said, we're doing more college recruiting than ever. We've got the growth. We've easily got double-digit growth for the next five years with everything we've got under construction. We're actually saying that we need 40,000 new ladies and gentlemen over the next four years, 10,000 a year. That's the new ladies and gentlemen we need to staff the new hotels, but it's also taking into account a high teen turnover rate. So anything we can do to reduce turnover reduces that number.

But, in saying that, we've also put together a much more aggressive corporate recruitment organization. We now recruit more heavily for the hotels than we did in the past. We used to be in much more of an advisory capacity. We now do college recruiting for them. We have one person who does nothing but sales and marketing recruiting. We have a person who does nothing but food and beverage recruiting. So we are out there helping individual hotels do the recruiting rather than have them doing it on their own or using a head hunter.

QUESTION: Do the individual hotels have autonomy to hire who they want?

COOPER: Yes, they can hire who they want, but they follow a selection process for the candidates.

QUESTION: At the end of the day this is just a people business.

COOPER: It's all people. Actually the model is pretty darn simple. A great product and great service equals an engaged guest. It's not that complicated. When you think about opening a hotel, there are three key elements, and two of them reside with my direct team. You've got to get the right location. Don't bother to put a Ritz-Carlton in the wrong location. You've got to have the right product. And then the third piece is you've got to staff it with the right ladies and gentlemen to bring it alive. But one and two take an awful lot of time and money, and are very, very important. Because if we don't position the product right for success, it creates a huge challenge. Great ladies and gentlemen can overcome shortcomings for a period of time. But they can't do it long-term. For a really successful Ritz-Carlton, you need great location, great physical product, and great ladies and gentlemen.

QUESTION: Your brand is one of those amazing brands that has become part of a lexicon. And living up to that and keeping that pristine is not a simple task.

COOPER: All the research shows that luxury guests have higher expectations of us than they do of anybody else. Those expectations are higher than our competition, partly because of the legacy you talk about, which is good and bad. One of the things that we've been doing a lot of work changing and evolving over the last three to four years is the brand. How do we make sure that Ritz stays relevant to luxury customers? We won't be successful if we only stay relevant to the customers that we had 20 years ago. We have to be relevant to today's luxury customers and tomorrow's luxury customers.

For example, take one of the well-known luxury department stores in this country. They started a completely new chain. And they will be the first ones to tell you that the sons and daughters of their customers won't walk across the threshold. It's not that they might not buy something inside, it's "That's where my mother and father went. It's not where I go."

Luxury customers are changing very, very rapidly, both demographically and psychographically. For example, if I'm trying to explain to a group of people about the tinkering we are doing, I say, "Okay, you cast your eye over the lobby of the Ritz-Carlton 20 years ago in Boston. What did you see? You saw mature men in suits. That's what you would see. A very homogeneous guest. It was very easy to understand what it was that turned their crank. And we came up with a prescribed service approach for that customer with our 20 basics. Do these things right and it will work."

You look now, scan across the lobby of a Ritz-Carlton today. You're going to see families, you're going to see diversity, you're going to see international customers. You're going to see gender diversity. And by the way, most people are going to be casually dressed. It's the same at the FOBs, the private jet terminals at airports. Look at all the families climbing out of their jets to go out to the Yellowstone Club. It's amazing.

Five years ago, if Goldman Sachs had a meeting and had 300 of their high-end sales people in a room, they'd all be in suits. Today they'll all be in jeans with a nice linen shirt and Gucci loafers. So our challenge is, with the very traditional perception of Ritz-Carlton, how do we continue to stay relevant? We've got a perception that's over there, and we need to be here.

QUESTION: How do you shift the perception?

COOPER: You'll see a lot of the focus in our advertising changing. We'll change our service delivery so the focus is more about outcomes rather than prescribed inputs. Rather than putting words in our ladies and gentlemen's mouths, they need to adapt to the customer because the customers are so different. It's the idea of scriptless service. Our problem is that we started with, "It's my pleasure" as one of the things that we're supposed to say. But today, you're going to get that at the checkout counter at Whole Foods. Another problem was that we put it in people's mouths. And even if they mean it, if you were in a Ritz-Carlton and it was the tenth time you heard it, you knew it was scripted. So we're trying to get away from that.

QUESTION: Do you have any role models in this whole area that you go back to and say, "I love the way these folks do it."

COOPER: Louis Vuitton. I love the way they do it. I use them as a great example of what we would like to do. They have adapted in effective ways. When they brought out their new graffiti bags, for example, the white bags with all the colors on them. It was fascinating because everybody knows the traditional sort of beige on brown Louis Vuitton colors, and then they came out with these colorful bags, which were highly successful. I use the two handbags in a slide show to talk to my people about staying relevant to your customer. I point out that when they brought out the new handbag, the sales of the old ones went up as well. I really admire the control they put on their products and more importantly, how they've managed to stay relevant. They've got something for the more traditional traveler who wants to continue to have that Louis Vuitton look, the traditional look. At the same time, they've got edgier products for the young buyers. They've done a great job and that is what we need to address.

Henri A. Termeer

CHAIRMAN, PRESIDENT, AND CEO
OF GENZYME CORP

The Purpose-Driven Company

Henri A. Termeer joined Genzyme, a biotech company, as its president in 1983, two years after its founding. He became CEO in 1985, and chairman in 1988. Under Termeer, the $3.8 billion company has grown from an entrepreneurial startup into one of the world's top five biotech companies. For the fourth year in a row, scientists named Genzyme a top employer in a *Science* magazine survey ranking the reputations of global biotech and pharmaceutical companies. Genzyme's culture is built around core values, including environmental sustainability, which makes the company especially attractive to potential employees.

Over the last 25 years, Termeer has turned the acquisition of talent into a science. He has cultivated relationships with local and partner medical facilities and universities that he views as feeder systems into Genzyme's talent pipeline. At the end of an interview with an applicant, Temeer wants prospective employees to leave thinking, "What are we going to do together?"

But it is the retention of talent that keeps Temeer focused.

Why do people stay? One reason, Termeer says, is that Genzyme employees consider the company "purpose-driven." When employees join Genzyme, they know they are joining a scientific and humanitarian activity whose capabilities are far greater than any individual can pursue alone.

Employees remain at the company to make scientific progress; to see the developments through; and to help the world. If they are aligned with the purpose of the company—in an environment that strikes them as having the right balance of competitiveness and collaboration—Temeer believes they will feel compelled to stay.

In the following interview, Termeer reflects on individualism versus teams; on horizontal organizations, and on the courage to do the right things when the quality of human life is at stake.

QUESTION: What is the secret for technology companies as successful as Genzyme to find and keep great people?

TERMEER: It is a continuous process. In this community in Massachusetts, we probably hire a thousand people in a year to replace people who are moving on or going back to school, and additional people for more tasks. To hire that many people you must see many people. Since we do this all the time, we have this connection with the community and a sense of where these people come from. That connection makes a company known and creates a reputation.

The company didn't suddenly reach its current size. We grew gradually as we hired more people. All this time, over 25 years, we have been in the process of finding good people, finding the connections for the different skill sets in the different environments in which we recruit.

Those connections have resulted in tremendous relationships with the academic community that surrounds us here. At the University of Massachusetts and the other schools in this area, we have programs that have been developed that are highly specific to those schools and are responsive to our needs and the needs of the schools. We have such programs at several schools such as Northeastern University, MIT, Harvard, and many other institutions around this area.

QUESTION: Explain those relationships.

TERMEER: Those relationships are multifaceted. They are tailored to specific schools within each university. We don't have a recruiting specialist who goes and gives a presentation about us. Instead, it is one of our employees, an alumnus of the particular school, who has the dual interest of supporting their school and making sure that the right people are being introduced into the company. And we foster that. I spend time personally listening to alumni of the schools around here. I give talks to classes. Others give talks at classes. We write cases that are being taught at these schools. We give examples of particular issues.

QUESTION: These are cases for the Harvard Business School, for example?

TERMEER: Yes, for the B School. And for Harvard's Kennedy (School of Government), and of course the Sloan School at MIT as well. So there is a real live relationship with the educational institutions in our area that is multifaceted, that has many different levels, where people that are in these institutions, who are proud of their programs, and want to improve their programs, ask for our help.

QUESTION: So you've created a powerful pipeline.

TERMEER: There's a pipeline that is continuously being evaluated by alumni who work here and came out of all those schools. They focus on what has worked and what hasn't worked, the characteristics of the individual who would work well here. So there are not many misfits, if you like, or complete surprises, because there is a lot of knowledge in this process.

QUESTION: By the time you actually speak about a job, you've gotten to know someone pretty well.

TERMEER: The criteria are high. This environment, of course, is an attractive environment. The purpose of meeting medical needs, trying to discover, and then actually creating access to these discoveries on a global basis, is a powerful attraction. Whatever it is, whether manufacturing or quality control, development of clinical trials or basic research or marketing, or the financial underpinnings, they're all interesting. They all work towards a purpose that is easily translatable. People can easily feel good about a sense of purpose. And the people within the company are very aware of that purpose.

QUESTION: Is that the corporate mission?

TERMEER: The word "mission" has never really stuck with me as a good word because it has something religious around it that I find more complex. But it is a purpose. The purpose is to come up with these treatments that work for patients, and to make sure that patients, wherever they are, get them. Add to that the process of doing all the other important steps correctly. It may take 10 or 15 years of failures before you get there, and that's okay, as long as you keep doing it in the very best way and learn from what you are doing. People in the community are somewhat aware of what this company does. Our people are motivated and they try to do this work in a very good way. You have to be serious. You can't just be flighty or uncommitted. Making that clear to everyone beforehand helps to select people who come for the right reasons.

There are other aspects of the company that are appealing. We haven't had layoffs or those types of things, so people feel comfortable that they can have a long-term career here. And the company's grown continuously. The internal promotion process is very visible. What's my career path? We don't have anything like AT&T. But we can point to many people who are growing and keep growing and do things that really satisfy their needs.

QUESTION: How many employees are there right now?
TERMEER: Between 9,500 and 10,000. Here in Massachusetts there are 4,000 to 4,500.

QUESTION: Just to step back a moment, you talked about the specific relationships with each university. Can you give me an example of how that might play out; say at a place like MIT?
TERMEER: At MIT, it starts with me being on the board.

QUESTION: That helps.
TERMEER: Actually it started with one of our board members being a full professor at MIT. So there was a natural, early connection there.

QUESTION: That was from the beginning?
TERMEER: From the very beginning, eight professors from MIT were advising me. And they had about 200 post-docs working for them.

That really got us a nice selection. They're right across the street, so we really have a lot of contact. That connection started at a high level. Within the different schools, such as the Sloan School in terms of MBAs, we teach there. We bring internships in. We have about 140 interns every year, not all from Sloan, but from the community, some from Sloan. We have an MBA program specifically to hire MBAs from schools such as Sloan, the Harvard Business School, Northwestern, Stanford, Darden, and Wharton in a carefully orchestrated process.

We go to these campuses and we talk to the students, not once, but a few times, to educate them about the company. We encourage Genzyme cases to be taught so students are familiar with and curious about the company. We participate in the on-campus recruiting program and we try to get resumes that are relevant to us. The best way is to get people to work here for a summer as interns so we get to know them and they get to know us.

QUESTION: Of those 140 interns, how many are likely to be offered full-time jobs?

TERMEER: I have asked that question but nobody is really sure, because some people go back to school for a year, then have work experience somewhere else, then come here. The percentage of people who come back to the company at some point in the first five years after graduating is pretty high. So we consider it a great investment. We ought to do that calculation more precisely. But regardless, I wouldn't want to do without this program because we don't want to lose that connection to our knowledge about these schools.

MIT also has an industrial program in the chemistry/biochemistry department in which people participate as members. There are other companies with similar programs but the difference is that we are here. A company in California must administer the program from a distance which is more complex and time-consuming. For us, it becomes a more natural connection.

Another connection in the pipeline is when we license technology. The technology might be developed by individuals at MIT and sometimes they come across to work here. That brings talent into the company that's highly specific to a particular situation.

The power of being within this geographic cluster is that it gives us access to the absolute top talent, which would be so much more difficult to get if you were in Peoria or in Cincinnati. The connection between the top talent and a corporation is not just at a recruiting moment. It's happening over time.

QUESTION: And you play a personal role in this?
TERMEER: Three weeks ago, I went over to the Sloan School and taught a class for a morning.

QUESTION: That's an innovation for the CEO to be teaching classes.
TERMEER: Yes, you couldn't do it if you had to spend a whole day, but if you spend an hour and a half, it's doable.

QUESTION: Is that something you've done regularly over the years?
TERMEER: Yes, I've done it for years. I've taught business classes and sometimes they have these keynote speeches. I also come in for programs the students organize. We do it at MIT; we do it at Harvard Business School quite a bit and at other schools such as UMass, Boston University, and at the Darden School at the University of Virginia, where I got my MBA. That's a high quality of life thing to do. If you want to have real fun, that's what you do, without having to design the course.

QUESTION: It's clear you didn't set up the company here in this area by accident. You obviously saw that this was fertile ground for talent. But even with that, given the competitive nature of biotech right now, you are competing with a lot of others right here for the best and the brightest. So being here is great but is it enough?
TERMEER: It's not enough. Because being here gets you access if you're prepared to be part of the community in the way that we described. Once people come onboard, however, the experience needs to be consistent with their expectations. Maybe the greatest value of these programs is that they have caused our retention to be very high and our turnover to be very low. We lose people that have a master's degree or bachelor's degree who go back to school for the next degree, because that's so attractive here. Or husbands

or wives move, or whatever. But we have very little turnover—its rave when somebody who works here, and is really engaged in something decides that they would really like to work for Biogen. That hardly happens, particularly on the science side. In IT, it's a little looser. But in science and engineering, in those aspects, it is a very stable environment. Even when Novartis came into Cambridge and hired 1,400 people, we lost just a few.

QUESTION: Few meaning what? Under one hundred?

TERMEER: Under ten. And in many cases, they've come back. It's rare that people leave for another company. It does happen, but that's really rare. And our senior vice president of human resources keeps telling me, "We are so fortunate." Now, why are people staying is the question.

I believe it starts with how we run the company. It is a purpose-driven company. What we get engaged in is important stuff. It's important to finish it, to deliver. It's much bigger than an individual's personal interest, to deliver a solution to a healthcare problem. And the feeling that you are making progress towards it, that it is not just an idea or a wish or a hope or an expectation, but you're actually getting there, that you're making progress. That's very compelling, too. So it's not easy to give up on if you're making progress on something with purpose that you really believe in. Also, the collaborative environment is competitive but it is very respectful. There's not much politics.

QUESTION: No politics?

TERMEER: There are always politics. But there's not much here. They don't overwhelm. The company is quite horizontal in nature. It's not very vertical with 20,000 committees and layers that you have to go through to get permission to come to work in the morning. It's a very horizontal environment. Of course, that is easy for me to say. I sit here in this ivory tower and what do I know? But I test it and I really make it my business to have a good sense for that. A certain amount of my time is dedicated to those kinds of efforts. I meet with people and know what they do and what they are engaged in. I don't know every one of the 10,000 people, but

I know what we do. And if they explain where they work, I will know what the work is and what it is all about.

I visit the factories. I go to all the sites around the world on a regular basis. When we had our 20th anniversary, I went to every site. I met every single employee, wherever they were. We're planning to do that again, not simply to have great celebrations and parties, but to really know what people do, and to explain the company and to allow a back and forth.

But the notion of a purpose-driven environment and how it translates to all our sites is the thing that's so consistent and so powerful, so absolutely convincing to me, which is not something I would have expected to have worked out that way. For example, we recently built a new plant in Ireland. We had zero employees. Now we have 350 employees. It was an empty building, now it's a building full of equipment and people.

QUESTION: How long a time period did it take to get staffed up over there?

TERMEER: It happened over a period of two years. We built the first plant and now we've built two more. The last time I was there, all 350 employees or most of them, were sitting in a basement of a hotel, the only space we could find in Waterford for all these people to fit in one place. It was 7 o'clock in the morning because they had to go to work at 8, and they were there for a meeting with me. I stood in the middle and they had breakfast, a good Irish breakfast. To a person, in the questions, in the remarks, and in the comments, these people understood what we were about. This was not because we had a mission statement sent up there or a manual to say, "Tell them this when you hire them." This was in the natural conversation, getting people onboard. The characterization of the type of people who fit in this kind of environment came across. And the quality of that organization was, from the beginning, absolutely excellent. The ability to build very complex engineering structures, get them to work, get them to be FDA-approved, was extraordinary.

That was Ireland. We did the same in Belgium. We did the same in Haverhill, Massachusetts. We're now building up in China. It translates so well to have a purpose that you can relate to.

QUESTION: Do you have a profile? Have you worked out over these 25 years, a sense of who's going to make it as a Genzyme person and who isn't?

TERMEER: It's almost self-selecting. We don't do profiling in any way and say, "This kind of background would fit us." But it will come out in the conversation; it will come out in the interview process. There are a number of people who have come across that are not very good in this somewhat unstructured environment. Here you take on a great deal of personal responsibility to do your part and you don't wait for your job to arrive at your desk. Much of that gets weeded out in the natural process, even before the interview takes place. Because most of our hires are through references, people refer people to us, through whatever connection. This is very true especially here in Massachusetts. It may be less true in areas where we have fewer people.

Of course we promote from within if we can, to the maximum extent possible. The management team has been around for a long time, so they know each other and the direction and the atmosphere don't change constantly. People aren't surprised by regular changes in direction: "What do we do now?" because there's a new person coming in. That helps. We also support significant training and education.

QUESTION: The training is ongoing through someone's career?

TERMEER: Yes, they train continuously, through many different layers, and in a very thoughtful way. We have meetings that specifically look at talent, unusual talents, and make sure that we understand how unusual talents progress within the company. But, again, that is not done in order to create an elite status and lesser status. No. It's an awareness of specific skills and talents and leadership. We promote the word "leadership" a great deal and individualism, more so than "team." Team is more an effect of our leadership and individualism. It's really what makes it happen.

QUESTION: That's kind of the opposite of what you hear a lot today. It's all about teams, building teams.

TERMEER: You can put a bunch of people together. It doesn't create anything. People tend to choose their environments and the company they want to work in, particularly people who have choices. And good people have choices. They choose their work. That's an individual decision. It's an individual decision to be in a very complex industry where there are natural uncertainties, highly regulated, et cetera, et cetera. Then those individuals choose other like-minded individuals who are also choosing their own career. They're not driven into a career. They form teams, teams that really work together.

There's the mountaineering equation. When somebody wants to climb a mountain, it's an individual decision. They say, "I want to climb that mountain." What route? "I want to go through the route that nobody has done." You say, "You're going to freeze your butt off." They say, "I don't care. I want to do that route." "Why do you do this?" "I don't know, but that's what I want to do."

That person is not going alone. He chooses another individual who went through the same personal process, made the same individual decision. Together they form a team. There are four, five, six more people and they put a rope between them and they go up. When you have a rope that connects you, you can't go your individual way. You have to make a choice. You have to make a decision. You have to figure it out, because you only can go one way. And when somebody's in trouble, you stop. You don't cut the rope. You become connected, in a way. If you can't get to the summit without killing yourself, you don't go there. You wait for the next day. You wait for a nicer day.

We use these analogies a lot within the company. We have an award that we call the Alpine Award. And this is a global award that particularly deals with the business aspects of the company. Everybody on the business side of the company participates. We have a separate award on the science and clinical side, and something different on the manufacturing side. But they're all somewhat similar.

QUESTION: How is the award given?

TERMEER: It is a team that may get the award and an individual. People get nominated by the leaders in their organization. Eventually it gets to my office. I get a recommendation of which team in

Brazil or Timbuktu or Cambridge, usually smaller groups, 20 people or so, and which individual, sometimes two individuals, who really are the right role models.

This process is visible and talked about. Whoever gets the award or whatever team gets the award, it is a massive victory. They all get the crystal Alpine and a slightly larger Alpine if you're an individual winner. In communication to them this notion of mountaineering is explained. The absolute need for excellence, the absolute need to do it right, the absolute need to not kill themselves in the way that they climb that mountain.

QUESTION: Is there a monetary reward with it?
TERMEER: For the individual, there's a monetary component to it ($10,000). For the team, there's no financial component, but it is a great honor.

QUESTION: It's a source of great pride.
TERMEER: Great pride. It's like the Nobel in the company. And people feel great about it.

QUESTION: And it's given out each year?
TERMEER: It's given each year and I do the presentation. I went to Brazil a year ago. I tell you, it is magnificent. There was not a dry eye in the room. People were just crying from joy and pride. It's a real global recognition. The description makes it clear that it's not that you have reached the summit and everybody else was stuck behind. But you became the role model, the example, the description of how we operate, what works for us.

This notion of recognition, there are many other mechanisms that we use as well . . . this notion of recognizing and identifying with what we do is maybe the most powerful way for people to feel emotionally connected to all this. Now, there's also a monetary side. Ever since I've been here, which is 25 years now and the company is 27 years old, we have given everybody equity at every level. So, all 9,500 people get options. They get options and restricted stock.

That has been a big commitment and it is not without controversy because there has been dilution associated with that and shareholders ask big questions and increasingly more questions about that. We think about it very, very carefully. Is it the right thing to do? Is it something that we can talk about to everybody, all stakeholders, the shareholders, and feel comfortable? So when I get questions at our annual meetings or wherever, it's okay with me. It's a fair question to ask. And we are able to give an answer.

The answer of course is that it identifies for all employees the value creation, that component of the company that of course happens only if we are successful in developing and reaching our purpose. That's a very important aspect, as well, in terms of retention.

QUESTION: So if you knew that a prospective employee was a real superstar, say, on the research side and somebody you'd love to have, and the first thing they're asking about is compensation, would that be a red flag to you? Would you assume the person is not going to fit in here?"

TERMEER: If that becomes an uncomfortable conversation or you can't get away from it, it could become a problem. You start to wonder if this person is really understanding or focusing on the right thing. But it is actually a fair question to ask. A person has a family, has a house to buy, has to possibly make a move, and there's a cost to making the decision. It's a totally fair question to ask, and we need to be able to answer it absolutely fairly and not just say, "Trust us." That's not how it works.

But it can't be the sole focus. You spend a very good amount of time getting to understand each other in terms of, "What are we going to do together?" and "What is the role you would play, and can you make that contribution?" At some levels, when it comes to my office, I give people a lot of time just to think about, "What is it that you really want to do now?"

Because if you start to do this work, you take on a responsibility. This is something that actually surprises people sometimes. When you are in a discovery phase in the research, you may find something important. Once you've found something in terms of a clinical benefit, something that works and can treat the patient with MS or with some horrifying disease that can't be treated otherwise, then it becomes a responsibility. Having found it, you have to utilize that finding.

If you can't get to it, find another way to make progress. Because you are dealing with a health issue here, the health of another person. Understanding that it is a responsibility once you have something that could be of value in that area rather than a financial opportunity or a way to shine individually, is key. If a person doesn't see that and continuously focuses on money and says, "I'd like to get a royalty if I make a discovery," they probably won't succeed here.

QUESTION: So that can't be the primary motivation.

TERMEER: It can't be your only motivation. Plus, we would say, you should work outside the company and we would license something from you. But within the company you would not get the royalties. We do have a bonus system. When there's an unusual performance by a group, we have an instantaneous way to reward them. We allocate 20% of all equity compensation of the company for recognition bonuses. So if a particular group has done something very well, and it works out very well, then the supervisor has the opportunity to give an instantaneous award. And that works very well. There are these ways to connect the equity piece, the financial piece, with the performance piece.

But back to your example, if somebody is too focused on only the financial side of the equation and does not ask many questions about the other side, then the conversation dries up.

QUESTION: Have you seen good people walk because of that?

TERMEER: In many cases, *we* walk. It's not comfortable. The conversation becomes clear. I'm very direct. It's okay, of course. You have one life to live and you have to make your choices and it can't be forced. You make a decision. If you're not ready to make a decision, take some time and that's fine as well. In some cases, we take quite a long time to recruit and nurture the person until the situation is right and then we connect.

QUESTION: Your investment into each individual that you've hired must be quite significant. You just talked about training. Have you measured what a five-year employee's worth is to you in terms of just pure investment?

TERMEER: I have no sense of that. The investment is definitely less than the productivity, so you get something in return. The payroll piece of our company is material. It's very large. But upon success, when you are able to bring to the marketplace something that really works, that investment is relatively small. The investment of course, the equity that many individuals develop by becoming knowledgeable on how things work, how to express ideas so that they can be acted on, that's a very important ingredient, too. You can't be just an individual. You have to be able to create an environment that brings people on board into an idea, so that others can help you carry it through. It is magnificently powerful if you find somebody that can do that very well.

Now if somebody can do it very well and has only bad ideas, it's not so good. And that becomes very visible as well. We are not only about research and development; we are about lots of other things that relate to manufacturing and to access of these medicines around the world, building factories, and so on. A person builds individual equity by becoming an expert, acquiring knowledge about a particular disease that is aided by the skill sets within the company and outside the company. That is a very powerful proposition. And that's where the risk is. A competitive company may look at those key positions and try to steal them. In the software industry, this happens all the time; whole teams go. We've had it happen, but it's very rare, very rare. This industry's still quite civilized by comparison. It happens but I must say, in the 25 years, I only have had two highly uncomfortable experiences.

QUESTION: Where you got raided?

TERMEER: Some other company came to take our talent and found some traction and we were damaged, not fatally, but we had some damage. It's very frowned upon in the biotechnology industry to do that.

QUESTION: The unspoken rule of gentlemanly conduct.

TERMEER: Yes, because you're vulnerable yourself. If you do it, of course everybody else will do it as well.

QUESTION: Has it changed even as the field has become more successful and more competitive?

TERMEER: No, not in a material way.

QUESTION: Your culture is built on a few key values including being environmentally responsible. Your headquarters building is considered a model of green building, for example. How does that play into the hiring process?

TERMEER: Those aspects of the company are known. The environmental side of the company is known and people notice us. Many people come into this building and say they're surprised about the marked attention that we paid to the environment in doing this. The thing that I find has traction with people is doing things right. There's no room for sloppiness. When you produce something that you put into the vein of a child, there can be no excuses. You can't say, "I was a little distracted here." No. You do it right. And to do it right, you have to do lots of things right. Not so over the top that you can't afford to do it, but do it and do it right. Don't lose the courage to do it because you don't quite know what right means. Keep moving and do it right.

It's a very important aspect for our employees, feeling good and proud of the company, being able to go home and talk to your spouse and children about what you do and how it's done, and how you take your responsibility seriously. Right is very functional; very to the point, very pragmatic but very high quality and very high standards and something that's visible. You can see it and sense it. You know it. Because when someone doesn't want to do it right, you make yourself an outcast, even if nobody may notice it in the beginning. Eventually it becomes noticeable. Certainly it's immediately noticeable to you.

QUESTION: There's so much at stake. Do you have metrics within the company on measuring talent and how people are performing?

TERMEER: We have the normal kind of evaluation system that you would find. Maybe it's more sophisticated or less sophisticated than some. But it is there and it's used for merit increases and for promotions. I like to know precisely what distinguishes someone and what needs improvement. Of course that's done with all the plusses and minuses that come together with these kinds of evaluations. Some supervisors are very good at this and some are not so good at it. And there we provide training, to help people do the best possible evaluations.

QUESTION: You would think that competitive people who would feel strongly about what they're doing and they really throw their whole life into it and they don't get the review they like, that would become an issue?

TERMEER: Yes, if you don't give a good explanation for the evaluation, there is a clear issue. But very smart people also understand good explanations. And we haven't had problems that have reached my desk. There are cases where a person feels, "Why didn't I get that opportunity? Why did somebody else get it?" Those are fair questions and often not so precise. I offer personal time to talk to whoever wants to talk about it. We try not to make anything a mystery or some kind of secret. If the appearance of that develops, then I like to break it down very quickly.

QUESTION: What about the issue of diversity?

TERMEER: Diversity is enormously powerful in terms of retention, in terms of how you feel about the community you're in. We do a lot of work on that. There's a chronic shortage of African-American entrants in the sciences and in these kinds of companies. So we are supporting many programs on the outside. I've been on the board of an organization for 15 years to try to help improve things in this area. We've made progress, but it is not enough progress. We're also supporting the teachers. We fund quite a few teachers programs in biotechnology, in our communities around this area and nationally. We've given a $2 million grant over five years to a very large program at Boston's Museum of Science that trains teachers. And we try and help spread the word in a good way.

Then in hiring people, we keep an eye on the diversity question. You know, obviously the skills have to be there, but diversity within itself, good diversity is a skill. It provides a skill. It creates a skill. So without it, we would not be as strong.

QUESTION: Do you incent your employees to recruit for you?

TERMEER: Yes, we do. We give a bonus for finding new employees. It depends on what kind of person you bring in. If it's a hard to fill position, then the bonus is higher. But typically, we give between $1,000 and $1,500.

QUESTION: Globalization is the hot topic now. With immigration issues and the difficulties of keeping foreign students in this country—presumably a key recruiting option for you—how are you addressing all this?

TERMEER: It is an issue. Immigration is an issue at every level. We have many Hispanic people employed in the company in other functions, not necessarily science functions. Many of them are immigrants. Many of them are impacted by these dynamics. *I'm* an immigrant. Of course I became an American citizen, but still I was an immigrant for a long time and I have an enormous sympathy for immigrants. In Holland, there were immigrants. The Turkish immigrants in Holland were there because work needs to be done. It is the same in Germany and so on. The immigrant issue is very important, very emotional, but very real. There's something very distasteful about the current discussion on the right side of the equation, extremely distasteful. I make it my business to be heard on this.

QUESTION: But what about the issue of globalization in the search for talent?

TERMEER: Of course we have a choice. We can set up an operation in China. We are doing that, not for outsourcing, but because China is a big market. There are 1.3 billion people there and obviously we need to be as active there as we are in Europe. We have many Asians, particularly Chinese people, working here who came out of the local schools and would love to go back. There are visa limitations for those skills. But that is almost manageable by allowing people with those skills to work somewhere else. You can bring it to where it's most manageable.

This is a little different from the Google or Microsoft problem. In those industries, you have a sudden need and you want to do it in-house because of some other proprietary reason. They need more access to these programmers from India. They run out of talent every year in terms of the quotas. We don't see it as much in our industry, and the numbers are smaller. Also the enormous production of really good people in this area through the schools, it gives us a leg up.

QUESTION: Do you face the issue of filling short-term needs but having to avoid overhiring for the long-term?

TERMEER: That is not so much the case in our industry. It used to be more the case. But in our industry, there are so many small companies that have almost no resources. They have become almost entirely dependent on CROs, contract organizations such as contract manufacturing, contract research, contract clinical, and so on. These contract companies were created because there was such demand from all these hundreds and hundreds of small companies that couldn't recreate all these resources.

So the competency to outsource is there. Now even China and India provide outsourcing capabilities, not like backroom groups such as in telecommunications or software, but more in terms of doing certain jobs that have a time limit. So we tend not to hire on a temporary basis, unless there's longevity to it. If something really feels temporary, then we would use a contract organization.

QUESTION: What about the opposite issue, hiring in areas now that you worry you might not be as strong in, but that might show promise in the early stages of research?

TERMEER: We have not run into a situation where we say, "We have to shelve that for a year or two and build the organization first." There are also a lot of transactions such as acquisitions. Most of the larger companies in our space, including us, have done transactions that bring in capacity for things that you don't have in a make/buy sense. And since you know a lot about a specific technology or function, you tend to know what you're buying. We recently bought a company in San Diego with the capability to make vectors for gene therapy.

QUESTION: Vectors?

TERMEER: Vectors. They're used to deliver gene therapy, so that they can produce proteins in the body. This particular company, we knew forever. We knew some of the people who worked there. Suddenly our needs grew to a level where we said, "We either build this plant or we buy that plant." We asked the people who owned the plant, "Would you sell it to us?" And they said sure. So it worked for them, worked for us. In that way we brought in 45 highly competent people who would have taken us a while to recruit.

QUESTION: What about the issue of executive hiring? You mentioned the executive team has been together a very long time.

TERMEER: For a long time. The last person we hired from the outside at the officer level was four years ago. And prior to that, I have to go back more than ten years. It's very infrequent.

QUESTION: Is that a blessing and a curse? Because there seems to be a block for young, ambitious people who want to feel there is an upward career path.

TERMEER: No. The company has grown so rapidly and it is very horizontal. So you don't have to get into this narrow path to the top. But the notion of lack of turnover, where it is a negative is in science, because sometimes technologies move and people get out-of-date or have biases. Something doesn't work because they tried it for ten years and it never worked, and then a breakthrough occurs. A skeptical person may not go there. You need new people. You need new blood in technology all the time, on the science, research side, all the time. So there has to be natural turnover. We don't force turnover. We kind of try and pull it apart a little bit and make sure that we don't have groups that have no new blood, new air.

QUESTION: Are there other organizations that have stood out for you as a role model in how you find and retain talent, do your work, and keep the best and the brightest?

TERMEER: That's such an unfair question. I like to learn all the time. I don't take for granted anything we do. I learn from wherever I am and how people do things. I don't think there is a perfect organization. But there are organizations that have done a fabulous job. Genentech has done a fantastic job in building skill, maintaining reputation, and really focusing on the science and good commercialization. They've done an absolutely great job. Gilead, which is in our space, has done a fantastic job in HIV, sustained the cause, done a really great job, and very high quality people as well. So there are clearly cases that I admire immensely.

QUESTION: How about outside the biotech world?

TERMEER: I'm on the board of the Massachusetts General Hospital (MGH) in Boston. I'm very impressed by the MGH organization and how they do things. It's an organization I'm exposed to because of my role there. It's fantastic how well they are able to have 19,000 people who are all underpaid; except for some physicians, most of the staff is underpaid. But they're highly motivated, highly competent, and do things where the margin of error is zero. The quality control is the patient. The patient will let it be known if something goes wrong. It's powerful. It's extremely descriptive from my view of the power of having a respect for what you do.

If you can create that respect in an organization, chances are that you will succeed. And if you get anywhere close to that in an organization, it becomes a bond that's understandable, it doesn't make it a mission statement with six bullets. It makes you pragmatic, makes you think about it in realistic terms, in terms of what you can do and what the organization does.

Another organization I'm very close to is MIT of course. And that is a magnificent example of a fantastic academic institution. You couldn't call it an organization. You can't even come close to describing how it works. It is just extraordinary people who are able to get together. They believe in teaching.

QUESTION: What's your biggest worry for the future in terms of your people?

TERMEER: I think the future will be bright if we don't lose our courage in what we do. What we do is not without risk. And there are simpler ways of doing things, particularly now that we have a base. We can take less risk. But that would devastate it. Then I can't keep the talent. Then I can't attract the talent and I can't challenge the talent. Then I can't challenge myself. Losing the courage for taking the risks, going in a place where you know you need to spend five years or ten years or fifteen years. Losing the courage to do so and becoming short-term, that kills what we do. And that kills the attractiveness of this organization to exceptional people.

CHAPTER 12

Gordon Bethune

FORMER CHAIRMAN AND CEO
CONTINENTAL AIRLINES

Set a Course, Stick to It,
Measure Your Progress Along the Way

Gordon Bethune is one of the most successful CEOs ever to run an airline. When he took over as president and COO of Continental Airlines, in 1994, it was the worst performing airline in the industry on nearly every measure—except for one: lost and mishandled luggage. Continental led the industry in lost and damaged bags. In addition, the airline had the worst on-time performance in the industry, suffered from low worker morale, and was losing money. Continental would have been a challenge for any CEO.

After being named CEO, Bethune in November 1994 acted quickly to turn around the company. He did so by enlisting the support of the airline's employees. One of his first initiatives was a policy to reward every employee whenever the airline scored first in on-time performance. When that occurred, every employee in the company received at home a check for $65. The idea in Bethune's mind was not just to reward good performance but to celebrate it. His goal? Make every employee feel like a hero at home whenever the airline was number one.

In less than a year, Continental went from *Worst to First*, the title of Bethune's book about his experiences leading the airline. In 1996, he became chairman and CEO of the company.

Bethune's turnaround of Continental was not just about making it a profitable and respected company. It was about changing its culture. In doing so, Bethune had something powerful going for him. He was one of "them," a CEO with airline credentials. Blunt spoken and often profane, Bethune was a licensed commercial pilot and airframe and power plant mechanic. Prior to coming to Continental he had been a vice president at Boeing.

Bethune's success could not have occurred without changing the airline's culture. As this interview shows, he did it by paying attention to people, rewarding them for success, and choosing metrics that really mattered.

QUESTION: You turned around an airline and rebuilt its culture from one of defeatism to success. To get people to change their behavior, what did you get them to focus on?

BETHUNE: It's pretty simple. You focus on the wrong things, you get the wrong result. If you were Airbus, and you thought your success was in making a bigger airplane than Boeing makes, then you'd be wrong. It's just not true. And what happened? Airbus built the wrong airplane. So, your definition of success has to be your customer's definition of success. That's what it has to be. Whatever the customer says, that's what it is. And, you've got to communicate that around your organization.

QUESTION: How do you find out what the customer wants?

BETHUNE: Well, you have to know something about the business you're in. If you're in the watch sales and service business, doesn't it help to know how a watch works and what they do?

In my business, the airline business, customers want to get to their destination on time. You can't be successful unless you do that very well. I don't care what movies or what routes you fly. It doesn't matter. People have to arrive at their destination on time or they won't fly with you.

QUESTION: So being on time was your primary metric?

BETHUNE: Timing drives everything. It's an orchestra. The timing in an orchestra drives the whole orchestra. One guy's off and it's like a part missing in a wristwatch. How many parts do you have in a watch? Which part don't you think you need? If one of them stops, the whole thing stops. How about if the crew doesn't show up, how can you board the airplane?

We're a complicated mechanism, a service business with a value system that's defined by our customers to stay reliable, on time, and all that, every day. Not just on good days, not just on days you feel good. Just like a wristwatch, it wouldn't have value if it stopped every couple of weeks. Let's say the watch has been running intermittently for the past two weeks and it stops. There's no value. So, the value in an airplane is the reliability and consistency of its delivery of what is a clean, safe trip for its destination. That's all it is from your perspective. So, that would be your metric and everyone would work around that.

QUESTION: How'd you change the culture to one of high performance?
BETHUNE: First of all, we said, "Who's the biggest beneficiary of an on time airline?" It's the employees that work there. They can go home when they're supposed to. And, when you're on time, you don't have any customers yelling at you because you're late. And when everything's on time, you're not missing any bags. So, we showed them how things are kind of nice when they run right. They're really nice when everything works on schedule. So, who's the biggest benefactor of a well-run organization? It's the employees. That drives a lot of things.

QUESTION: Were there other changes?
BETHUNE: When you look at why you're late, you ask, who wrote the schedule? Turns out it's marketing. Now, marketing ought to decide where we're going and when we're going, but not how long it takes. The time it takes to fly a leg is different in the summer than it is in the winter because of weather. So the time it took to fly a leg went to operations. That's who determined that.

See, like I said, marketing tells you where you want to go, "We want a two o'clock flight to Albuquerque." But operations flies the airplane. So, operations says if we leave at two, this is when we arrive at Albuquerque. So to make this work, you get everybody together: the airport people, the pilots, and they all kind of say this is what it takes to go to Albuquerque on Tuesday on a summer day if you leave at two o'clock.

QUESTION: How did you get everybody to work harmoniously?

BETHUNE: All right, now if you say you're going to act like a team and reward everybody based on your metric of on-time performance, then they know either they all get paid or nobody gets paid. That creates a big incentive to get people to work together. Everyone's in it together.

So, the overall metric we use to celebrate our performance is the one where the government ranks all airlines by on-time performance. Every airline has to report its performance under law. We needed to be in the Top 5.

So, in February 1995, the first month of the program, we came in fourth place. We had payroll cut a separate check, not part of the paycheck, and no direct deposits. The checks were sent home. These checks weren't big, sixty-five dollars, and on the memo it said "thank you for helping us be on time." So, sixty-five bucks just dropped out of the sky, right? And everybody got it at home. In March, we came in first place, and everybody got a check in the middle of March. In April, we came in first place again, and everybody got another check.

QUESTION: So, you used the check as a kind of communication system to tell people they had done well and to let them do a little bragging at home, too?

BETHUNE: Yeah. So, first of all, you say something—set a goal—and then you do it. And then you reward the behavior you need to get you there. Very simple. The idea is that people realize that because they're all in it together they can solve the problem on their own. If the plane fills up and you find you're short a couple of meals— which can happen—rather than waiting for those meals to show up and be late, the flight attendant can just make the decision to go. She knows being on time is what's important. Instead of finding fault and passing the buck, they solve the problem. That's the power of "everybody gets paid or nobody gets paid."

QUESTION: What about the person who didn't get a meal?

BETHUNE: Not everybody is going to eat on that plane. They don't all necessarily want to. So, the flight attendant can finesse it. She can tell a couple of businessmen, "Hey I'll buy you drinks if you skip the meal." She can do that.

QUESTION: She has the power to make those decisions?

BETHUNE: Sure, I let her do whatever she wants. See, the dynamics change. Everyone's suddenly in it together.

QUESTION: And, how does she know she can make those decisions?

BETHUNE: She works here. She knows. And I told everyone they have that power. See, you've got to let the people run their own show, but the goal is to be on time. I mean, here's a nineteen-year old flight attendant, maybe working here only three months. Everyone sits down, they close the doors. We go. You know why? She wants that money. It's not a lot, but to her it's a pair of shoes or a car insurance payment. So, now I've got people who normally don't give a darn and they give a darn.

We put our 800-number in to solve these kinds of problems and we staffed it with a woman who later became our senior VP of Flight Operations. If there was always a truck in the way in the parking lot that caused delays, you'd call it in. It's a tool to get you to be on time, because there are a lot of barriers to being on time.

We communicate what we need to do, we measure it, and we talk about it every day. A daily news update would come out everyday. A bulletin board, a voicemail you could listen to, the 800-number I mentioned. We constantly told people how we were doing regarding on-time performance, what we were doing with our baggage, what our stock was doing, who did what to whom in our company.

QUESTION: Was there competition between teams? Cities?

BETHUNE: No, no, no. There's no competition. We're all on one team. There's only Continental. We're beating United, American, Delta. We don't beat each other. That's important.

QUESTION: How do you make it known that you're one, single team?

BETHUNE: Like I said, you only pay them when you beat them. That's the way we're measured as a company. Your customers, they don't give a darn about your budget. We're Continental. What's Continental's reputation? Are they clean, safe, and reliable? Do they get us there on time? That's what our customers want. If we can't provide that to them, they'll fly somebody else. So, we became the most on-time airline in America. That's what happens when you get focused. When you are all on one team. And, when people fly a lot, they notice.

QUESTION: What was the next step after that with regard to changing the airline's culture?

BETHUNE: It's not sequential. You do things concurrently. So, we put in profit-sharing. Fifteen percent of pre-tax income gets distributed to employees based on their levels within the company.

QUESTION: Everyone gets the same share?

BETHUNE: No. It's per your earnings. If you earned less than I did, I would get more than you did.

QUESTION: So you segmented the workforce?

BETHUNE: No. We don't do that because that's not the way teams work. You want to know how that changes the culture? I'll tell you. You're a flight attendant and you're working flights everyday. If it's half full, you work less than on a full flight. Let's say that your company is jamming the heck out of it and running full flights a day. If that's the case, then you're working a lot harder. You say, "darn! That guy's got three bags!" But if you get a percentage of the money that comes in from running full flights, you're really glad to see that guy with all the bags and you're happy to find a place for his bags! So, you've got to put the workers into the equation. Why would they be glad to see you if there was nothing in it for them besides more work? That's the psychology of success. If you want to modify the fish's behavior, well, it's incumbent on you to figure out what the fish likes then, isn't it? Maybe if you know enough and study enough about how to motivate a fish, you might get it to do what you need it to do.

You think our employees are any different? Why would they want you to be successful? I had a guy on my board who said, "You know, your employees ought to be happy to have a job." But my answer was, "Hey, I have a job, everybody has a job. You want me to bust my rear end at your job so you can be successful? What's in it for me?"

It's like a horse race. The measure of success in a horse race is the first horse that starts *here* and gets *there* is a winner. The rest don't win. Does the winning horse get things that the losers don't? You bet they do. That's why they work harder. Motivation isn't always money, but you've got to have something in it for the horses.

QUESTION: What are some of the non-financial motivations?

BETHUNE: Recognition. Being the best they are in the world, being proud of who you work for, and having people say, "Hey, we're a J.D. Power award-winner." Telling someone from United Airlines, they're in second place and you're in first. Telling your competitors that you beat them every day at the same game they plan. I mean, we all fly to the same cities and we're on time and they're not! All that helps.

QUESTION: What about individual recognition?

BETHUNE: To me, that's not key. Eventually you might get a promotion or something, but that's a different issue. We're not talking about individuals, we're talking about teams.

QUESTION: But were individuals rewarded as well?

BETHUNE: The good ones moved up and got promoted, the bad ones got fired, and the rest of them got to keep their jobs. I mean we also had recognition of great behavior. We had Pizza Day, for example. Is that recognition? I mean, free pizza is better than no pizza, right?

QUESTION: Did they get time with you?

BETHUNE: I had a weekly voicemail: I'd go to the crew rooms. We had Thanksgiving dinner in the crew room, Christmas dinner, when people had to work. I think the leader has to be visible. Also, any rewards have to be simple and well-understood and well-articulated. That's another reason for choosing on-time performance. Because —guess what?—will we ever have good baggage numbers if our on-time performance stinks? No. We'll misconnect more bags, right? So, when our on-time got to be good, what happened to the lost bag count? What happened to complaints? They went down too. Isn't that a miracle? Customer complaints went down, employee complaints went down, and overtime went down. All that stuff went down. Why? Because we were very focused on what we had to do.

QUESTION: So you always emphasized teams?

BETHUNE: Yes. Business is a team sport. A team of thousands because you can't do it on your own. What happens if any part of the wrist watch doesn't work? What part of the watch don't you think you need? You have to let everybody know they're important. That's why everybody got paid or nobody got paid.

QUESTION: How long did it take to turn around the airline?

BETHUNE: In February of '95, we wrote our first check for being in the Top 5 of the government rankings. We were first place in March and first place in April, how fast is that? I started as CEO the previous November. That's behavior modification 101.

QUESTION: So you really changed everything in a period of a few months?

BETHUNE: We didn't have a lot of time. We were going broke. In fact, we didn't even know if we were going to make the February/ March payroll. When I became CEO the board didn't really want me. They wanted me to be Office of the Chairman. I told them I wouldn't do it. I was President and Chief Operating Officer. So I asked them, "Have you ever been in a Boeing airplane and you look in the cockpit and there's one pilot seat. Somebody needs to be in charge. People look for leadership. You can't have an office in charge." So they gave it to me.

QUESTION: Did you have a special advantage leading the company because you worked with planes?

BETHUNE: I'm not sure that the background is that important. I think it helps. But I think your personality helps you more. Look, I was the tenth CEO at Continental in a very short period of time. There were nine guys before me and some didn't last a year. So, here you are, another CEO in a company with no money. So, for me communicating with everybody was really important. They had to know I was going to be there. I started with messages from me on the voicemail system that you could access from anywhere in the system. These messages were set up so you could send a message back to me. Back to the CEO! So, everybody had information from me every week. My point is, you have to work at communication very, very hard.

So, we had an 800-number that you could call, we also did it with employees from marketing to operations. My point to everybody was, "You call Gordon, he calls you back." And, if you're a customer—we started an 800-we-care. Do you know how we reduced customer complaints to the Department of Transportation? Because customers could just call us instead of the government.

QUESTION: What other metrics did you look at?

BETHUNE: You want to know what's important to look at? Sick leave. It's a good way to measure employee morale. You watch sick leave start to drop and guess what? It means it's easier to go to work. In fact, they kind of like it here. If they don't like work, they don't go. If they do like work, they find a way to go. So, I guess we measured everything.

QUESTION: What were some of the critical people metrics you used?

BETHUNE: Like I said, attendance. People vote with their feet. If they don't like work, they don't show up. What does it cost you not to show up? We put up a perfect attendance award. I said we'll give every employee group a free car every six months, pay the federal gift taxes, and all the other taxes on it. All you've got to do is show up for work for six months without calling in sick. Flight attendants get a car, pilots get a car, reservation agents get a car. It was a drawing. One car for each employee group with perfect attendance.

And why not? The ones that don't call in sick for six months didn't cost us money. It's very expensive and disruptive when people call in sick. So, you know what happened when we did this? Sick leave went down. People showed up for work. We also gave people trips with their spouses for perfect attendance.

QUESTION: Did other airlines follow you with programs like these?
BETHUNE: No. At least not immediately.

QUESTION: Why not?
BETHUNE: Because they're smarter than we are. Go and ask them and they say they are smarter than Continental. But I know United, a couple of years later, offered an on-time bonus. It was $65, ironically, which was our figure. That $65 was derived by the number of employees we had by half of the money we thought we were losing by being late. We gave half the saving to our employees, we kept half.

I'd rather give it to them, anyway. They help me be on time so I don't waste money on hotels and cabs and putting people on American Airlines. I'll give you half the money you save us by being on time. That turned out to be $65.

Well, when United announced that they were going to implement an on-time program, they said they were going to pay $65, but only to managers! Another good idea screwed up with faulty implementation.

QUESTION: What was the result of all this?
BETHUNE: Collective behavior and the recognition we got in the marketplace and the recognition from our customer base got us on J.D. Power and 100 Best Places to work list. And you know what? We went to the same cities with the same airplanes and the same crews that couldn't get there on time before. That's the kind of changes we made.

QUESTION: How do you keep the morale up?
BETHUNE: Well, you make the place work on time. The whole system.

QUESTION: How did you come up with these metrics?

BETHUNE: I sat down with my COO, over a series of dinners and kind of laid things out on a tablet. It was what we called our product plan—to make reliability a reality. Not talk about it, do it. Then, I borrowed from my people plan from my days working at Boeing. We had to decide where we were going and how we were going to get there.

QUESTION: After you began being first in on-time performance, was the rest just fine-tuning?

BETHUNE: No, it's implementation. I mean, yeah, it's fine-tuning, because the macro things don't change. Not everybody is skeptical when you start coming in first. But old habits die hard. Before people really trust you, they have to say Gordon is going to be here and we better do what he says because it works and we better stick to it. Then they say, "We better show up." It takes time.

QUESTION: Which is what you call behavior modification?

BETHUNE: Yeah. All these things are behavior modification and some of it is peer pressure. You're sitting on the plane five hours together and you'll have the nay-sayers and the positive people who say, "We better start to do this." At first, its 50-50. Then, the mix starts to be 80% positive and 20% negative. And guess what the 20% do? Ultimately, they shut up. It's a process that takes time. In the end, I had to have credibility. People had to trust me. Look, you can't lie to your own doctor, that's kind of stupid. You can't lie to your attorney, that's also stupid. And you can't lie to your employees, because they're all you got. So don't screw around with them. Tell them the truth.

QUESTION: Did financial results follow the cultural change?

BETHUNE: We made so much money in '95 it was obscene. Continental hadn't made any money in ten years and now we got a profit. My predecessor had told the guys on Wall Street that the reason for the failure was we were broke so we had second-class citizens as employees.

So, we were flying the same airplanes to the same cities and winning J.D. Power awards. What changed? Just the leader.

QUESTION: When did you feel everything had gelled?

BETHUNE: Well, '96 was a good year. But we had a 20-year reputation to overcome in the industry. Traffic overall was up and they say a rising tide lifts all boats. But it didn't lift the ones with the holes in them. TWA went broke in '97. And we made a fortune in '97. So, you know, the answer is we have a theory of the way you run a business and the way you treat people.

CHAPTER 13

Linda A. Hill

WALLACE BRETT DONHAM PROFESSOR OF BUSINESS ADMINISTRATION, HARVARD BUSINESS SCHOOL

Linda A. Hill, Wallace Brett Donham Professor of Business Administration at the Harvard Business School, has spent her career researching, writing, teaching, and speaking about the art of management and issues pertaining to leadership and the development of leadership talent. She is Faculty Chair of the Leadership Initiative and High Potentials Leadership Program at the Harvard Business School.

Professor Hill is the author of *Power and Influence Customized Course Module*, and *Becoming a Manager: How New Managers Master the Challenges of Leadership, Second Edition*. She is also author of two e-College course modules: *Managing Your Career* and *Managing Teams*, and of the award-winning multimedia management development programs *High Performance Management and Coaching*, and *Managing for Performance*.

Professor Hill's consulting and executive education activities have been in the areas of managing change, managing cross-organizational relationships, globalization, career management, and leadership development. Professor Hill is working on two projects: leading in emerging markets and leadership as collective genius, in which she explores the relationship between leadership and innovation.

QUESTION: You have written extensively about issues pertaining to human capital, managers, and management. You've also written about how a good manager becomes a great manager. How do you think about talent innovation?

HILL: Let me tell you about what's influencing my thinking right now. One of the things that I have been studying is leadership development or talent management practices across the globe. How they manage in India, for example. In fact, we've written some case studies about it, including one on HCL Technologies. I think *Fortune* magazine described them as being one of the most innovative talent management companies in the world. What we described in the case in great detail was how HCL thinks about talent management. The first phase of their change strategy is, "employee first, customer second." Fundamentally, what HCL is doing really goes back to what we know from the research on service management— that you only get customer loyalty if you have employee loyalty. And, to the extent that we are seeing more knowledge-intensive and service businesses, getting the employee piece right is going to be the real competitive differentiator for companies. Because HCL believes in transparency, they share their strategy with their customers "employee first, customer second"—a practice that makes many of the executives to whom I have taught this case nervous. And, by the way, in places like India, the challenge is not attracting talent but retaining it. It is not simply a matter of providing the right pay and perks.

QUESTION: Okay. That's HCL technologies. What are other innovators doing?

HILL: Well, at Pixar, the computer animation and production company, there's the belief that the manager's job is to create a world in which other people want to belong. They too are thinking about what really makes work intrinsically motivating. A number of people have talked and written about how little attention is actually paid to designing work that is *intrinsically* motivating for people. Instead there's so much effort put into making sure that you have the *extrinsic* motivators right—how you pay them, recognize them, and so on. So I think the real innovators are trying to design work and the work environment in ways that tap into things that we know talented people look for. Talented people look for autonomy, challenge, development, a sense that they can contribute. We know that this is what makes work intrinsically motivating, but very rarely do companies step back and try to design work so it aligns as closely as possible with that kind of reality.

QUESTION: Is there a difference between designing work and designing jobs?

HILL: Well, one of the things I know they do at Pixar, if this is what you mean by your question, is that their executives design work around the talents of their people. They talk about the fact that "everyone has a slice of genius." If you don't believe that people have a slice of genius, they don't belong in the company. But once they are in your company your job as a manager is to find their slice of genius and design their work so it plays to that slice. Now, at Pixar, they continually rework, in a very dynamic way, the way in which groups are organized around individuals' capabilities and passions. Jobs are sculpted as much as possible to capitalize on people's strengths.

Companies recognize they need exceptional performance from people. How do you get exceptional performance? It's going to come from really helping people learn to capitalize on their strengths as opposed to correcting weaknesses. Now, of course, you need to correct weaknesses that are truly going to derail someone. But even great leaders are imperfect people, because we're all human. And so, people are not necessarily as well-rounded as we'd like.

QUESTION: If you do that, do you get the bottom line results too?

HILL: Yes, I think you do. Or, you're much more likely to. But I'd like to add that the challenge companies face is not simply selecting talent, but rather it is about developing talent. As my colleague Boris Groysberg's work shows, stars are more made than born. What you see is that they're going to work for companies where they think they're going to learn and have opportunity. Given the talent shortages across the globe, good people know they can command high salaries. They want more.

One piece of the innovator's puzzle that is very clear in companies that have been able to retain talent better than others is transparency. Why is transparency so important? I think there are lots of reasons. HCL, for instance, relies on a very content-rich intranet to share information with their global workforce and encourage candor and transparency. The CEO puts his 360-degree feedback up on the intranet for all to see, and to role model that he is open to feedback and needs to be a life-long learner. And obviously you could game or fake real transparency. But one reason why I think transparency is so important in a lot of these settings is that the more information people have about what is going on in the company, the better able they are to assess their impact and ability to contribute. You get to understand the link between your effort and results and whether the results get you the rewards you want. So, what I'm seeing in some very innovative companies is that much more information is being provided to people about a whole range of things. About what are really the drivers of the business, what's really going on with various competitors, and so on. Now, you have to trust that when you put this information on the intranet people will keep it inside. But I think we've reached a whole new level of transparency in some organizations and that that helps make work intrinsically motivating.

QUESTION: Several companies that were very innovative in creating flexible organizations ended up vanishing. How do you create an environment in which the business and people are all trying to achieve the same goals?

HILL: My coauthors and I on our new book about collective genius believe that there are a set of five paradoxes or tensions that have to be managed. On one side, there is *unleashing* diverse talent. On the other side, there is *harnessing* it. So, what we're saying is that, yes, you need to unleash, and even amplify people's individual identities, their passions, their talents, their genius, and so on. But then you have to harness those diverse identities, passions, talents for the collective good—take a pot luck and turn it into a mosaic (to mix my metaphors). Another paradox is that you have to provide structure, but you must leave space for improvisation. It is not easy to manage these paradoxes.

Now, frankly, for many organizations, there is simply not enough unleashing. Companies don't release the diverse slices of genius that they have embodied in the people that work there. But, having said that, once you get talented, exceptional, diverse people working, you do have to have some way to control and bring together those talents. You need to harness it. How do you do that? Well, there are a variety of ways we have found in our research. IBM, for example, does it be leading from its *values*. That shows they hope to hold a global organization of over 100,000 together. The idea is that these shared values will provide the mechanism for alignment. So, on the one hand if you want innovation, you have to amplify the differences or diversity in your company, then the question to ask is, "What do we all have in common?" "What is our common identity or what makes the whole more than the sum of the parts?"

QUESTION: How do those tensions play out in the organization?

HILL: Well one of the other tensions is support versus confrontation. People aren't willing to take risks and innovate unless they experience some degree of psychological safety. But we know you don't get innovation without confrontation. There has to be some abrasion or conflict between diverse perspectives to get creativity. If you just let people go off and do what they want and there is no confrontation such as challenges of their ideas or high standards they must meet, they will not produce innovative work. So, none of these environments that we've been looking at are stress-free. In fact, some of them are quite stressful, because very, very high performance is expected. That means the standards are quite high and so is the level of debate and confrontation. So, if you want people to volunteer to put their 360-degree feedback or performance on key metrics up on the intranet, they must feel they are part of a supportive learning community. When everyone can see how you are doing the performance pressure can be intense.

QUESTION: How else do you avoid situations where you have loose management oversight but high expectations?

HILL: It goes back to values. There's tremendous reliance on trust in these organizations. Managers have to have a sense of control and ways to ensure that people comply with policies and standards. Transparency helps managers monitor behavior. In addition, the high performance organizations we're looking at are very selective about who they bring in. Hiring is a very, very important part of the puzzle. Getting the right people into the game is critical. And so, as I've said, if you don't have the trust then these organizations can't work. But of course, companies must build in checks and balances around key policies or practices. But back to unleashing and harnessing, the reason why many organizations don't do it probably is because it is hard work and requires skilled leadership. It's difficult to develop leaders who are capable of—and comfortable with—conflict management among diverse, highly talented people.

QUESTION: It sounds like what you're saying is that not everyone is going to thrive or be accepted in an environment that is designed to really unleash and also harness people's slices of genius.

HILL: That's right. In fact, people will leave. They'll self-select out. They'll do it because its pretty clear what the values are and how intense the internal competition is. No one wants to be at the bottom of the heap every time. In a lot of the organizations we've looked at, it's very transparent about who contributed what and who hasn't and who has been carried. There's a lot of generosity on the part of people to let you take risks and make mistakes, or even have periods when you're not so successful. But in these organizations also you have a high need for achievement.

QUESTION: What about metrics?

HILL: At HCL there are tons of measurements and there are different ways these systems get played out. I mean, this whole issue of what are the appropriate metrics for white collar work and, in particular innovative white collar work, is difficult. But most organizations we've studied have a fair number of metrics. Mostly, these are generated by using balanced scorecard approaches. Although in many of the organizations we see that they want to do cutting edge work, make it a point not to overrely on the views of their current customers who may be too conservative in their tastes and preferences.

QUESTION: What do you see them using at creative companie?

HILL: I was recently interviewing someone at a company where innovation is key. It was a large company and, as it had scaled, a fair amount of structure had been built in. To keep some agility and to hold the leadership accountable for "people management," the company had instituted the following practice. Every quarter, people could resign from their particular project team. As a result, each manager had to convince people to continue to work with him or her. And if too few people chose to reup with him or her, then they had to try to get their work done with inadequate staff. Now, I think this is highly innovative. Now I don't know what this company does when the imbalances of work to staff become great. But what they described was that this system basically lets each manager know immediately if they have a problem managing.

QUESTION: With a system like that, can they recruit the people they need?

HILL: Yes. Because of how well they're doing and what they do, they can attract talent. In fact, I think they are really making sure the work is interesting and that the managers know their people. But in a bigger sense, I don't think you really have much choice. You have to make work engaging. When you're talking about knowledge-intensive businesses, making work interesting is an asset because it helps with retention. And if you don't keep people, you've got a problem. Now you do need to help people have reasonable expectations.

QUESTION: In high-performance, high-talent environments, is there a difference between leadership and management? Or is everyone asked to be a leader because the environment is pushing them in that direction?

HILL: To the extent that leadership is about being willing to innovate, then you need people who are leaders. I mean, in business you have to execute a strategy, then adapt it and innovate as circumstances change. How do you create a context in which people can do that? In my view, in these environments, you do need more leadership. And, I think you probably do see more of it in these high-performing, high-talent environments. But you also see people bringing more of themselves to work, in general. When they are allowed to do that, they tend to bring more of what they're good at to work. What they bring are their slices of genius.

CHAPTER 14

Billy Beane

VICE PRESIDENT AND GENERAL MANAGER, OAKLAND ATHLETICS BASEBALL TEAM

The People Against Whom You Compete
Add to Your Value

QUESTION: Baseball is all about talent. No one is hired, fired, or rewarded without taking into account their ability to contribute to the team and the game. Given that, how do you think about talent? What's your philosophy?

BEANE: In my game—in my business—you are evaluated first by your public. They do it on a minute-by-minute basis. So, I'm dealing with emotions that come with decision making at a higher level then probably just about anybody else. I mean if you're running a mutual fund, most people check on a weekly, monthly, or quarterly basis. But it's different in my business. My "shareholders" are 60% of the country. They cross all industries and classes. They are people who go to the sports page first to see how their home team did.

So, my biggest challenge is that my shareholders—the people who follow the game—are checking in on me minute-by-minute. That means when I make talent decisions, I'm dealing with a lot of emotion and a lot of noise. There's noise in the financial markets, but there's probably no greater noise than there is in sports.

So I think of my philosophy this way: The better I am at ignoring the noise the better my decision-making process will be.

QUESTION: How do you ignore the noise?

BEANE: Good question! We're very much data-driven here and objective in our decision making. That being said, it's easier said then done. I mean if I get in a car right now, there's going to be somebody on one of the local radio stations who's going to be evaluating how I did my job the previous day. And they're going to add permanence to yesterday's temporary results. I've got to be disciplined enough to ignore that as much as possible.

QUESTION: What would be the downside if you actually let that noise affect your decisions?

BEANE: In sports you have two choices. You have the ability to try and manipulate the next day's articles and you have the ability to write the next six months' worth of articles. What I mean by that is that in this business, a lot of times you make moves because you're hoping for a reaction the next day. When you win games, you essentially write the articles yourself. So we do a lot of things in this business hoping that we get one or two days of press, like signing a guy that would have public appeal but not necessarily playing appeal.

Now, if we ignore the noise, then we ultimately do things that are going to lead directly to winning regardless of what is perceived in the initial public reaction. When we do that, we have the ability to write articles for the next six months.

QUESTION: Are you talking about players?

BEANE: Absolutely. You see, when you sign a player he may be a popular player but as you evaluate that player, you may find that while he's popular, he might not be particularly good anymore. Yet, he may have value by virtue of his name. He may bring in fans. And, you may get kudos or one or two days of good coverage in the papers when it really doesn't mean anything because ultimately, you have to go out and play and win games. And, if the player isn't helping you win games, then the articles shift and become not very pleasant for the next five or six months during the season.

The reverse can also be true. You can sign a player that you know might not necessarily have initial public appeal but will help you win games. When you start winning games, there are daily positive articles based on the fact that you're winning. When that happens there's a lot of noise because there's a sense of relief when people are clamoring for your organization to do something and it does it. That's when you get six months of good articles.

QUESTION: Are you talking perception versus reality?

BEANE: Exactly. When you sign a player that the public perceives as being a good player, even if he's not, maybe just the perception is there. And when you sign a player that's not perceived as a good player, you know the initial reaction will not necessarily be positive. But if you know that player is going to help you win games, then it gives legs to the signing and it repeats itself throughout the course of the season while you're winning.

QUESTION: Some teams have a penchant for signing high-profile players. Are you saying that's wrong?

BEANE: No! No! No! Not at all! The unique part of my business is that there are 30 teams, each of which is a micro business. Each of them is run differently for different reasons.

QUESTION: What are some of those differences?

BEANE: Let's take the Yankees. The Yankees is one of the few teams that is an international brand. Their brand is built on a lot of things beyond just winning games on the field. New York, for example, is part of their brand.

If you travel to Europe or China, there's a good chance you'll run into people wearing Yankee hats. So part of the reason the team is able to spread its international brand is the way they do things. There's an investment that the Yankees make that's beyond other teams' capacity. They have a lot of resources to invest.

QUESTION: Can't you use your resources the same way the Yankees do?

BEANE: The Yankees use their resources at the highest level. They get a return in a different way. The Oakland A's don't have an international brand name. If I go to Europe or China, it's very unlikely that I will see an Oakland A's hat even if I spend three weeks over there. But it's very likely I'll see Yankee hats.

Now there are limitations that I have in creating an international brand name. I've got a much smaller business and a much smaller niche. My city—Oakland—isn't a global city like New York. So, what I need to do is take advantage of the niche I have and maximize it.

But the Yankees are good for us too. Each time the Yankees invest in their brand name, I also benefit because I play them. In baseball, we have 30 businesses that are independent but are also affected by each other. When the Yankees become an international brand name and their franchise value goes up, my value goes up because I'm in the same business.

QUESTION: So you're arguing there are 30 different teams and 30 different business models and 30 different ways each team can succeed?

BEANE: Absolutely. Positively. But it's funny because the question and response that's typical represents a very linear view. It is: "Well if I do things this way, why don't they do things that way too?" The answer is that my business approach has to be more formal and more myopic than the Yankees business approach. There is a kind of cachet the Yankees have that I don't have. Part of it is simply their large investment for which they get a return on the dollar that just isn't necessarily tied directly to winning games on the field.

True, they do win a lot of games and they do win a lot of championships. But they have also built an international brand–based business. Which is arguably—along with probably Manchester United and maybe Real Madrid—one of the largest sports franchises in the entire world in any game. You see, baseball is really only played in a very small part of the world but the Yankee's brand transcends that. So when I play the Yankees, I gain a lot. Some of their investment actually ends up boosting me.

QUESTION: So the players, the strategy, and the business are ultimately about brand?

BEANE: Yes. Think about it for a second. The Yankees have built an international brand name in a business that's really very limited in its scope, as far as where it's played. That's pretty phenomenal.

QUESTION: Can you emulate what the Yankees did with the Oakland A's?

BEANE: I think it is possible and the reason I say that is because with the growth of media—the fact that we can be in the U.S. and talk about Manchester United and Real Madrid—gives us scope. It gives us impact. The media is helping us blast a product like a baseball or football team out internationally. I mean, we're still used to a time when we would choose a team because of a specific geography. If you grew up in Boston, you were a Boston fan by virtue of its proximity. That's changed because of the media.

That means that right now, because of the media, I can have a favorite English Premiere-League soccer team and I don't have to live anywhere near London. The fact is, I now have the opportunity to reach people who have not yet chosen a favorite team and are not limited in their thinking by geography. And, if it's true for sports, it's true for everything. That means there's going to be someone in Taiwan who will get on his cell phone in the next couple of years and will punch in a number and watch an Oakland A's game. That's incredible! So, can I emulate the Yankees? Absolutely. I can do it with the media.

QUESTION: What does that mean with regard to your talent strategy? Does it mean you have to align it with your business model which is now global?

BEANE: That's absolutely, dead on, right. And understand that my star appeal is that—for lack of a better description—I'm a mutual fund and the Yankees are a mutual fund as well. They are made up of large-cap proven businesses—their players—while my mutual fund is made up of small-cap businesses, my players. My players are small-cap stocks hoping to become mid-cap and then large-cap. So I have to understand that a lot of my players are only starting with me in order to grow within my organization into something bigger. Ultimately, some of my players will become stars and outgrow my team. But for now, they are building their resumes. When they grow from small-cap to mid- or large-cap players, I will have to sell them off and go find the next crop of small-cap players.

QUESTION: Sounds like what you do is what companies call succession planning. They develop high-potential people who can go into key roles and maybe even one day become CEOs.

BEANE: Yes. It is similar.

QUESTION: If that's the case, how do you evaluate players?

BEANE: Well, it doesn't only relate to the playing field. It relates to our infrastructure as well. We've lost as many executives as anybody in the game by virtue of promotions and opportunities elsewhere because of our success. I'm not only talking about players who go onto bigger and better contracts, I'm also talking about management. We're like every other business in that way. Think about Berkshire Hathaway. Certainly the most anxious moments they've had over the last few years is when they think about who is going to succeed Warren Buffet.

As a result, we're constantly managing our own internal portfolio with the idea that everybody is going to outgrow the business here and go for greater opportunities. So we're always playing the shell game when it comes to succession. Fortunately from a CEO standpoint, we've had a very stable business.

So we've had a tremendous amount of stability and the succession that we had here was very linear. My predecessor ran the team for 17 years and I trained under him. I'm running the team with no desire to leave at this point and I don't see myself going at any point soon, certainly not for any other sports job. So there has been stability and we've been able to maintain it. And when we needed succession in other areas, not just players, we've been prepared for it because we planned for it and then saw it on the horizon.

QUESTION: How many players in general do you like to have lined up for each player that might leave?

BEANE: Well you like to have as many as possible but that's not always possible. I mean the one thing that you think about when you talk about players on the field is that you have other risks that are involved. It's almost like an actuary looking at things. I mean we know when there's a possibility that a hurricane will come up the coast. But we don't know when it will happen. So, we prepare, but we can only prepare so much.

QUESTION: That's how most companies operate.

BEANE: Yes and in our case, we're never in a positive where we're completely covered at every level.

QUESTION: In the corporate world, the Board of Directors would say, "What happens if our CEO gets hit by a truck or something?

BEANE: Exactly. That's what we face. I mean, I've lost my right-hand guy. He went to Toronto to run the Blue Jays. I had another right-hand guy and he went to run the Dodgers. My scouting director went to the Rangers. So, there's no question that we've had a brain drain over the years. And one of the things that we've tried to do is maintain depth. Call it bench strength.

QUESTION: Young talent probably views you as a good training ground to go on to bigger things too, right?

BEANE: Yes. Maybe foolishly so, but it does help because we get them for awhile.

QUESTION: Is baseball a team sport or is it just sort of a collection of individuals that are good at what they do?

BEANE: It's funny and I'll give you a little story to illustrate what I think, which is that it's a combination of both. In my day, I played with a number of players and managers. Lenny Dykstra was a player and Davey Johnson was one of my managers. Now, Lenny was one of those guys, who tried for as many individual statistics as he could get. If he was at the plate and he took a walk and he wanted to steal a base or two bases, he did it for individual reasons. I remember someone said that they thought he was even selfish.

But, Davey Johnson who was the manager back then—and one of most underrated managers that we've had in the last 20 years—he saw it differently. He looked at Lenny and said, "I wish I had 25 guys who took that view because then we'd win every game." He saw Lenny's individual orientation as a plus.

So, I think it is a combination of both. The individual performs and certainly the sum of his performance adds up to a series of wins or losses. So could that really be perceived as being selfishness if you're playing on a team? If you take care of yourself and do your job and everybody does theirs times 25, then ultimately you have a winning team. One guy alone doing it is not going to make it work. But if 25 guys individually take that attitude, you're going to have a great team.

QUESTION: That sounds like it could almost be a cultural issue. Is it something that exists among teams in baseball?

BEANE: No question about it. I think winning is a habit for an individual and I think winning is a habit for an organization. And I think winning—the experience of winning and knowing the process of how to win—is what success is all about on a team or in business. In other words, people say they're going to reorganize and then after a year, if that reorganization hasn't had immediate success, they pull the plug on the whole process and they start again. That's not developing a habit of success.

The point is that you really have to build a culture of success. If you do, you're not as apt to pull the plug on what could be a successful plan. But if you've never had a culture of success, then you don't know what to do. Success is a cultural issue.

I mean if you think back to what Warren Buffet said in 1999, it was that he wasn't investing in tech stocks. He said he wasn't because he had the experience of knowing he'd never be part of a business that couldn't prove that it had revenues and earnings. As a result, he didn't invest in those stocks. In the middle of the tech boom, he even said "I don't understand this, I don't know it, therefore I'm not going to invest in it." And ultimately he proved that he was right because of his own experience. He went from supposedly being left behind the curve to accelerating far ahead of it. But it was all based on his previous experience. So culture is very important.

QUESTION: Culture counts.

BEANE: Yes. Part of it may be that certain teams adopt certain styles of play. Those styles will lend themselves to being either more attractive or less attractive to other people. And let's face it, as much as sports is about winning and losing, the teams that have been able to take it to the next level from a media standpoint are also ones that are able to combine it with star power that transcends the talent in the league that they're playing in. You know the Bulls were one of the greatest franchises of all time but they also had arguably the greatest player of all time, which put a multiple on their business.

15

Micky Arison

CHAIRMAN, CEO
CARNIVAL CORPORATION

Your People are Part of Your Customer's Experience

Micky Arison is the Chairman and CEO of Carnival Corporation and the Miami Heat basketball team. Carnival is the world's largest cruise line that includes, among others, the Holland America Line, Princess Cruises, and the Cunard Line. The company, founded by Arison's father, Ted, who died in 1999, took ocean cruises—once the domain of the elite— and brought them to the masses.

As a business, cruising is more about the experience and less about ships. What that means is, to be successful and to have repeat business, Arison's customers must have memorable times. Carnival's employees have to deliver a memorable time to tens of thousands of people, and they must do it again and again.

One element that makes a memorable experience is fun. Because people on a cruise are on vacation, they have to enjoy themselves. But training a Carnival employee to be a *fun* person is a dubious enterprise. As a result, as Arison says, a great deal of Carnival's emphasis is on the recruitment of its talent. In addition, because the company has a number of cruise lines, each of which offers a different experience, Arison gives the leaders of each business unit a great deal of freedom to create unique experiences.

In this interview, Arison talks about how he manages the company and develops its talent.

QUESTION: You grew up in the company that became Carnival Cruise Lines, didn't you?

ARISON: The company that became Carnival was founded by my father in 1973. I got involved in the early years. I was basically in school but I worked around the office all the time and went full-time around 1974 or 1975, working in various departments in the company and eventually became president of the company in 1979 when my father stepped back.

QUESTION: As you look around the company now, how important is it to have a very strong culture in the company?

ARISON: It's critical. Our company was a very family-oriented group. And we were a very small group of young people at that time. That's pretty much just what we were. A group of young people who worked together and really believed in what we were doing. We believed we were creating a product of delivering great vacations to a broad audience. We really had a great belief in it and we worked to perfect it over a long period of time. And we stayed together.

QUESTION: That's a really interesting point. Why do you think the people stayed together for so long?

ARISON: Well, it's a business where our job is to make people happy and to create dreams, and it's been great. It also had tremendous potential, which means that a lot of people were able to make very good money. And so the company grew; and it's a business, an environment that people kind of get hooked on.

You know, it actually becomes addictive, making people happy. So, we don't see a lot of people leaving the cruise industry. It is a really fun business. You know, you can be in the business of buying or selling or creating things, but we're in the business of selling and creating dreams. And that's a fun thing to be doing. So people stay.

QUESTION: Would you say that the culture at Carnival and the various businesses you have under that umbrella have a different kind of a culture from your competitors?

ARISON: Yes. I don't think there's any question about that. We're a multitude of cultures now, because, you know, as we became successful, we started acquiring other brands. Our company is 35 years old, but we own brands like Cunard and Holland America. These brands are over 100 years old.

Those brands have a distinct heritage, tradition, and also cultures. We're not really one culture anymore. We're a global group of cultures that are unique and different, and have a need to be different. You see, unlike an airline seat or a hotel room, when people go on a cruise, they really live in your home, your cruise ship, and eat, drink, and play there. They do everything on board. So, you're responsible for a floating city, and the various brands having various cultures are required to have their own corporate cultures because they are all distinct products.

QUESTION: Do you give the leaders of each brand the autonomy to create and keep their cultures intact?

ARISON: Absolutely. Clearly, a company such as AIDA, which is a growing number one brand in Germany, has to have a totally different culture than Costa, which is our number one brand in Italy, or Cunard line and P&O, which operates globally but has primarily U.K. passengers, or Carnival, Holland, America, and Princess, which would operate in North America. All of these have different cultures and all need to be really specialized in understanding their customer base.

QUESTION: What's your main role in the organization?

ARISON: I think of it this way. I do whatever needs to be done to make the CEOs of the various brands successful and to give them the kind of support they need to stay successful.

Of course, the critical area for me is allocating capital and deciding where our investments go from the standpoint of new buildings and new ships. We have 20 ships under construction right now. So, how we allocate those ships and where they go is a critical element for me to work on.

QUESTION: Do the CEOs of those various brands interact at all? Or, are they pretty much on their own?

ARISON: Oh, no. They interact. And many of them are on our board. We also have CEO conferences and meetings. They also meet and talk on a regular basis. It's critical. They have to know what each other is doing.

QUESTION: With all you business interests, you're one of the busiest people around. Do you have time to get to know some of the rising stars in each of the organizations?

ARISON: Probably not as well as I would like to anymore because we've gotten so big. I mean, we're now almost 80,000 employees, so it's not, you know, obviously 20–25 years ago when it was just Carnival Cruise Lines, or just Carnival Cruise Lines and Holland America. Back then it was a lot easier.

QUESTION: Do you encourage CEOs of each brand to get involved with the rising stars in their brands?

ARISON: They do it and I think they try hard at it. The cruise industry is very, very much a people business. The interaction between the manager and their people, and their people and their guests are critical. So, clearly each CEO needs to be aware of the best people in their organization and encourage their growth.

QUESTION: How does leadership in the cruise industry compare with sports?

ARISON: It's just as important in both industries and I think the management skill sets are similar—other than from the athletic point of view. I mean, from the business point of view, the skill sets are similar and the desire to win and be competitive is critical in both. You know, people that are very, very competitive in business are also very, very competitive in sports whether they're owners or players.

QUESTION: Would you say a basketball team has a culture just like a business does?

ARISON: Absolutely. I think our team's culture was clearly created and developed by Pat Riley. He came 11 years after I bought the team. It was in February around the All-Star break. By August, Pat was already with the team. And he had a real strong outlook on how he wanted the franchise to operate. The culture he built permeates the team today. There's no question about that.

QUESTION: How much does the coach or manager create the culture?

ARISON: The person or people that run the business create the culture. I'm not involved with the business of the Miami Heat. I mean, I am the owner. Pat—on the basketball side—reports to me. So does the business side. But clearly, I spend more time being a Heat fan than I do being involved in the day-to-day operation of the team. So, Pat really created a culture for the team. He's been working hard and doing whatever it takes to win. I mean, that's been the culture of the team for the last 11 years.

QUESTION: Okay. He's an incredibly hard worker, but what else does he do that makes him such a good leader?

ARISON: He's totally committed to what he's trying to achieve. And when you're willing to work as hard or harder than anybody in the organization, and you're totally committed to the success of the organization, whether it's sports or business, you're going to succeed. And you're going to send a message. Pat is all of that and that's what the culture is based on.

You see, he's absolutely committed. Committed to winning, committed to working hard, and committed to having a very disciplined outlook for the way the organization should operate. I think that's a culture and a formula for success.

QUESTION: Do you think the players on the Miami Heat take pride in their work?

ARISON: They're just like any group of employees; you got those for whom the answer to that question is absolutely yes. And, you got those where the answer is not quite as much. It's just human nature.

In any company or team, you have people that are completely committed and understand how the organization works. And you have others that are just there for the ride. That's true of every organization.

There's only so many Alonzo Mournings. There aren't very many people as committed as a person and as a player as Alonzo. There aren't a lot of people who are willing to go through all the stuff he goes through to accomplish what he's accomplished.

So, you have those kinds of players and you have other players I don't want to mention by name. But those players don't really care what happens as long as they get a paycheck.

QUESTION: Do you have a lot of Alonzo Mourning-type people at Carnival? People who go all-out?

ARISON: I do. That's what makes our cruise businesses so great. It's because we have so many people that are absolutely committed, hard-working, and who really believe in what they're doing. You know, we have a group of great people throughout the organization in Carnival Cruise Lines and all the brands. And that's what really makes the difference.

QUESTION: Can you name your stars in the other businesses like you can in sports?

ARISON: I'll probably get crucified if I said who. I'll probably get crucified for isolating Alonzo from any of the other players. I mean, we've really had a lot of great players who are hard-working guys in our sports organization. And, we've had a great many on the cruise side of the business.

QUESTION: What are some of the other similarities between the Miami Heat and your other businesses?

ARISON: Well, the key element to me is to get the right people, and give them the latitude they need to do their job. That means give them the tools they need to do their job. And then just let them go to work. You have to give people the opportunity to be successful.

If you have an area of weakness and you can strengthen that by bringing in the right people or consultants or whatever to strengthen those areas, then you have to do it. There may be some weakness that undermines your effort. But those can often be overcome as long as you're absolutely committed to what you're doing.

CHAPTER 16

Linda Smith

FOUNDER, PRESIDENT, AND CHIEF EXECUTIVE OFFICER, FOUR-D COLLEGE

When Linda Smith founded Four–D college in 1992, she dreamed of creating a school to train nurses and allied professions. But even more than that, Smith's objective was to create a business that would unambiguously serve the needs of its students, not just when they are succeeding in class, but when they need help. Further, it would serve student's needs not just to turn a profit, but as part of the school's mission.

To make certain that her dream stays a reality, Smith continues to take a hands-on approach to running the school, even though more than 6,000 people have completed programs and the school has won numerous awards, including the most coveted award, full accreditation by the Accrediting Bureau for Health Education Schools (ABHES), the United States Department of Education, and the State of California Bureau for Private Postsecondary and Vocational Education (BPPVE) bodies. It also has accreditation from other organizations operating on the state and Federal levels.

To make certain that the school—which now has two campuses—really does serve the student's needs, Smith herself runs in-service programs for the staff and faculty. She also reserves for herself final decision-making authority on all new hires during which time she discusses Four-D's values and her personal vision. What does Four-D stand for? It stands for **Desire, Determination, Drive** and the ability to **Deliver,** qualities shared by students, staff, and faculty.

Since students come from diverse backgrounds, Four-D works with them to create specialized curriculums. The point of tailoring the curriculum to the students' needs is to help all students succeed, even those who come from disadvantaged backgrounds. And, when students have concerns or problems that impede their progress, the school often forms "encouragement committees," to analyze a student's problems and take a team approach to solving them.

Four-D is a unique institution and Smith is a unique leader who views herself as just another Four-D employee. And, while she may be Ms. Smith to her colleagues when the issues are professional, she's Linda to those same colleagues, when the issues turn private and personal. Through intense interest, caring, and involvement, Smith has created an outstanding and innovative environment that fosters the success of students, staff and faculty.

QUESTION: You're the CEO of the nursing and allied health care professional school that you started. Are you also responsible for the curriculum?

SMITH: Not at this time. The department managers are responsible for the curriculum. I'm an integral part of the review process with them to make sure that the content and the flow meet the standards for the school. But I don't do the initial development. I do sit with each director and review with them the content and the layout of the curriculum as well as the lesson plans in order to make sure that all of the ingredients fit together and to make certain we have a sound training program.

QUESTION: You're at a milestone. You now have over 6,000 course and program graduates.

SMITH: Yes. That's the population of students who have gone through our career development programs; the licensed vocational nurse, pharmacy tech, medical billing, and related programs. In the past, when I started, I had a department that was listed as continued education. In this department, we developed 30 or more different courses for individuals who want to maintain their licenses, and for nonlicensed and licensed nurses. We also had people coming to take our director of staff development programs or the IV therapy training program, which are for licensed individuals. And then we had courses on CPR and congestive pulmonary artery disease. So we had a number of courses that individuals took in order to maintain their licenses. In our program, in our early years, we would have as many as 1,000 individuals come to our classes. So, it has been estimated that we've had over 6,000 individuals go through our school in various programs.

QUESTION: You operate in a very hot area where there are real shortages of qualified and trained people. What's your philosophy with respect to hiring and working with your talent?

SMITH: When I review resumes, I understand that resumes are there to give me a synopsis of who a particular individual is that is sitting across from me. So, I try to analyze the resume and look at the content and the flow of the information the person is providing to me. I try to be astute and look at their timeframes and at when they worked at all their jobs or performed certain functions. If they just give me a month and a year, that'd be very ambiguous to me because it could be that they started at the end of December, and they're trying to claim a whole year's worth of work experience. So, if I don't ask specific questions, I may be misled. So I really look carefully at work histories and then I ask key questions about their histories. I don't just look at a resume. For me to hire them, they have to have dialog with me, tell me exactly what they did at their various jobs. And then I ask questions to ascertain their communication style. Do they look at me when they talk to me during the interview process? Do they really have the language to describe the job duties that they were responsible for?

QUESTION: Do you make all the hiring decisions?

SMITH: I make all the *final* decisions. Our process is that our HR department reviews all of the applicants and does a telephone screening, or sees an applicant in person. If HR feels that the applicant warrants the next level, then they are interviewed by the Director of Operation. The Director then makes a determination whether or not they are referring a candidate to see me. In addition, if the applicant is coming through the various departments, their department manager would do the selection and make a hiring determination before I would see the applicant. But I do make the final determinations because I want to get a feel of the individuals that want to come to work here. When I see them, I share with them what our operating philosophy is, what my expectations are, and I give them the opportunity to ask me any questions that they want because I do feel that an interview process should go both ways. Not only are we selecting the candidate, they need to be assured that this is where they want to be before a final decision is made.

QUESTION: So you function as the chief talent officer?

SMITH: Oh, absolutely. I interact with my staff. We have over 100 employees and I think I know 90 of them by name, and whom I actually know and talk to. And so I stay in contact with them. I'm a very hands-on person and I try to learn the activities that are going on in every department, from HR to the registrar's office to the admissions. I mean, I try to understand the basics of what they are doing so that I know when I need to ask questions and make sure certain things are done. I also interact with my faculty. I give in-services to the staff when I determine that Four-D is getting a little off-kilter. I do that when I look at the relationship between the faculty and our student population, and see that something is not going right. That's something that I felt last year. So, I had a mandatory in-service workshop that I put together for the entire staff.

QUESTION: What did you do during the in-service?

SMITH: The first thing that I did was to address the managers and I talk to them about the core values of Four-D College. I started off with our philosophy. Then we went and addressed what the core values of Four-D were. What were their opinions of the core values? Who is Four-D College, or what is Four-D College? And I had them develop and discuss *their* core values as managers. And then the next step of this process was to have each manager write the core values for their departments. What I was looking for was to see if there was a tangible flow—are we all thinking the same and are we all on the same page? And then, following that, I had a mandatory in-service with all of our staff and our faculty, and I explained to them what we had done at the meeting establishing the core values and that now I wanted them to participate in developing core values for their departments. Then, each director went over this training process with their staff members, and they all developed their core values. Then we listed all of the core values from all of the programs. From all this, it was really amazing to see that we're still on target with regard to being a very service-oriented company and that we were still very mindful of our mission statement and our philosophy and the underlying spirituality of Four-D.

QUESTION: What happened after that?

SMITH: The managers and their staff review their core values, if not monthly, in their meetings on a quarterly basis. They also do it at all staff meetings. We constantly go back and review our core values, making sure that as a team we're keeping a focus on Four-D with students in the forefront. That was one in-service that I provided to the staff. Another one I did was called Reposition Your Mind. I wanted them to stop and think about who they were and to integrate it into Four-D College and look at how they were viewing our customers, who are our students. Are we being as mindful as we should be with respect to how we talk to them, how we determine who stays and goes academically, and are we being fair? And I felt that there had to be an attitude adjustment to get them to think differently. We can think about retaining students or we can think about saving students. And I wanted them to think about saving students.

QUESTION: What's the difference between retaining and saving students?

SMITH: If the attitude is, "We have to retain students to maintain a particular financial base," then it becomes very dangerous to me. We can come very close to crossing the line of not looking at what's in the best interest of the student. You retain that student, even though they may not be performing. They may have excessive absences and you've done everything, and you say, but if I let this student go, we will lose the revenue. So am I going to keep a student in a program if they had excessive absences? Do we keep that student because we want to keep the tuition? Or do we say, we want to save that student and not worry about the tuition? That's a different mental position because if I start thinking about saving a student, then I'm going to reach out and try to figure out why that student is not coming to class.

QUESTION: So saving a student is looking at him or her from the perspective of their needs?

SMITH: Yes. I brought a process to Four-D called the Encouragement Committee. The Encouragement Committee consists of a director of a program, it could be a member from the registrar's office or the Director of Operations—or even myself. And we identify students who are having difficulty. And rather than make an assumption that a student is not performing academically because they are just not capable of learning, we look to see if there are some social or financial issues going on so that the student is not able to adapt to the educational environment. So, through our Encouragement Committee, we bring that student in to a very confidential meeting, that's structured, and we talk one on one with that student to find out what their problem is. And our question is, "how can we help them? What can we do?"

So, the student is brought in and the first thing we say is that this is not a disciplinary hearing. We have identified that you have an attendance problem. We want to know, what can we do to help you? And that totally changes the relationship between that student and the management or the faculty of staff at Four-D College. Now, we're not adversaries. We're there to help them. And when we reposition our minds to think like that, it has had tremendous success because now that student will open up to us and tell us about very confidential information, whether it's a home life situation or financial situation. And we start strategizing together about what we can do to help them. Once we know what the problem is, it's easy for a team to come up with a resolution. And if we're able to do that, then we're able to see the success of that student. And for me, that is the ultimate. Four-D College was started as the result of a prayer that I wanted to make a difference in someone's life. When I can reach out with my team members here and save a student, then that's what it's all about. That's the essence of this place. And that's the essence of the workshop on encouragement. You know, after I gave that workshop, one of my team members came up to me with tears in her eyes and thanked me for the workshop. She said, "Now I know. I am the problem. It's not the student. I am going to reposition my thinking."

QUESTION: Can your approach be transferred to other businesses?

SMITH: I think it can. I know an unsatisfied customer can do damage. But we strive very hard to satisfy our students. We have standards that they have to meet. But I let students know that Four-D is not about putting you out of school; we're about educating you. And I expect students to meet us halfway in their educational journey. But I do think that if companies looked at *saving* their customers, I think it would enhance the overall level of performance and enhance the quality of who they are. You may not be the biggest in the industry, but your quality would become better.

QUESTION: You talked a lot about the values. Can you teach people your values, or do you have to find people who share them to begin with?

SMITH: I think you can teach values, but I think some of it has to be demonstrated. I value my staff, and I think the fact that they have heard me speak so often regarding Four-D College and the values that are at its core has helped them buy in. Now, if you buy into something, you can learn. But if you don't buy in, then that thing becomes irrelevant to you. In our core values, I stress spirituality of who we are as individuals and collectively. I stress the foundation of Four-D. Now, I don't waver from who I am as a person and how I treat others and what I expect Four-D College to be able to do. And so I have really been blessed here because I have faculty, and particularly my managers, who understand the value of Four-D. And they will not allow me as the CEO or President of Four-D College to cross over a certain line. But I also think I'm no different than any other president who understands that you have to make money in order to stay in business.

You see, what's unique within our organization is my relationship with my staff. They're not afraid to talk to me. And we really get along great. That's why I know so many of them. And when you have that kind of comfort zone that you can sit down with the president of the company and talk with him or her about anything, it makes a difference. I know which of their kids has a broken arm, and so it is that kind of relationship. And I think that's very unique. So, I really feel blessed to have the opportunity to work with the individuals that I work with who feel comfortable enough to come and talk to me. While I'm Mrs. Smith out of respect, I'm also Linda in a private session. In fact, while I may be CEO, in reality I'm just another employee.

QUESTION: What is the relationship between the mission of the school, as a business, and the values?

SMITH: They both come together. The ultimate *goal* for our students is that they will have employment and become financially independent, at least more financially independent than they were, especially if they come to us relying on the social services for some sort of their financial livelihood. When we look at our mission statement and how that ties back into our philosophy, our mission statement is about providing education in nursing and the allied health professions and for continuing education. But we put in our mission statement that we want our students to have a level of care and compassion towards the clients or patients they serve. I think that if you deal with people from the spirit of positiveness and love, it is reflected in the outcomes you have with the people who receive your services. In other words, the quality of life of your patient is going to be enhanced by who you are as a service provider, even if your job is working with medical records. So, when I can talk to my staff and my faculty about how we communicate to each other and treat each other, it's really about what kind of outcomes their students will have.

QUESTION: Can everyone share the same values even if they have different personal beliefs?

SMITH: When I interview individuals and I share with them our philosophy and our mission statement, I inform them that I never ask and I never have asked a student or a staff member about their religious background. However, I do share with people seeking employment about where I stand. I let them know that by faith and birth, I am a Christian. But I tell them, if my mother had been Jewish, I would be Jewish. The religious process is not important to me. I tell them that it's like the freeway. We're all trying to get somewhere and we all have different cars. As an individual and as a nurse, I am very respectful of that fact. I also share with them that when I was a practicing nurse, I understood that I would be taking care of people of different religions and that it's important to know what our differences are so that we can respect those differences. And so when I talk with individuals who want to come to Four-D, I share my beliefs with them and ask what they believe in.

QUESTION: By charter, you're a secular school?

SMITH: Yes. But we are a private school. But I look at each person individually and I look at their performance. And I want managers and directors of various departments to be fair. Right now, we're looking at salary raises. Each manager has to critique their employees. But I want to review their reports on how they view their employee. And then, when we sit down and discuss their next financial step increase, I like to get a feel of why they would recommend a certain amount for one person and not for another, if those persons are equal in their performance, attendance, and overall attitude and work relationships. So I think that when you're dealing with values, it heightens the level of being fair with individuals within the company.

QUESTION: What are your metrics for making personnel decisions?

SMITH: Attendance. I get a report every month on everyone's attendance. If I'm dealing with a faculty member, I review evaluations from their students which we do every quarter. I also look at whether the faculty member is starting their class on time, are they following the curriculum, do they have positive relationships with their students, are their students allowed to make comments? So I scan those to get a feel of how that person is performing in class, because I don't see them all every day, of course. And so, that's an excellent tool for me to be connected to see how they're doing out in the field. If they're working in the hospital, I want to know whether they are competent at providing clinical instruction to the students in the hospital. So, my goal is to get a good feel of pretty much everyone's level of performance from the students' perspective. That's what our values are about.

CHAPTER 17

Ilene H. Lang

PRESIDENT AND CEO, CATALYST

How Inclusion Heightens Competitiveness

Catalyst, a nonprofit corporate membership organization, began advocating for women in the workplace in 1962. Over the years, as more women entered the workplace, Catalyst's mission changed—from helping women enter and re-enter the workforce, to helping companies compete by utilizing a broader pool of talent that includes its women employees. Today, Catalyst is a global organization with offices in the U.S., Canada, and Europe. It helps companies build inclusive workplaces while expanding opportunities for women and business. With more than 400 members, Catalyst conducts research, collects data on women in the workplace, and on their leadership roles.

Over the years, the Catalyst Award has also changed. Initially, it was given to women of achievement and to corporations for initiatives like adding day care centers to their campuses and offices, and for diversity training programs. Today, this highly coveted award is given for broad-based initiatives that create measureable change inside organizations and enhance advancement opportunities for women. The award's strict criteria, which link the awards to business strategy and require a business case, means that the rigor of competing for the Catalyst Award is a change-and-educational program itself.

Ilene H. Lang was named President of Catalyst in 2003, after a successful career in high tech that included being CEO of a software company. She is an expert in the advancement of women in organizations and in the placement of women on boards of directors. Under Ms. Lang's leadership, Catalyst has continued its global expansion and released a number of important research papers and studies. As President, Ms. Lang is both a visionary and a pragmatist—two qualities she indicates are necessary to be a talent innovator. Ms. Lang and Catalyst believe that change is possible, but that it takes commitment and work. They also believe that without accurate metrics and a systematization of processes, real change won't occur. In this interview, Ms. Lang describes the relationship between inclusion and competitiveness.

QUESTION: Your organization focuses on the workplace and issues relating to diversity. What issues do you see facing companies right now?

LANG: Globalization is perhaps the biggest trend that we are seeing. Because of that, there is a real imperative for companies to consider talent no matter where it comes from. And, while the term globalization makes you think about the entire world, we have to remember that doesn't mean you can have a double standard with one set of rules for inside the U.S. and one for outside the U.S. That doesn't fly. So, it's really important for companies to realize that they have to overcome stereotypes about leadership and about talent. They have to look beyond their own traditions and biases. What that means in practice is when people talked about someone who did a really good job they might say they want to clone that person. They might say they want to hire another person just like the first one. But the fact is that everybody is different. And, if you think about it, you can't find people who are exactly the same. So, what companies really want to be able to do is look past a desire to clone somebody and ask themselves whether they are recognizing and nurturing talent wherever it is. If you're looking for clones, you're going to be very superficial in your search.

QUESTION: Are you seeing some innovative new ways companies are using to recognize leaders?

LANG: Yes. When I look at the most diverse hiring, I see it's usually at the entry level; it's the people right out of school. It's at college campuses and graduate school campuses. Today, these campuses are very diverse. Young people today, wherever they are receiving their educations, are in a much more diverse environment than in the past. So companies do pretty well when they make college hires or graduate school hires. But, if you look out over time, they don't do that well.

QUESTION: Why is that?

LANG: It's because the leadership of companies is less and less diverse the higher you go. People at those levels start looking more and more alike. Now part of it is there is a corporate culture, and so typically corporate cultures are one way and people are expected to behave that way. So that's a problem. Second, there is a view—and we've documented this in our research—which says that the default assumption is that leadership is male. So, getting women into the leadership ranks is still really very challenging. And, when they do get there, our studies show they are confronted with stereotypes. This is particularly true for women of color—African American, Asian, and Latinas. What we found is that they are excluded because of these stereotypes. Excluded because people think Asian women are demure and not aggressive enough to be leaders. Or, they think Latinas are too family-oriented or too frivolous and that if they speak with an accent then they're not considered sufficiently intelligent. With African American women, they are considered too direct and abrasive. Now, of course, these assumptions are not true. They're just stereotypes. But people still have a lot of stereotypes.

QUESTION: So companies are getting better at hiring, but are not so good at developing leaders from their more diverse pool of workers?

LANG: Absolutely. And it's well documented.

QUESTION: Are you seeing any indications that this is changing among leading-edge companies? Do you see any new programs emerging?

LANG: We put a lot of confidence in the Catalyst Award and the Catalyst Award process. The Catalyst Award is given for initiatives.

These initiatives are within companies. But the whole idea is that they follow a change process—and there are several criteria that we think are important in order to have a real change process—that produces measurable results. Now, when we say measurable results, we mean that there are lots of numbers and metrics around the award process. So here are our seven criteria, which I think are relevant.

First, there must be a business rationale, which is to say that the initiative has to fit with the business strategy; in fact, it has to be tied to a business case.

Second, there must be senior leadership support. Senior leaders in a company have to be fully behind the initiative, including the CEO.

Third, there must be metrics. Change programs can't be fuzzy. It all has to be measurable.

Fourth, there has to be accountability. Managers and others have to be held accountable for changes.

Fifth is communication. Initiatives have to be communicated widely throughout the whole organization. People have to know that this is a priority in the company.

The sixth criterion is originality. That's really important when we give the Award. But it's not so important for companies. In fact, we don't really care if they copy each other, because that makes change. But with regard to our Award, we are seeking out new, interesting and vital ways of creating programs.

The seventh criterion is replicability. That's because we want these programs to be role models. We want others to copy them. We want companies to be able to systematize their initiatives so they can be rolled out throughout the whole company.

Those are the criteria we use and then we measure performance towards goals of the initiative. So if it's a pipeline initiative, then we want to see remarkable improvement in the representation of women throughout the pipeline. And, if it's a global initiative, we want to see results reflected globally. If it is a senior executive initiative, we want to see results at the senior level. We look at the numbers. Those numbers typically focus on women in general and women of color. It's not just white women.

QUESTION: Your awards process really does track with change programs inside companies. Do you look at other things as well?

LANG: Yes. Retention and attrition, because those always go together. Now, the reason companies do this in the first place is that there's a very strong business case for doing it. The business case fits into a framework. And the framework is that either the initiative will grow the business, which has to do with the top line and new markets. Or, it is about the bottom line, which means costs will go down. And that's where you get into retention versus attrition since attrition's very expensive.

Now, related to that is the fact that as employees become more engaged, which goes along with retention, customers become more satisfied. Employee satisfaction and customer satisfaction go hand-in-hand. That also improves the business, and it's also part of a very strong business case. It has also been proven by a lot of research over the years that diversity and innovation go hand-in-hand. Diverse teams produce better results.

In my view, there are a lot of elements here that are really strong and have a strong business case, including becoming an employer of choice for employees. As you know, that is very important as we face a future where we really need exceptional talent, particularly in the knowledge economy. It's not just about people who can do repetitive work. Companies need people who can program and run equipment, who can run computers, and they need people who can bring innovation into the workplace to help them stay ahead. They also need people who can be close to the customer and who understand what's going on out there. Companies need people who can work as part of creative teams, and develop products and services that can be deployed globally and be successful locally. To do all that, you really need to have a tremendously diverse team that can work well together. So teamwork is a key part of what we look at. And if you have a group of people that you call a team, and they are all the same, with the same strengths and weakness, and they all look the same, then probably they're going to fall off a cliff in the knowledge economy.

QUESTION: What else do you have to do to build teams in an innovative way?

LANG: You really need to raise different opinions; you need to have teams that will wrestle issues to the ground; that will talk about the hard subjects; that won't make assumptions about people that aren't like them. The best way to do that is to have diverse team members that bring to the table a variety of opinions from a range of different backgrounds.

QUESTION: What types of initiatives have won the Catalyst Award?

LANG: This year (2008) one of the winners was Nissan of Japan. Now, if you look at Japanese culture you've got a lot to deal with. So Nissan developed an initiative for getting more women into management and leadership positions in the company because 2/3 of all car purchases in Japan are influenced by women. But they just didn't take the easy route. They looked at all functions. They increased the number of women in engineering, manufacturing, design, in marketing, and in sales—which they call "car life advisors"—which is very unusual in Japan. In the Nissan-owned dealerships they now have a lot more women than any of the other dealerships, either non-Nissan owned Nissan dealerships or in dealerships of other manufacturers.

Nissan also opened up its manufacturing to women—that includes manufacturing workers and the manufacturing leadership. They did it by adjusting a lot of the equipment and making it more ergonomic and comfortable for women so that women could be successful there. That's pretty interesting.

QUESTION: Have they gotten good results from the initiative?

LANG: They've gotten great results. Some of those numbers are on our Web site, and we'll have more numbers over time. But in addition to the numbers, Nissan tackled some really entrenched stereotypes about what women can or should do from a Japanese cultural perspective. When we did site visits, which we do for the Catalyst Award, we had Japanese cultural advisors with us on the visits. All of the people we spoke with, many of whom were men, confirmed that even though it is difficult for them to make change, they have to do it because it is how the company will succeed. They understood that getting women into leadership was a key success strategy for the whole company.

QUESTION: What else have you seen other talent innovators do?

LANG: In 2007, Scotiabank, which is probably the most international of all of the large Canadian banks, was one of the winners of the Catalyst Award. Theirs was an advancement of women initiative. The Scotiabank initiative was based on making the whole performance management and promotion process transparent. To do that, information was posted throughout the company. Everybody knew exactly what they had to do to get promoted. They stuck to their business case which was about really thinking about the customer and the business, and they realized that they had a lot of women working at the bank but that they weren't rising as fast as the men. They felt that there was something wrong because the women were as smart as the men, and they were performing well. So, they had to get people to break down whatever the perceptions were about women's performance to make sure that every job—branch manager, for instance—had women candidates. Over the course of three years, they dramatically increased the women in leadership.

QUESTION: Have all of the winning initiatives been led by the CEO and top management?

LANG: They're not always top-down programs. They're often bottom-up as well. But the leadership at the top has to be supportive, and has to articulate the business case, and has to be a role model.

QUESTION: Are you saying that for real change to happen, top leadership has to be involved?

LANG: Yes.

QUESTION: So, what is it about the leadership at Scotiabank or Nissan that enables them to see the importance of these initiatives? What makes them talent innovators?

LANG: Two things. First, they are values-driven. They have a very strong sense of fairness and what's right, and they believe in meritocracy. They know that when they look at traditional representation inside companies and at traditional programs, they see that something is wrong. They also understand that you can't have diverse teams at the bottom and in the middle and not at the top.

So if there are a lot of women in companies, they know there's something wrong with the system if it keeps women from getting to the top. So that's one thing. In addition, they also know that to have a meritocracy they've got to be playing with a full deck. They have to be choosing leaders from all the talent that's there and that they need the system to support that. So, that's the first thing.

The second thing is that these are very strong business people. They believe in the business case. They want their companies to get better and better. And so, even if they're cut-throat competitors, they know that if their customers are women then they've have to have women in their leadership too. They have to reflect their customers at the very top.

QUESTION: If you think about Japan, for example, it has a crisis when it comes to its worker population. Demographically, it is the oldest country in world and simply doesn't have enough workers. Was Nissan looking to widen its pool of high-quality workers?

LANG: Yes.

QUESTION: So, would you agree that in many cases, decisions about inclusion are often just the pragmatic thing to do?

LANG: Of course. I always used to say that women were the guest workers in Japan. And here they are—very well-educated, hard workers, that want to work and have jobs. The company that gets them is going to have a bigger, better-educated workforce. On that point, I often quote a CEO from a Fortune 100 company who responded to my question of, "What do you think is the competitive edge for your company?" by answering, "Women." He said, in fact, that he thinks women are the competitive edge for the American economy. That's because we have more women in the workforce and more women who can achieve. He also said any company can take advantage of that fact. He said it's a kind of enlightened self-interest.

QUESTION: Women in the work force also have more discretionary spending power.

LANG: That's true. Impoverished women who get a job and are just entering the economy are making a difference and they're also becoming consumers.

QUESTION: What's Catalyst's role as an organization? How is it changing?

LANG: Our role is to be a catalyst, so we're aptly named. Catalyst was founded in 1962. The focus was to help women, and particularly mothers, enter the workforce, and then to help mothers re-enter the workplace. In the '60s and the '70s, women were going to work and they were getting well educated. That was the time when women started obtaining a much larger percentage of college and professional degrees. Through the mid-to-late '60s, the '70s, and '80s, there were more and more women seeking careers. They didn't just want to be in the workforce for a few years until they got married and had children. They wanted careers. This represented a shift in the entire U.S. economy. In its first 20 years or so, Catalyst used to give an award to women of achievement—women who were advancing. We really focused on individual women. But in the mid '80s, or so, Catalyst stepped back, and our founder said, "You know, the problem isn't about fixing women, the problem is fixing the workplace." As a result, we shifted to become a corporate membership organization that looks at change initiatives that aim to make the workplace more female friendly. Initially, Catalyst was a domestic organization. But then some of our members, which were global companies, asked us to take a more global focus.

QUESTION: What other changes have you seen in the initiatives that have won the Catalyst Award?

LANG: The initiatives changed from being these one-shot, let's fix one piece of the problem, like professional development or day care or elder care, to let's start looking at the processes and the systems within the company to attack the whole challenge of diversity much more strategically. That's what we see now—highly integrated initiatives that are built on the business and tied to the business case. For example, Goldman Sachs, which was a winner in 2007, had an initiative to get more women into partner-level roles. It was a multipronged initiative with business development as one of the roles they wanted to develop. So Goldman began helping women develop business with women clients. They did it in corporate finance, because there were women who were CFOs, and asset and wealth management, because there are a lot of wealthy women out there, and they did it in trading services, because there are women who run hedge funds. They developed programs that helped build businesses for women so that they could achieve the kind of scale in their own portfolios that would allow them to become partners.

The other part of the initiative was to look at the promotion process and to rout out stereotyping and any kind of feedback that was dismissive of women or that didn't treat them as individuals, or that said, "Oh, you know, she has sharp elbows." Well, what do they say about men who are aggressive? It's usually positive. So, there's a double standard of behavior here. Goldman went about it on both of those dimensions and women of partnership rank increased dramatically over a period of about four or five years.

QUESTION: So, is diversity really about increasing a company's competiveness?

LANG: Yes. It's about improving businesses because of a change in the make-up of the labor force and of leadership. It stands to reason, that if the women are as well educated, and sometimes better educated, if women are more than 50% of the graduates of the best schools and graduate programs at the professional schools, and if women are not on a par with men, then the company is just not a meritocracy and the few are advancing at the expense of the many.

You know, in a lot of companies, they said, "Well, hey, that's the way the cookie crumbles. Women probably just aren't as ambitious, or they don't want to be, as the men. They don't want to play the game the way the men want to." But when they realize that they're choosing their leadership of the future from half the deck of talent, or if they look at who is in the fastest growing segment of the educated workforce—which is people of color and women of color especially—and, if after looking at that, they say, "Oh, you know, our leadership isn't going to look like our employees of the future," then they're going to lose out. They won't be the employer of choice.

But I don't want to give the wrong impression. Companies that work at this, and it is work, are getting better. If you think about what makes a strong business leader, they have to inspire others, right? They have to do it with regard to the mission and with regard to business success. But, you need them to inspire all of the people and not just a few. That means they have to have a style and a perception that's very broad.

QUESTION: It is hard work. Are there ways to measure incremental success toward achieving the goal?

LANG: Yes. Many companies measure progress and they're pretty careful to have metrics that are concrete and reflective of what they want to achieve, so they don't have the unintended consequences of rewarding the wrong things. And they also have accountability mechanisms so they can hold people accountable for what they said they're going to do and so they do what the business needs.

QUESTION: What are some of the qualities that talent leaders need today?

LANG: There are a few things. They have to be good listeners. They have to challenge assumptions. They have to have credibility. That is, they have to be honest and direct. They have to have integrity—they need to walk the talk. They're good role models. And— it's very interesting—you can't get to the vision and you can't lead innovation unless you have big ideas or unless you can mobilize the people with the big ideas. But you also have to mobilize the pragmatists—the people who can actually make things happen. Because if you're good at making things happen, then you can also be good at making the wrong things happen.

QUESTION: What about institutionalizing the vision?

LANG: You can't really institutionalize anything. I mean, we're not talking about bureaucracy here; we're talking about systems that actually help make change. And, if you don't have a certain degree of systemization then it won't be fair because it will be ad hoc and you won't have a credible foundation. Several years ago, Shell Oil won the Catalyst Award. It was wonderful because at the time, the CEO of Shell Oil was a woman. It was the first time a woman had accepted the award. At the time, Shell did something very, very simple. They had diversity targets for all their departments and they published the numbers on their intranet so everybody could see them. It was completely transparent. Now, I can tell you, nobody wanted to be the losers on that score. There's an internal competitiveness that gets started.

In 2007, one of the winners was PepsiCo. Their initiative was a multicultural women's alliance that was about women of color. PepsiCo found from employee surveys that they did every year, that when they looked at the intersections of race, ethnicity, and gender, women of color lagged in many areas of employee satisfaction. So, they started looking at that, focusing on it, and they built an exceptional initiative that resulted, a few years later, in increasing the numbers of women of color at the senior management and director level and stemming the attrition of talented women of color. During the time that they were working on this initiative, and while we were doing our analysis and site visits, Indra Nooyi was named CEO. She's living proof that paying attention to a company's talent and embracing authenticity can really pay off.

CHAPTER 18

Ron Sargent

CEO OF STAPLES, INC.

It's Not Just About Having the Right People,
It's About Having Them in the Right Jobs

Ron Sargent is Chairman and CEO of Staples, a Fortune 500 office products retailer. Sargent became chairman in 2005 and has served as CEO since 2002.

Sargent has had a long career at Staples. He was appointed president and chief operating officer in 1998. At the time, he led a number of the company's major initiatives. He expanded its worldwide operations, developed its retail superstores, its supply chain management, merchandising, and its marketing initiatives. In 1991 Sargent launched Staples' delivery business. Sargent began his career at Staples in 1989, as regional vice president leading the company's market entry in Ohio.

But while Sargent focused on these initiatives, his primary concerns were Staples' bottom line—he has a reputation for frugality—and its people. Sargent understood early that Staples' success is dependent upon how well its talent performed. To get Staples employees, called associates, to treat the customer well, they must also be treated well.

As this interview shows, Sargent developed a number of important recruitment, training, and talent measurement initiatives.

QUESTION: Obviously, hiring the right people is the first step in talent innovation. Tell me about Staples hiring practices.

SARGENT: One of the things we've done well is reconsider our recruiting efforts. We've morphed our efforts into becoming a kind of internal search company within the company. I just learned this statistic recently, that only three times in the last seven years have we paid a search fee for executive talent. So when you look at the tenure of our executive search group—and it's a fairly small group—they've all been here more than ten years. They get the company. They understand the culture. They know what we're after. After ten years of doing that kind of search, they're very good at what they do. I'm not even sure what those three times were when we looked outside but we've gone outside only for a very unique, specific job. So changing the focus from recruiting to an internal search is one thing we've done well.

QUESTION: When you say "internal search" be a little more specific. It's an internal search organization, but they go outside to find people?

SARGENT: We treat them like we're calling on Heidrick and Struggles or Russell Reynolds. Basically, they come to me or the other executives in house and they interview us and ask, "What do you want? What are you looking for?" They create a job spec. And then they go out and work it.

I also think that finding great people has been tremendously impacted by the Internet, which has really changed the world in terms of search. Because there are so many wonderful sites out there where people can post their resumes and let us know who they are. We also have our own portal where we can post anything we have an opening for, and that has really caused a flood of internal response. So I'm not saying the search firms are obsolete, but I believe the Internet has really leveled the playing field in terms of finding great talent.

QUESTION: Is this internal team just for executive recruiting? How low into the organization do they go?

SARGENT: They focus anywhere from manager level all the way up, because we don't have a lot of turnover at the executive level. We also have a college recruiting team that does nothing but acquire folks from college. We also do significant diversity recruiting because we want to make sure that our company management is as diverse as our hourly workforce is, and as our customers are. We've built a pretty sophisticated recruiting operation here over the years. And we found that we've just had much better success with people who know us doing the recruiting rather than people who don't know us. We've also got a pretty good employee referral program. If you refer somebody that we hire who stays for six months, we give you a $1500 cash bonus.

QUESTION: What other methods do you use to ensure that you hire the right people?

SARGENT: We do a behavioral assessment test, not unlike the Myers-Briggs test, when we hire people. We've done probably a thousand of these by now and it gives you a sense of whether somebody will fit into the culture of Staples. We've got our own model of what works. So, for example, if you know somebody is very process oriented versus output oriented, they're not going to be successful here. Because we tend to focus on getting things done and output is really important. So if somebody scores two on a scale of one to ten in terms of output orientation, we know that they can't make it here. We believe they need to score six or better. It's a very sophisticated model that we use for management. And we also have another model that we use for hourly employees such as store employees. That test focuses on different qualities such as whether you're outgoing, whether you're friendly, whether you've got a positive attitude, those kinds of things. So we've got a little science in the recruiting side, as well as connections and referrals.

QUESTION: So if somebody comes in for a management job and they are really terrific, everything about them feels right, their referrals are great, but they don't score that six on the test, they're just not going to get the job?

SARGENT: Well, there have been times when people have gotten the job because of all those things. And I don't think there's ever been a case where I haven't gone back in six months and said, "Mistake."

Those people tend to leave. Every time I've overruled the science, I've regretted it. So now I don't overrule the science anymore. To me it's a non-starter if they don't have the right kind of qualities for Staples. Because you just know, they might be great people, great employees, but they're not right for us.

QUESTION: What other specific qualities might there be in that Staples fit from your perspective?

SARGENT: Interestingly enough, analytical versus nonanalytical is another differentiator. Obviously it depends on the job. For most jobs here, the analytical side is important. If you are working in the advertising or marketing areas, the creative, nonanalytical side would be more important. We also look at the introvert vs. extrovert qualities and the maturity of an applicant. You want somebody who's more mature and displays more team-oriented behavior versus "What about me and my ego?" There are probably five or six different kinds of metrics that we use.

QUESTION: So you've come to rely on these metrics?

SARGENT: In terms of hiring, I always ask for that information and then we make a decision. I tend to go by the metrics. And our metrics are certainly different from any other company's metrics. Having been here for 20 years, having hired thousands of people, we know what works for us. Not that we're trying to create robots, but we do know who's going to be successful, or has a chance of being successful here.

QUESTION: What about retention? Once you've found them, how do you keep them?

SARGENT: Our first priority is to hire from within. And I think that's probably something every great company does. Competitive pay is important. We tend to be in the 50% percentile with salary. But with incentive pay, bonus pay, we shoot for the 90% percentile. So it's really pay-for-performance. If the company performs, and you perform in your role in the company, then you're going to be well paid. If the company doesn't perform, you're only going to receive average pay.

QUESTION: So you try to make it an ownership culture?

SARGENT: Yes. We try to get stock in everybody's hands. From the guy who is running a register in the store, all the way up to the senior executives in the company. When I look at my pay, 75% is equity based, 25% is cash and bonus based. So I would say probably 90% of it is at risk, but probably 10% is salary; 15% is bonus, 75% is stock ownership. I think from the early days, one of the things that (founder) Tom Stemberg did a wonderful job with was making everybody feel like owners.

In fact, in Tom's original document on the culture he was trying to create when he founded the company in 1986, he talks about the ownership culture. And when we went public, we started giving stock options to sales reps, to people on the delivery side, to store managers. There are not a lot of retailers that give stock options to people who run stores. Typically, it's all piled at the top. In our case, we give stock options to the store manager all the way up. It's great to visit stores and hear people say, "I bought my house with my Staples stock options." Or, "I put my kids through college with my Staples stock options." I don't know how many millionaires have been created here with stock and stock options. But the stock is up 30 times since the IPO.

QUESTION: Nothing like creating millionaires to create long-term loyalty.

SARGENT: As our CFO tells our management team, "We want you to get rich slowly." And I think the stock ownership culture is really, really important.

QUESTION: That's an interesting point, "get rich slowly." So you don't get a lot of young retirees like in Silicon Valley or in Redmond, Washington.

SARGENT: How do you keep people like that? There are people who probably made a lot of money if they've been here for any period of time. But they've got a whole lot of money left on the table. So it's in their best interest to stick around and continue to vest their stock options, stock ownership.

QUESTION: What is your vesting period?

SARGENT: In some cases, over three years; in other cases, over four years. But you get options every year. So you always have those options. You always have this rationale, "If I stay another year, I'll get to this vesting." And you stay another year, and you say, "Well, if I stay one more year I'll get to this vesting." We try to have options that vest every year, and also options at risk every year. You've got ten years to exercise and sell those options.

QUESTION: What about nonfinancial incentives?

SARGENT: That brings up the whole issue of culture and team culture. I think everybody wants to be on a winning team. And we really try to focus on the fact that we are a team. We want everybody to get the values. I was just working on performance appraisals and 40% of your performance appraisal is based on how well you fit with the culture. So 60% is how you did versus your objectives for the year; 40% is how you fit with the five cultural values. We call it Team CARE. The "C" is customers and how you interact with customers. "A" is associates, which is what we call our employees. "R" is results, and "E" is easy, which refers to our ad campaign and also whether you are making things easy not only for our customers outside, but also for your colleagues inside.

So we really try to push this cultural dimension, that we're all in this together, and we all have to do these five things in order to be successful as an organization.

QUESTION: How do you reward on something as fuzzy as cultural issues so that people really make that connection the way you want?

SARGENT: We score for the performance appraisal. If you're a great cultural fit, you're going to get more money on your annual increase than if you're a lousy fit. Our bonus system, on the other hand, is based on financial metrics for the most part. It's 20% sales, 30% earnings per share, and 30% return on net assets (RONA), which is something we've really focused on. And then the last 20% is customer service.

QUESTION: I know customer service is a huge issue for Staples.

SARGENT: We measure customer service as any retailer has to. How you interact and how you deal with your customers is really important. So 20% of my pay, my bonus pay, is based on how the customer thinks I did. We have metrics that the customer scores us on. And last year, we missed our target a bit, so I didn't get my full 20% bonus, that customer service portion of my bonus.

QUESTION: You base this on customer satisfaction surveys?

SARGENT: Yes, both in our delivery business and our retail business. This year I think we're doing better on our customer service metrics. In fact, we introduced what we call the Bonus Calculator which tells people on a quarterly basis how we are doing with customer service. Each quarter, you know where we stand and we publish that information on the same day we release quarterly earnings.

QUESTION: That kind of transparency is probably unusual for retailers.

SARGENT: I think so. And it's quick too. It's a pretty slick little tool. It's very quick and immediate, and you know how you're doing on sales, profits, and customer service metrics.

QUESTION: The customer service metric seems pretty hard to impact by any single individual. It is clearly a team-driven issue.

SARGENT: It is. One of the things I changed five years ago is we, at one point, had something like 48 different bonus plans. So everybody was trying to optimize their own bonus plan. People might end up fighting about which merchant was going in an ad because their bonus was tied to that merchant's products in our stores. It didn't make sense because you wanted to put in the ad what would sell the most from a customer standpoint, not who was trying to optimize their own bonus.

So I killed that, and we went to eight bonus plans. But they're all basically the same. And they're all based on the metrics I mentioned earlier: 20% sales, 30% EPS, 30% RONA, and 20% customer service. The reason there are eight variations is because the Europeans' sales and RONA are based on European results. North America, it's based on North American results. Canada, it's based on Canadian results.

QUESTION: So it's geographic.

SARGENT: But the metrics are the same companywide. And the downside of that is that I'm one of 79,000 employees; how do I affect this stuff? The upside is we're all in this together and we're one team. And if teamwork is a big part of our cultural norms, I want everybody else to do well. I want the Europeans to do well. I want the delivery guys to do well. Because if they do well, I do well.

In the early days, when I joined the company, you wanted every single person to do well, because that made your bonus better or your stock go up. I think the problem today at a lot of big companies is that people are trying to feather their own nest, and they don't feel like they're part of the big team. So there's pros and cons.

QUESTION: Are there real measurable results that you can say, this really does pay off?

SARGENT: Yes. Five years ago, when we changed the bonus system, we were a $10 billion-dollar company. In '06 we'll be an $18 billion-dollar company. In that time, we've tripled our earnings. Whether this is because of the bonus system, who knows.

QUESTION: But it's certainly not a coincidence either.

SARGENT: I don't think so. The cultural thing is really big and powerful in our company. And those are the ways we keep people. It actually follows pretty closely with what Tom Stemberg wrote in 1986 in a one-page statement: "Here's how we're going to behave and act as a company." He talked about being the low-cost operator and we're still there. He talked about operating as a team, not as individuals. It's really not so different than today.

QUESTION: In a retail operation like Staples, the people who are on the lowest rung of the salary ladder and the power structure of the company are the ones who spend the most time with your customers. This makes them arguably the most important people in the company. How do you find, keep, and motivate people in these circumstances?

SARGENT: Five years ago, we felt we were losing the focus on customer service and at that time, we put every single hourly employee in all our stores on a bonus plan. I visit a couple of hundred stores each year and meet with people. If a store did particularly well, we did pizza parties at the end of the month. And when you talk to people, they said, "These are not highly paid jobs. And if I've got a choice between a pizza party with people I work with all the time on a Friday night here at the store, or just paying me more, I'll take the pay every time."

People are not in high-paying jobs. They are trying to make their rent payment, or gas payment, or insurance payment. So what we did was put everybody on an incentive plan where if the store did well and our customer service metrics were strong, as measured by customer satisfaction surveys, then they would get an incentive payment at the end of every month. Probably 70% of our employees earn that incentive payment every month.

QUESTION: How does the bonus system work?

SARGENT: That payment varies based on how well you do. In some cases you might make 25 cents on every hour you work that month, which wouldn't be that great. But in some cases you might make three bucks for every hour you work that month, and that's a good-sized check at the end of the month. We pay this out monthly, not quarterly or yearly, because there's an immediate reinforcement of the behavior. And you know, in the break rooms, that's a powerful thing to think "I only get 25 hours a week, so that's 100 hours a month. And if I can get $2 bucks more for every hour I work that month, that's $200 at the end of the month that will cover a lot of my expenses." I don't know of any other retailer that does it. I can't think of a single one.

QUESTION: And the attrition rate—has that been impacted by this?

SARGENT: Yes. In terms of hourly workforce, we used to run 100% a year, 110% a year attrition, which is probably industry average in retail. The fast food industry has the highest attrition but retail is probably right after that because a lot of times, people are seasonal students working in the summer. But this year, our rate in the hourly workforce has dropped to the 65–70% range. It depends somewhat on the economic environment. If times are really good, you have higher turnover than if times are tougher. But we have kind of steadily brought down our attrition rate on the hourly side. On the management side, we've probably gone from the low 20's to mid-teens, 15% a year, something like that.

QUESTION: When you look outward, how do you address the idea of not over-hiring qualified people who might end up finishing a project and sitting around bored and anxious to leave?

SARGENT: Some people don't want a future with the company. They want to put in their 30 hours a week, 40 hours a week, 45 hours a week, and be done with it. But good retailers paint the picture in terms of where you can go from here. And the nice thing about retail is we're still opening two stores a week all over the country. And now we're in 23 different countries. I spoke to an employee this morning who wants to transfer to Shanghai. She's from there originally and has been in the U.S. for ten years. She wants to go back and we have an operation in Shanghai where she can do a lot for us. That is painting the picture that you can grow with the company. Another fellow who runs our U.S. stores business, which is an $8 billion-dollar business, started out as a store manager in store number 11 in Manhattan. So here's a guy who was a store manager, and moved up in the organization. We've got a lot of examples of people who started as hourly workers, in some cases part-time workers, who ended up running stores or running districts or running zones.

QUESTION: Is there a clear path for advancement?

SARGENT: The structure is fairly well defined. Typically you go from a part-time hourly employee, to a full time hourly employee to a management trainee, to an ops manager, to a sales manager, to a store manager, to a district manager. There's a very clear path in retail, like there is in the grocery industry. I visit store managers all the time, and they say, "I started as an hourly employee when this store opened." And now they're running the store.

QUESTION: I've always felt that the hourly workers in Staples, when I walk into a store, seem to be more engaged and serious about what they are doing and how they treat people than in other retail outlets. I'm not sure it's an innovation, but getting your hourly people to feel some sense of pride and ownership seems like a significant advantage.

SARGENT: You've got to hire the right people. You've got to train them well. And you've got to get them to buy into the culture. And I think if you do that—the company is full of great examples where people have done incredibly well.

QUESTION: You've also instituted some off beat ideas, like encouraging and rewarding employees who come up with new ideas for products.

SARGENT: Exactly.

QUESTION: Do those kinds of programs make a significant difference?

SARGENT: Yes. We do a lot of these kinds of things. We have a meeting we call Steak and Staples where we send executives to visit stores all over the world. Tom Stemberg used to go to every store every quarter to talk to the employees. We're too big for me to do that alone now. But we send the executives out, 20 years later, three times a year, and it's a Steak and Staples meeting where we talk about what's going on with the company and we also talk with employees in the stores to see what they think about what's going on in the company. When an executive visits a store, he or she has to shake hands with every employee in the store, spend a minute or five minutes or whatever with each employee. You can't ignore the lady at the checkout counter or the guy in the back room. You wait until they are finished with a customer. We ask our store employees to say hello to every customer who comes in the store and this all reflects respect for individuals. When I was in the grocery industry, when the zone manager came, he talked only to the store manager and everybody else just cringed hoping he didn't ask them anything. In our company, everybody talks to everybody. That's how you find out the good stuff.

QUESTION: Do you admire other companies who've done well in this regard?

SARGENT: Wegman's does a great job. The Container Store is a little operation but they do a good job. Starbucks created a passion around coffee but it's not just the coffee, it's the experience. Publix in Florida has done a nice job.

QUESTION: Talk about the idea of holding people accountable and communicating that all this matters.

SARGENT: The thing you have to do is measure everything. And the nice thing about retail is everything's measurable. We can measure customer satisfaction through scores, and we rank them high or low. We measure payroll, sales. I get that data every day. What we try to do is measure everything and rank everything. It's a great motivation when you're saying there are ten district managers and I'm number ten and I've been number ten for six months. You know that you're either going to have to get out of that bottom rank or you're probably going to be losing your job.

As tough as it is to manage by metrics, and that's not the only way you have to manage, or can manage, but it is a measurable business. And we're here to make money for our shareholders. I always say you've got to let people go and become successful somewhere else, because they're not being successful here. It's tough to make those kinds of decisions. But if you don't deal with it, you're going to risk all the jobs, not just that job.

QUESTION: Do you have metrics to help you determine when it's time to let someone leave?

SARGENT: It's very clearly defined by human resources. You have a warning, written warning, and then termination. It's really crystal clear. If you get the first warning, you don't want to get the second warning. In some cases people respond to that, and in some cases they don't. But we do measure. We look at our numbers every day, every week. We also look at them monthly. We do a monthly operating review with every part of the business. And then we make decisions. But it's not just metrics. If people don't fit in with the culture, you have to make some decisions. Even people who are pretty good performers but aren't treating the people the way that you want them to be treated, and aren't showing team-like behaviors. Occasionally, you have to make changes there too.

QUESTION: So part of the secret is to really pay attention to the mission statement?

SARGENT: If you don't, you're sending the wrong message to the 95% of your employees who are right with the plan. You know, "They say it but they don't really walk the talk, because they let this guy or this lady hang around." Usually when somebody is forced out, people understand or are cheering about it, depending on what the issue was.

QUESTION: How do you deal with the issue of hiring for need now, versus looking to the future?

SARGENT: The management level or the store level?

QUESTION: Start with the management level.

SARGENT: With short-term needs we would probably hire short-term people such as contractors. There might be an IS project that's going to be gearing up and we would use contractors or consultants. If it's an expertise that we don't have, we'd go outside and get it.

QUESTION: What about at the store level?

SARGENT: Our stores are a different story. When you're trying to gear up for back-to-school, for example, which is when our customer service metrics dip every year, it's a difficult problem. So we've tried to bring technology in as much as possible. A year ago, we introduced what we call line-busting technology. If there are 14 people in line during the back-to-school period, we have somebody with a small, portable register in their hand. They essentially walk up and down the line and check you out. They scan all your items and put them in a bag. They close the bag and all the cashier has to do is take your money. We try to make the customer experience a little better, a little easier. We did the same with rebates. People always complain about rebates and how cumbersome they are to fill out and send in. So we introduced "easy rebates" which is an online form on our Web site where you can fill in the rebate easily and it gets sent to you. No more cuttings things off the boxes and filling in endless copies of receipts.

So we're trying to make things easier for our customers, but we're trying to bring technology to the party because it's really hard to staff up that quickly, especially since you know, by the first of October, you're not going to need those people.

QUESTION: Another challenge you've had in assessing talent is in the online space. Staples has made a big presence on the Internet.

SARGENT: It's amazing. Six, seven years ago we did virtually no business on line. Now we've just found that we're the second largest retailer on the Internet today after Amazon. We'll do $4.9 billion dollars of our $18 billion dollars in sales online. When you look at our back-to-school ads, we've given customers a choice. They can either fight the crowds or go online. A lot of people are now opting for online for back-to-school supplies.

QUESTION: How will this impact how you will be hiring and finding talent? Is it going to change the profile of the Staples employee?

SARGENT: I don't think so. In general in our stores we want people who are technologically savvy, because we sell a lot of technology in our stores. We also have an online presence in our stores. So if we don't have it in the store, or if you need 100 binders instead of 10, we can order it on the kiosk in the store and have it delivered to you the next day. But a lot of people just love to shop retail. And you know, we try to get them shopping both channels because they spend more if they shop online and retail. But, try as we might, if you're a retail shopper and you like to go to stores, and you want the immediacy of I need it now, and I want it now, and I'm going to go get it now, that's almost a different kind of customer than somebody who orders through the catalogue or through the Web. Usually bigger customers tend to order more delivery; smaller customers want it now. Our new stores are opening stronger than ever. And there are still about a dozen big markets we don't have any stores in. So we're still growing. We just entered Miami last year and we're going into Denver this year. We still don't have stores in Houston, San Antonio, Las Vegas, St. Louis, or Minneapolis.

QUESTION: What other ways have you addressed long-term hiring needs?

SARGENT: What we tried to do is create these little businesses within the company. In the last year, for example, we've created a copy center business because we think it's a big opportunity to grow. We have copy centers in all of our stores, but we're only doing about $300,000 dollars per copy center. Kinko's does about $2 million dollars per copy center. So we created this entrepreneurial team that said "How do we grow this into a million dollars a store, not $300,000 dollars a store." We've got a team to do that.

From that team evolved another team. They said, "Why don't we do freestanding copy centers?" So we just opened freestanding copy centers in Boston. And we're going to open a bunch in New York this coming year. We see this as a big opportunity.

We've also launched our Easy Tech effort, which is the Staples version of the (Best Buy's) Geek Squad. We're getting into new retail channels, which are selling Staples products to grocery stores. So we're trying to seed all these little new businesses for talented people to come in and run. Typically, we bring in talented folks in our strategy group, and they stay in strategy for one to two years. Then we move them, as well as other people, into these entrepreneurial opportunities to let them grow a business.

QUESTION: How are you spreading the word to let people know this is an opportunity that Staples has?

SARGENT: Internally, we have a succession planning process every summer. We spend the summer going through each department to identify high potential people. We say, "If we've got a business that we are creating, this person will be a natural to either work for the business or run the business." We try to move people around, particularly the high-potential and the high-talent group. Because those are the people that are typically most likely to leave. The guy who is running Asia now started in the Strategy Group. The guy who's running our outside copy center business started in the Strategy Group. The person running Easy Tech started in the Strategy Group.

QUESTION: So you're tapping into people's inner entrepreneur?

SARGENT: Everybody wants to be an entrepreneur, and it's hard to be an entrepreneur in a $20 billion company. That's why we created these ideas and opportunities, and it adds a lot of pizzazz and growth and excitement.

QUESTION: How is this business going to change in the next decade?

SARGENT: We've got to have more global skills and more of a global mentality. Five years ago we were in six countries. Today we're in 23. The six countries we were in were basically North America and Western Europe. Today we're in Brazil and Argentina in the South, we're in Eastern Europe which is kind of a different animal. We're in India and China, which are very different. We're even in Taiwan, which is very different than China.

So the creation of a global mentality is going to be really important. Right now we're a U.S. company with international operations. We need to evolve into a global company. I also believe that at some point, our delivery business (catalogue and Internet sales) will become bigger than our retail business because of the relative growth rates. In 2013 everybody is going to still know us as a retail business because they see our stores everywhere. But the big hidden jewel is the delivery business. It's still growing very fast, and it's more profitable than our stores, because you don't have the long-term leases and the bricks and mortar and the fixed cost that you have with our stores.

QUESTION: Hiring people and placing people in these exotic locations is a significant challenge. It is difficult to find people who understand the local business climate and the local culture. How do you address that?

SARGENT: We make probably every mistake you could make internationally that a U.S. company could make. Even Wal-Mart in Germany and Wal-Mart in Korea, they had to close the doors and leave. I think we're probably the only U.S. retailer making money in Germany today. But that only happened when we got local people and international people to run the operation.

The reality is that this idea of a united Europe doesn't exist and probably won't, certainly in my lifetime. Maybe in my grandchildren's lifetime it might. So you really have to be wildly sensitive, not only to the language, but to the cultural issues.

QUESTION: To be global, you have to behave globally?

SARGENT: Yes. Because we're such a big player in a big economy here in the U.S., we don't have the talent to really succeed in all these venues. That's why we're trying to partner. We've got a joint venture in China. We own 90% of it, but it's a joint venture because we want local expertise to help us run the business. In India, I think we own about 40% because we don't know a thing about doing business in India. India has a middle-class that's 300 million people. So that's where we will focus.

But we need to evolve that international sensitivity here. We just brought our first class of people from other countries here for three months to teach them the Staples Way, the Staples culture, and best practices. Then we send them back and we'll continue to do that. We also need to send our U.S. people out into the field for three months to bring the Staples knowledge out to them. Global issues are probably among our biggest issues going forward.

QUESTION: It feels as if Staples has been very innovative on the basics but has an opportunity to stretch the thinking in terms of talent innovation.

SARGENT: We've evolved the culture in many ways over the last 20 years, but in some cases we haven't evolved the culture at all. Every month, we have what we call The Breakfast Club where I invite 20 people to have breakfast with me. There's no agenda, there's no reading, no preparation. It's basically just to talk about the business. And they can ask questions. Someone just asked me, "Are we ever on the (*Fortune* magazine) list of Best Places to Work?" And I told them the whole saga that for years we ignored it, and then we said maybe we should do a little better trying to respond to the questionnaire. This year we said, you know, let's go all out and try to create a marketing document that would help us.

People here are very willing to tell you what's on their mind. I visit so many stores and most people don't even know I'm the CEO. They think it's just someone from corporate. They tell you what's on their mind. Our tuition reimbursement program, for example, is a whole lot better today than it was two years ago because of the Breakfast Club. We heard it loud and clear that our tuition reimbursement program stinks and we needed to upgrade it. So we did.

QUESTION: The challenge is to never let your guard down.

SARGENT: The challenge that all companies have is you've got to look at one year, you've got to look at 10 years, and you've got to look at 100 years. And even though I'm not going to be here in 100 years, you have to figure out what you've got to do today so that the company will be here 100 years from now. Tom Stemberg used to say it's like knitting while water skiing. You have to sweat the details every day, but you also have to water ski.

CHAPTER 19

Jerry (Yoram) Wind

THE LAUDER PROFESSOR,
THE WHARTON SCHOOL
FOUNDER, WHARTON SCHOOL PUBLISHING

Managing Creative People:
Break Down the Barriers

At the Wharton School of the University of Pennsylvania, Jerry (Yoram) Wind wears many hats. He is The Lauder Professor, Professor of Marketing, Director of Wharton's SEI Center for Advanced Studies in Management, Academic Director of the Wharton Fellows program, and Founding Editor of Wharton School Publishing. He is also a prolific researcher and writer, and creator and lecturer of Wharton's MBA course, Creativity.

Wind's recent work focuses on what he calls "mental models." Mental models are those constructs through which we view the world. For executives, mental models are especially important because they form the basis of what they believe they can and cannot do. They also form the basis of a company's culture.

Do people in an organization believe in themselves and in their abilities? Do they think they have the power to change the world? Do they feel ready to compete against the best companies in the world? The views people in organizations share about their own abilities and chances for success are based upon their mental models.

One of Wind's recent books, *The Power of Impossible Thinking: Transform the Business of Your Life and the Life of Your Business*, which he coauthored with Colin Crook, focuses on how companies can create positive change. In that book, Wind and Crook challenged their readers to alter the way they perceive the world and by doing so change their companies and their lives.

As the following interview shows, Wind's research-derived point of view has given him an upbeat, even enthusiastic perspective regarding what companies can achieve. All it takes is a willingness to challenge a company's assumptions and the courage to throw away any view that imposes limitation on success. In Wind's view, to succeed you must challenge yourself, challenge your company, and challenge any idea that holds you back.

QUESTION: When you are trying to build an innovative organization, where do you start?

WIND: You start with asking, "How do you recruit your talent?" One interesting framework to think about in doing this is the whole field of positive psychology.

QUESTION: How do you define positive psychology?

WIND: This is primarily the work of Martin E.P. Seligman, Director of the Positive Psychology Center at the University of Pennsylvania. The basic premise of positive psychology is that most social sciences focus on problems and ills and try to fix them. So, if you're depressed, how do we fix your depression? Positive psychology takes the reverse approach. It asks the question "How can we improve the happiness and satisfaction of people?" Seligman developed a model that has three components to it. Feeling good and happy about what you do, have meaning in what you do, and be engaged in what you do.

The beauty of Seligman's approach is that he developed specific Web-based instruments that allow you to improve yourself or your employees on all three dimensions. So, it's a very practical tool that focuses also on how to improve.

QUESTION: In practice, what does that mean? How does feeling good produce results at work?

WIND: That's a great question. That's what we're in discussion with him about at Wharton. We're looking at how to experiment with this in a corporate environment, linking the principles of positive psychology with a focus on client experience and engagement and its corresponding employee and partners engagement program.

Focusing on positive psychology principles in the context of engagement is expected to help in the attraction, development, and retention of creative people, and the creation of a more productive corporate culture.

QUESTION: So, people use these instruments to help them see the meaning in what they do? Feel good about what they're doing? And be more engaged? Do you expect this to result in higher productivity?

WIND: Yes. This is the expectation, but we are trying to find out if it will lead to higher levels of attention, development, and retention of creative people, and their engagement to higher productivity and overall better results.

One of the biggest problems facing most companies is how to sustain the level of engagement throughout the lifecycle of the company. You start with a new product or new idea and everybody is excited. You have a small group of people and you have the feeling of engagement, connection, and involvement. But what happens once you start growing and become a more mature business? The passion goes. The excitement goes. How do you recreate it? How do you get engagement back?

QUESTION: What about using incentives to enhance engagement?

WIND: The findings vary on that. While I have not done a systematic analysis, my guess is that the picture is mixed depending on the level and type of people you're dealing with. And, if you're talking about creative people, giving them financial incentives is not enough. You can have golden handcuffs and all types of ways of keeping them there, but if you do not create enough of a sense of engagement, meaning, creativity, and freedom, they're not going to stay. You'll lose them.

Let me go back to the fundamentals. One of the toughest areas is how to identify and recruit creative people. And, part of the difficulty is the question of whether creativity is taking place at the individual level or the group level.

QUESTION: What's your theory?

WIND: You need both, but you knew I would say that. In reality, the challenge is that when you're recruiting, most individuals are reluctant to recruit people who are dramatically different from them. I'll give you an example.

I know a guy who is a genius at teaching math. But he looks like he walked out of the Bible. He wears sandals and has a big beard. I don't know the last time he changed his clothes. How likely do you think it is that he will get a tenured position? And if a genius professor has difficulty in an academic environment, how do you think he would do in a corporate environment?

QUESTION: Are you arguing that creative groups are formed from a mix of behaviorally diverse people?

WIND: Yes. But I'm also asking if you are willing to take the risk of hiring a genius—or someone truly creative—if that person looks out of place to everybody in the company?

QUESTION: Are you talking about personal risks inhibiting an individual's ability to build really diverse teams?

WIND: Yes. And there are many explanations about why that is, including the fact that members of a team do not always feel comfortable with someone who doesn't fit this mold. I'm not talking about gender or ethnicity or religion. I'm talking about how we think. How we behave. How we form groups.

Another problem is that increasingly, the hiring process is done by a group process and the method is through consensus. As a result, it's getting tougher to recruit really creative people because they are not very likely to be approved by the consensus view of the people interviewing him. These are two of the ways we limit our organizational creativity and innovation.

QUESTION: So you don't believe in consensus as a way to hire people into companies?

WIND: No. It reduces the likelihood of hiring creative people.

QUESTION: What if you're looking for technical people, let's say accountants or software engineers. Don't you want people who have the same technical skills as the other members of the group?

WIND: Let's take accountants. Just look at the accounting firms. The accounting practice was developed in the precomputer era. Today these old structures and its old thinking do not make sense.

Let me give you another example. Just look at how people are treated by financial accounting. While every manager says people are their greatest asset, when times are tough people are the first to go because financial accounting treats people as an expense. That's a 19th-century—or earlier—mindset.

Similarly with inventory. Inventory, in financial accounting, is an asset. But Michael Dell taught us twenty years ago that inventory is really a liability! So, if you want people to start challenging financial conventions, if you want them to start developing the next generation of meaningful audits, you need to have people who are different. But if you use a group hiring process you will not hire them.

QUESTION: So, if you need a different hiring process, what would it look like?

WIND: I don't have a complete answer, but I do know that the current consensus-based approach isn't working. The right solution would be to experiment with different approaches. Different approaches produce different results. So, you would get different types of people.

By the way, there are also a number of studies that show that interviewing leads to worse results than hiring without interviewing! I know how that sounds. But in interviewing, what you're really doing—according to the research—is role-playing. So, what you're seeing is how someone role-plays. And, you're looking for similarities. You went to Yale, the interviewee went to Yale, bingo! You know, immediately the person must be good. So, you start forming impressions in your mind that have nothing to do with performance—they're not predictive.

QUESTION: So when you interview someone, you rate them higher the more they are like you?

WIND: Right. The whole recruiting process is flawed.

QUESTION: So what is the solution?

WIND: Another solution to the recruiting challenge is to rethink the corporation. Instead of hiring, can I connect to the needed competencies? Can I form strategic alliances with them? Can I encourage someone to start his own firm and then contract with it? What are the alternatives to a full-time relationship? Can I treat them as free agents?

QUESTION: Can you develop creativity?

WIND: Yes. You can develop creativity. There are many tools that help people enhance their creativity, and there is a rich literature on enhancing one's creativity. It can be done!

QUESTION: By creative you mean someone who produces value? Not someone who is simply novel?

WIND: I mean someone who comes up with new and better solutions.

QUESTION: New and better solutions that ultimately create measurable value?

WIND: Absolutely. But keep in mind that I'm including artists, curators, choreographers, scientists, and creative people in all disciplines. In this context, value creation is a multidimensional process. It's not necessarily just creating traditional economic value for the firm. Talk about an artist like Picasso. Forget the fact that his paintings now sell for over a hundred million dollars—one measure of value. The aesthetics of it and people's enjoyment of his creative genius also has value.

QUESTION: So it's a very holistic process? And that adds value?

WIND: I would hate to narrow it down to a monetary value alone. But when you see an iPod that is aesthetically pleasing, you're more likely to buy it than when you see something that isn't, like a generic MP3 player.

Now the iPod is a great example, because there is creativity in the design, in the functionality, and also in the revenue model. It's a perfect example of the recording industry needing an outsider to solve its problems of people downloading music for free. The record companies were defensive and not creative. Their primary view was to sue people downloading music! They took a legalistic approach and decided to sue music lovers rather than figuring out how to turn them into paying customers.

QUESTION: Building on your earlier thought, do you think that part of the problem in the record industry is that it is made up of people who are largely the same in the way they think?

WIND: Yes. And also that the industry, which caters to young people, did not have enough young people working in it! A lot of developments today relate to understanding youth culture. Yet, if the record company executives that have been doing their job forever look at Napster, their first instinct is to sue rather than try to figure out how to capitalize on the emerging trend. It does not mean that only young people should lead, but it does take an exceptional older person to challenge the mental models and recognize such new opportunities.

For a great example, consider IBM. When confronted with open source, the head of R&D at IBM Research invited the inventor of open source to discuss open source with IBM. Now think about the courage of doing it at a time when the initial reaction of everybody at IBM would have been, "open source, bring the lawyers, sue them!" But he brought them in to try to understand what was going on. As a result, IBM decided to adopt open source platforms and build proprietary applications on top of it. This was a very creative solution. It would never have gotten there with a traditional approach that says oh, let's sue them.

QUESTION: So how do you develop people to be creative?

WIND: People have to recognize that we have to develop both at the individual and the group level. A lot of companies work in teams. You want to make sure that the development is not limited to one or the other. You want to capture both and create the right creative corporate culture. In this respect, I always like the 3M philosophy of doing anything that is legally and ethically permissible that upsets the status quo, changes the rules of the game, and increases the value to customers, thereby resulting in a novel and powerful competitive advantage that is difficult for the competition to respond to.

QUESTION: Are you talking about developing people to keep your competitors off guard?

WIND: I'm talking about creating a culture. The point of the 3M philosophy is the creation of a culture that encourages and constantly pushes for developing new creative solutions.

That is easier said than done. But one way to do it is by using the culture values also as criteria for evaluation. So, you come to me with a new idea. You say, okay here is this new pen. Based on the 3M model, they would ask you these basic questions: Does it upset the status quo? Does it change the rules of the game? Does it offer increased value to the customer? Does it offer a differentiated product?

To create a culture of innovation, the same criteria should be applied both to the individuals and to the group.

In addition, having the right performance measures is also critical. 3M for example requires that a certain percent of revenue comes from new products.

That's one aspect of developing a creative, innovative culture that helps talent flourish. Another thing 3M and an increasing number of innovative companies do is to encourage skunk works and to provide every individual with time off to work on whatever they want. Providing free time for people to work on whatever they are passionate about is really important. I believe that passion and engagement are the keys.

QUESTION: Are you saying there should be some unstructured time?

WIND: Not exactly. If somebody's passionate about wanting to develop a new type of pen or a new type of ink, yeah, let them develop it. Give them the resources; give them the time to try to develop it. It may not work. But give them the time and opportunity to invent.

While passion is important, having the right competencies is key. Consider, for example, the failed initial transformation of Xerox from selling boxes to selling integrated digital solutions. While Xerox's thousands of salespeople were very comfortable selling to the traditional buyer of the "boxes"—the office manager didn't know how to sell to the CIO, the new buyer of integrated digital solutions. So, while they had a great strategy and vision for moving the company into the future, the salespeople did not have the needed competencies to pull it off. The result was the near collapse of Xerox. So, at the end, it's all people. And, in this case, not the innovative R&D people, which they had, but the salespeople.

QUESTION: So, if you're talking about developing people, don't you need structures to train them?

WIND: It is more than just the structure. You have to think about the entire organizational architecture. You have to deal with the culture and the values. You know, in many companies, it's still unacceptable to make a mistake. You make a mistake and you're out. But there is no way you can encourage creativity in this type of environment. You have to continuously encourage experimentation. If you have a culture of experimentation it can only be a culture that realizes that not everything you do succeeds. At the same time, it requires measurement of outcomes because you must know what works and what doesn't.

QUESTION: What else is needed?

WIND: Well, most innovations are really cross-functional. They primarily require cross-functional, interdisciplinary perspectives. They require taking technologies from different fields and bringing them together. Most organizations are still in silos. Having a VP for marketing, a VP for product development, and a VP for content—you have three silos. So, you have to create processes for empowering people to share ideas across disciplines/silos and for bridging the silos.

QUESTION: Companies have been talking about doing this for a long time. Isn't that true?

WIND: Talking, yes; doing, no. Now, the reason it's difficult is because you need in-depth knowledge in a lot of fields or technologies.

This in-depth knowledge often resides in silos. So what you need is both the in-depth knowledge and the ability to work effectively across silos.

QUESTION: In science you have translational research. This is when you share experiences and knowledge and even work together from different disciplines to achieve a single goal. You bring together biologists with computer specialists with geneticists. Can this be translated into business?

WIND: Absolutely. It is a great idea! But you need the process. You have to do it as a truly interdisciplinary process from the start. From my point of view, I would design these processes within the organization as a whole but I would start doing it in a well-defined area focusing on a specific project/experiment.

QUESTION: So, if you want to design the next iPod, how would you do it?

WIND: I'd get an open space. I'll get rid of all the offices. I'd select the best people in the world and give them that space to play in. Then I would use that to demonstrate to the entire organization how to work. And, if it could not change the whole organization initially, I would at least have a place where I could demonstrate what works.

But all this has to relate to the customer. It goes back to the fact that consumers are actually the ones that create many of the innovations. It also relates, for example, to a company that does this extremely well, which is Microsoft. Microsoft has its consumers—its actual product users—play with and fix their products. If Microsoft had to hire the people to try to do that and do all the bug fixing and improving, it would have cost them about a billion dollars. They save when they make their customers a part of the process. And their customers are happy because they get the product they want.

QUESTION: How does this relate to the talent within the organization?

WIND: We have to redefine the pool of talent. We're not limiting it to the people who work in the company. We're including customers and partners as part of the talent pool. If I have customers involved, I don't need to hire as many people. And, I may not be able to hire people who will actually know what the customer wants in terms of a product, service, or experience. But in addition, I would define my talent to include my suppliers, distributors, and other partners. Traditionally, neither group is considered part of a company's talent base. And you know what? I may have to educate my suppliers, distributors, partners, and even my customers and, at the same time, be open to learn from them.

QUESTION: How do you get people to think differently about that?

WIND: They have to look at all aspects of the organizational architecture of the firm and its networks. We haven't really talked about the critical rule of incentives and performance measures nor of the increased importance of network orchestration. But the key is trying to make sure that the value and culture of the organization encourages innovation and creativity; that everyone knows that they are rewarded if they challenge the current mental models of the company as opposed to just accepting them. People also have to know they can challenge what others are saying. To achieve creativity, challenging the status quo is a must!

But you have to sell these ideas effectively inside a company. One way of selling them is with data. For example, there are some fascinating studies showing that most new product innovations come from outside the industry. Incumbents rarely develop a radical new product. Diet Coke was not invented by Pepsi or Coke. And, as I mentioned, the iPod came from outside of the music industry. Why is it? The reason is it that the incumbents are often stuck. They are stuck in protecting the current offering and in striving for a standardized, single incentive system for everyone, rather than rewarding heterogeneity and recognize the need for flexibility. People relate to things differently. Some value time, some value money, some value titles. So why in the world would I want to come with a single approach? It just doesn't make any sense. Markets are not homogenous. Why try to make companies run that way? Homogenizing everything takes out the passion, the engagement, and the fun. That's why we have to go back to Seligman's work to try and rekindle happiness and engagement and passion. It's because the organizations in which people work beat these things out of them.

But there is one more thing that companies need to do to allow their creative talent to flourish—ownership. I'm a big believer in stock options. I think people like to feel that the company is theirs. They also feel that ownership is to a large extent a matter of fairness. So is compensation. If I'm a creative guy and I'm doing all the work and someone else is getting all the rewards, I feel I'm being left out. That's the reason people leave and become entrepreneurs. To retain them in your company, people have to feel they are getting a fair deal. They have to feel like passionate owners.

CHAPTER 20

Howard Behar

FORMER PRESIDENT,
STARBUCKS NORTH AMERICA

FORMER PRESIDENT,
STARBUCKS INTERNATIONAL
MEMBER, STARBUCKS BOARD OF DIRECTORS

It's Not Just the Coffee,
It's the Experience

The brew that is Starbucks is only getting stronger. By transforming what was once a commodity product into a luxury good, Starbucks has built a premium, global brand that offers more than coffee, pastries, food, and music. It offers the "Starbucks Experience." Since opening its first store in Seattle, in 1971, Starbucks has expanded to 16,000 stores worldwide, and employs about 172,000 people.

Howard Behar, who has held a number of leadership positions at the company and is now a member of its board of directors, says Starbucks' executives work as a team of equals. The company's senior-most executives share a set of values and a vision without having identical points of view. They add to each other's strengths and make up for each other's weaknesses. At Starbucks, the top-most team is engaged in a continuous conversation about the company, its future, and its people.

Behar joined Starbucks in 1989 as vice president of retail stores. His first responsibility in that role was to conceive, build, and deploy scalable people systems; with the aim of creating what Starbucks' chairman, Howard Schultz, called a "people first" culture.

Starbucks has a highly decentralized business model that values culture. As a result, culture is one of the forces that holds the company together. What type of culture did Starbucks' create? The company created a culture that gives its people sufficient autonomy and authority to solve problems, take risks, learn from each other, and take action. It helps decentralized units set their direction while maintaining impeccable standards and providing everyone with sufficient support. Though its products are important, Behar believes the people at Starbucks are what makes the company great.

QUESTION: What's your philosophy regarding managing talent?

BEHAR: In a lot of ways, managing talent is a lot like raising kids. You bring your values to bear. You try to create the right kind of environment for them. You try to help them flourish. But different people respond in different ways. You just do the best you can, and in the end you discover it's just an unpredictable journey. It can be fun and rewarding, and it can be a big pain.

QUESTION: You've had a number of different jobs at Starbucks, both operational—as president of North America—and also as a board member. You were also president of Starbucks International. Did you see much change?

BEHAR: When I started at Starbucks, things were a lot different than they are today. It was right toward the end of the roaring eighties, around 1989 I think. Howard Schultz, the company's CEO and Chairman, was a fiery entrepreneur and he did a great job building out the franchise and building the brand. We had something like 20 or 30 stores in America when I started, although we were also starting to get somewhat of a global footprint. We had some smaller competitors, but by and large, it was a very fragmented industry at that point.

So, Howard Shultz recognized that we needed a different skill set at the leadership helm to get to the next level. He was not comfortable with his own abilities getting us to the next level. But he was very

secure in that he wanted leaders around him that were even better—
or maybe I should say had a very complementary skill set to him. And
he was clearly still very driven. In other words, 30 stores were just a
blip on the screen for him—even back then—when he could have
very easily sold out and retired comfortably. I mean, that was a lot of
money back then. Still is. It's all relative I guess.

QUESTION: What was your background?

BEHAR: I had a fairly solid background in systems and controls and
processes. I had come from a very large accounting firm. My career
was doing very, very well and a lot of people were surprised that
I left. But I guess I, too, was an entrepreneur at heart. And frankly,
the stock options dangled in front of me didn't hurt either. So
I joined Starbucks with another fellow named Orin Smith. Our
collective names became H2O—the two Howards (Shultz and I),
and Orin. And boy did we make a nice leadership team. Not always
do people gel together at the top, but we seemed to make a pretty
good go at it. It wasn't an office of the CEO, per se, but we made
a lot of decisions together. We would debate issues thoroughly—
with me usually playing devil's advocate—then we would present a
common face to the troops.

QUESTION: What was your focus?

BEHAR: Our focus was to grow the business. The goal was to make
the pie bigger for all of us. That was a central driving force, because
it meant we could all put our own personal egos and ambitions
behind the overriding goals of the company. It was a win-win if
we could pull it off. The thing to remember is that we set a trend
early on. By not being an egotist, Shultz recognized that he needed
to round out Starbucks' leadership capability and hired me to get
the job done. Well, that was a philosophy we extended throughout the company. I hired a lot of people that I thought were "better than me." We always looked for people that were talented,
smart, and humble. Don't get me wrong, Schultz had an ego and
was very confident, but he never let that get in the way of the
company and the greater good.

QUESTION: Did you focus on building a unique Starbucks culture?

BEHAR: Yes. We set our culture very early around people. That's where it began and ended. It was all about culture. And because we recruited good people—and believe me, we took a lot of time looking for and evaluating people to make sure they were good. But equally important, we wanted to make sure they would fit into our culture. But again, because we hired good people, we felt very comfortable giving them a lot of autonomy and power to accomplish goals *their* way. Of course we gave them broad operating procedures, but we encouraged them to do what it took to satisfy their own customer base. That's exactly what Howard Shultz did for me. He hired me, respected me, gave me space, gave me some real authority, gave me autonomy, and let me do my job. To accomplish that, he had to have some level of underlying security. Not surprisingly, because we were growing so fast, building a great brand, serving our customers well, and growing the pie, we had very little turnover at the top. That was one of our hallmarks—low turnover. But why should people leave? We created the kind of place where people could succeed. That's really the heart of good leadership. Human resources policies need to be centered on that goal.

QUESTION: What else does human resources have to do?

BEHAR: Okay. Let's dig a little deeper on the human resources side. My job was to conceive, build, and deploy systems—particularly people systems that could scale, and scale fast and efficiently. That was the post start-up goal. It's a tough job. It's where a lot—and I mean a lot—of companies fail. They just can't or don't create the kind of systems that can scale fast and efficiently—especially the people ones. I never thought there was a tradeoff between scale and empowerment. If you're smart you can do both. You can give people the space they need, while having the underlying "backup" systems to support them so they will succeed. By that I mean support the leaders, the regional managers, all the way down to the baristas. For example, we helped our people understand specifically how to recruit, where to look, and how to evaluate. But ultimately, the hiring decisions were very decentralized. We trusted our people to make good decisions. It's all about the decisions. And I think it still is at Starbucks.

It's not just about human resources. We looked for diversity. Not just diversity of ethnicity or skin color. We looked for diversity of ideas and thoughts. We didn't want to get stale. That sort of gets back to my background. I haven't shared it too much with the press, but I am a big fan of poetry and philosophy and I fundamentally believe that taking a multidisciplinary approach to leadership is much more effective.

People are very complex. The more ways you see them and the wider the lens through which you view them, the better off you are and the more effective a leader you are. That said, there is no substitute for zeroing in on the critical issues and framing problems correctly. That requires some digging. And frankly, when I joined Starbucks, a lot of people, especially our leaders, were afraid to dig too deep. We didn't like the awkwardness associated with asking tough questions. We were very nonconfrontational and a bit too homogenous. But respect comes in many shapes and sizes. I believe it is a sign of respect to question the status quo. That's how you improve as an organization and improve customer satisfaction.

In the end, the central human resources goal is to create a stimulating environment for our people to succeed. That's the secret sauce. That's the main leadership lesson I can impart. If you don't create an environment for them to succeed, you're just another mediocre copy. That's not going to win.

QUESTION: Did you question everybody?

BEHAR: Sure. I even took on Howard Schultz. Daily. I don't think there was a day that went by—at least when we were in the same town, that I didn't challenge something he said, or question one of our operating procedures. It's all about getting better—and I know that Howard Schultz appreciated that.

QUESTION: What kind of questions did you ask?

BEHAR: Well, one thing I questioned pretty hard when I got to Starbucks was, believe it or not, our focus on coffee. I thought we were too "product-centric." I used to say people make coffee, right? Products are inert, but people are dynamic. It's the people that will make or break us—not the coffee. So it was a major initiative of mine to focus more on the people than the beans (even though the beans were of course important). I just didn't see it as the biggest point of our differentiation.

We used to all say, "We're not filling bellies, we're filling souls." To that end we had to become more customer focused. I initiated some policies that are still around. For example, I started a procedure called, "Snap Shots," which was a human resources policy to make sure that our people were treating customers the right way. We would have our senior managers go into the retail stores and make sure that employees were treating customers the right way. Again, this was yet another human resource policy that reinforced our culture. It's such a simple policy, but so underused at most organizations. I could never understand why more executives didn't go out and kick the tires. It's the best way to reinforce the kind of culture you aspire to.

QUESTION: What else did you do?

BEHAR: Well, another human resource mantra I was proud of was a play on Nancy Reagan's *Just Say No* to drugs campaign. I used to say, "Just Say Yes." I guess our neighbors at Nike kind of got wind of it, or maybe it was vice versa—I'm not sure. But Nike had their *Just Do It* campaign. In any event, "Just Say Yes" was designed to bias our people toward action. It fit so well with empowering our people and giving them autonomy and hiring the right people. Once all of those things were in place, the worst thing we could do was not leverage the advantage. So I always said, "Just Say Yes." Do something. Take action. Fix problems. Solve customer needs. Go above and beyond the call of duty. It really worked for us.

QUESTION: What else?

BEHAR: I also encouraged our people to speak their minds—just like I did. They were of course nervous at first to vent their frustrations and talk about their concerns right off the bat—particularly to the president of the company. But believe me, once they started, it was hard to get them to stop. It really paid off. We got so many great ideas from the front line.

We also had what I called Open Forums each quarter. We used to invite our customers to these forums. All our senior managers would interact directly with the customers and get their ideas and act on their feedback. It was a great, complementary tool, just like the "Just Say Yes" and the "We're Filling Souls, Not Bellies" mantras.

And of course I would always throw in some grenades. I used to spark debate. Maybe it just got people mad when I would say or suggest things like, "Why don't you guys open the store ten minutes before the scheduled opening time?" Believe me, the store managers that were already getting there at 4:30 in the morning were not too keen on that idea. But the idea was to spark dialogue and look for productive change.

QUESTION: So you saw your role as *agent provocateur?*

BEHAR: In a way. But one more thing you should know. The rest of the senior leadership team and I took succession planning very seriously. Not just at the CEO level of course, but also for key positions throughout the company. We had a very deep bench. And we always looked to promote people into more challenging roles. And believe me, since we were expanding so fast, we had a lot of cool opportunities for people. I think that is one of the reasons that our turnover and attrition was so low. We recruited good people, created a great culture, had a strong brand, and had plenty of opportunities for our stars. I doubt that any of our competitors took succession planning as seriously as we did. I doubt many companies in any other industry did. We really tried to get a bench of two or three possible candidates to rise into key positions. Trust me, that's hard when you're growing fast. It's even harder if you're not growing at all.